Rise of the False Gods

By

Alicia-Leslie

NOTE: Cover Art

The beautiful image on the cover of this book was found in a Google search for images marked for reuse without copyright permission required. While I searched diligently, I could not find its source. I do want to acknowledge the creator of the perfect image to express the essence of the message I wanted to convey.

Copyright © Rev. Alicia-Leslie

All rights reserved. No part of this book may be used or reproduced in any manner whatever, including internet usage, without written permission from the author. Such usage is punishable by law. Publications are exempt in the case of brief quotations in critical reviews or articles.

Dedication

I dedicate this book with love and gratitude to the Living Spirit of Truth that changed my life through an understanding of Universal Principles of Truth. . I pray that the words I share will touch hearts and change lives for those who are new to metaphysics, as well as those who have made metaphysics a lifelong study and lifestyle.

Acknowledgements

I would like to acknowledge Unity School of Practical Christianity—now Unity Institute—and the ministers and teachers who helped me build the strong spiritual foundation on which I stand. I would also like to thank those who have inspired and encouraged me on the journey we share. This includes, but is not limited to Rev. Eileen Douglas, Rev. Helen-Jean Nelson and Rev. Leddy Hammock. Also those who have sat in my congregation, and have been fed by the teachings I shared, because it gave me the courage to write this book.

RISE OF THE FALSE GODS
INTRODUCTION

In our country and around the world, false gods undermine the best of all that we are, and all that we can be. Over eons their presence has ebbed and flowed, yet never been completely overcome. Two thousand years ago, Jesus said: "In this world you will have tribulation, but I have overcome the world." He also instructed us to follow him, assuring the things He did and even greater things could be done by us, if we would believe. I believe. I believe it is time for the false gods to be transformed by the light of Truth. Will you join me? This is what you need to know:

False gods are everything God is not. They are states of mind formed through error thought of humankind. God is all-good, false gods are misperceptions of good. In the Bible, we can find two primary false gods. One is Baal, the nature god. We worship, or give worth to this false god through our carnal or lower nature. It is idolatry and includes sex and senses. The other is Mammon, or materialism. This is the worship of money and things, material riches instead of inner riches of the mind, spiritual substance, life, and intelligence behind every outer manifestation. (Pg. 14)

False prophets, or prophets of the false gods are deceptive thoughts built up by error, or selfish desires. They are the rationalizations—rational-lies we tell ourselves, or hear and decide to believe. They allow us to live under the illusion we can find a loophole in spiritual law. False prophets appeal to what we want to be true, not what is true. The Lord, or Principle, will not be fooled. We will reap what we sow. We, the citizens of the United States, are reaping the effects of our own mistakes. Yes, the false gods led us, but we let them. (Pg. 24)

WHY I WROTE THIS BOOK—WHY ME—WHY NOW?

We all share the basic needs for survival: food, clothing, and shelter. We want love and acceptance. It seems so simple; we all want the same things. How can it be there's so much hate and evil among people? A great deal of suffering would vanish if we could just learn to love and accept each other. But unseen forces drive us apart. Some people say it's *the devil,* in reality it's false gods. *These are not beings.* They are states of mind—errors, lies, and false beliefs that block our good.

For the past few years, Spirit has been moving me to write a book about false gods. Long before that, I've been observing humankind walking on a slippery slope, sliding away from God, church, and foundations of faith. I'm not an expert in psychology or anthropology, but I have walked my own slippery slope, often careening perilously downward, rescued by the Grace of God. I emerged with a message and a mission.

As far back as I can remember, I have prayed without ceasing for world peace. I've experienced the thrill of spiritual victory, and the agony of regret. My dreams crumbled before me. I faltered and hit bottom, but didn't fail to get up again, and heal. Through it all, as a lifelong Truth student, I've explored orthodox teachings, unorthodox teachings, and those considered taboo, including astrology and reincarnation. My goal never changed: seeking God, peace, and love for all.

At one point, like Dorothy, returning from Oz, I came to realize I was home already. Through introspection, the study of traditional religion, and metaphysics, I achieved clarity about my beliefs. Now grounded in my beliefs, I have been able to release what I was taught by others but never believed. Questions I'd never had the courage to ask were answered. I am being compelled to share this with you.

The good news is, I won't try to change what you believe. You will decide, and will recognize the Truth within you. How you worship is up to you. I only ask that you open your heart and mind to the possibility something I share may bless you. Armed with knowledge and enlightenment, together we will overcome the false gods.

What I have to share, is a metaphysical solution to very human problems. Because of this, you may disagree, or be challenged by what I say. That is understandable. All I ask is that you continue to read and consider the possibilities.

In her book, *Lessons in Truth*, H. Emilie Cady asks that the reader set aside their current beliefs long enough to consider what she wrote. She assured they could pick it right back up afterward. So can you. As you read, you will find examples and exercises that prove the teaching. Try them. Consider them experiments and watch the results.

A truth that is hard to accept, is that the dark times we are experiencing today, June 26, 2018, is the product of our collective consciousness. We manifested this through our own thoughts, words, and feelings by actions we've taken, and actions we have not taken but should have. To overcome our problems, we must change the mindset that created them. We make the changes as we practice the Principles.

My spiritual path is Unity, Christian by culture, but unlimited spiritually. We see God in all faiths. Since my primary path has always been Christian, you will find many scriptural references and the teachings of Jesus. Yet Jesus taught: "In my father's house there are many rooms…" which I interpret as faith groups (religions/denominations). We may each live in a different room, but it's all the same house. It is Oneness in Spirit.

New Day

Anonymous

This is the beginning of a new day.

I have been given this day to use as I will.

What I do today is important,

Because I am exchanging a day of my life for it.

When tomorrow comes, this day will be gone forever,

Leaving in its place something I have exchanged for it.

I pray it will be good, not evil,

Gain, not loss, and

Success, not failure,

In order that I will not regret the price I paid.

Anonymous

CONTENTS

PART ONE—FALSE GODS 1
    THE EMERGENCE 1
    TRUE OR FALSE? 6
    FACT VS FAKE 8
    GOD, GODS, AND FALSE GODS 11
    WHO OR WHAT ARE FALSE GODS? 14
    FALSE GODS AND THE ANTICHRIST 15
    IF THEY ARE FALSE GODS WHERE DO THEY GET THEIR POWER? 16
    THE HIERARCHY OF FALSE GODS 21
    PROPHETS OF THE FALSE GODS 24
    FALSE GODS ~ ARE YOU UNDER THE INFLUENCE? 28
    A QUESTION OF EVIL 31
    THE CRUX OF THE MATTER 34

PART TWO ~ SIN 39
    THE TRUTH ABOUT SIN 39
    SIN, SIN, AND MORE SIN! 41
    NAME THAT SIN 42
    THE BIG TEN 42
    SINS OF COMMISSION AND SINS OF OMISSION 51
    CORPORATE, OR COLLECTIVE SIN 52
    MORTAL VS VENIAL SINS 54
    THE SEVEN DEADLY SINS–PLAYGROUND OF THE FALSE GODS 55
    (AND THEIR ANTIDOTES) 55
    BUT WAIT–THERE'S MORE! 57
    MONEY, SEX, AND POWER 59

PART THREE – SPIRITUAL LAW 61
   LAW OR GUIDELINES? 61
   SPIRITUAL LAWS AND FALSE GODS 62
   ONE GOD, MANY FACES ~ ONE LAW, MANY EXPRESSIONS 64
   SPIRITUAL LAW AND THE LAW OF THE LAND 66
   THE DOGMA AND DOCTRINE OF FALSE GODS 68
   LIES OF FALSE GODS 69
   TAP DANCING ON THE SLIPPERY SLOPE 71
   WHAT'S KARMA GOT TO DO WITH IT? 72
   IS OUR CURRENT WORLD CRISIS KARMIC? 75

PART FOUR–AWAKENING 77
   HOW DID WE GET HERE? 77
   A SEARCH FOR TRUTH 82
   CAN YOU HANDLE THE TRUTH? 84
   THERE WILL BE SIGNS 85
   SIGNS OF FALSE GODS AT WORK 86
   HIJACKED HOLIDAYS 93
   SOMETIMES THE DRAGON WINS 96
   BEWARE OF THE WOLVES 99
   RELIGION AND SPIRITUALITY 100
   EVIL AS A CONTAGIOUS DIS-EASE 104
   THE PIT AND THE PENDULUM–IMMORALITY VS RIGID RELIGIOSITY 107
   VERSUS ~ SORTING IT OUT 110
   PRIDE, PREJUDICE, POPULISM, AND POLARIZATION .. 116
   HEAVEN, HELL, AND HOLLYWOOD 119

WORDS, WORDS, WORDS 122
PART FIVE–HOMEWARD BOUND 127
   WAKE UP AND BE VIGILANT 127
   IT'S ALL IN YOUR MIND 130
   WHERE THERE IS NO VISION..133
   THE CREATIVE PROCESS 136
   CREATIVE VS FORMATIVE 139
   TRUTH OR CONSEQUENCES..141
   GETTING TO CAUSE 144
   AUTOPSY ON THE ELECTION 146
   WHAT'S NOT WORKING ~ WE'VE GOT TO THINK OUT OF THE BOX!..152
   SOME THINGS THAT ARE NOT WORKING, OR NOT WORKING WELL: 153
   WHAT'S YOUR EXCUSE? 164
   A MATTER OF AUTHORITY 165
   SURRENDERING TO VICTORY 168
   IT'S NOT ME ~ OR IS IT? 169
   YOUR CREDO: A POWERFUL TOOL FOR TRANSFORMATION 172
PART SIX – CLEANSING AND RESTORING THE TEMPLE.175
   A TIME TO HEAL...177
   WHY CONFESSION IS GOOD FOR THE SOUL 179
   SONS OF LIGHT VS SONS OF DARKNESS 180
   LOST SHEEP–OUR SEARCH AND RESCUE MISSION........181
   FROM FATAL ATTRACTION TO FAITH-FILLED ACTION 184
   RAISING THE BAR...186
   FROM PEOPLE PLEASING TO PLEASING GOD................189

NOW IT'S GETTING PERSONAL! 192

CLAIM YOUR POWER OVER FALSE GODS 193

REVENGE OF THE FALSE GODS 197

FOUNDATIONS AND FRAMEWORKS 199

THE POWER OF FAMILY–SACRED BUILDING BLOCK OF THE TEMPLE 200

MARRIAGE–FOUNDATION OF THE FAMILY 200

FAMILY–BUILDING BLOCK OF OUR FUTURE 202

BEYOND FAMILY–IT TAKES MORE THAN A VILLAGE . 205

BUT WHAT ABOUT *"THEM"* 209

PART SEVEN - EMERGENCE OF THE WARRIORS 211

ARE YOU THE ONE? 211

CHARACTERISTICS OF SPIRITUAL WARRIORS 213

THE DUTIES OF THE SPIRITUAL WARRIOR 215

GOD: WHO SHALL I SEND? US: HERE I AM, LORD. SEND ME! 215

YOUR MISSION, SHOULD YOU CHOOSE TO ACCEPT IT… 217

SIMPLE–BUT NOT EASY 218

USE YOUR GOD-GIVEN TOOLS! 221

THE GIFT OF GUILT 224

THE POWER OF FORGIVENESS 226

HARD QUESTIONS AND LIVING WITHOUT THE ANSWERS 228

PART EIGHT–RETURN TO PARADISE 231

ANOTHER DAY IN PARADISE 231

THE REMNANT–HOPE FOR THE FUTURE 233

CAN WE GET THERE FROM HERE? 233

SMALL FOOTPRINTS 236
ABUNDANCE, TO HAVE AND NOT HOLD 236
TALK TO ME: COMMUNICATION IN PARADISE 238
GOVERNMENT/LEADERSHIP 239
BUILDING BRIDGES NOT WALLS 239
A GUIDE TO CONSCIOUS VOTING 241
ARE WE THERE YET? – HOW WILL WE KNOW 246
EXERCISES 249
GLOSSARY 290
RESOURCES 297
SUGGESTED READING: 297
ALSO BY THE AUTHOR..300
COMING SOON..300

PART ONE—FALSE GODS

THE EMERGENCE

NOTE: This is not a book about politics. It is a book about spiritual growth on the individual and collective levels. Politics are presented as they relate to spiritual law, or Principle, not political parties. There is neither Democratic nor Republican preference, only a desire to help others to live meaningful lives, in fullness as our Creator intended. While the concept of politics is neutral, our perceptions and usage, determine our experience.

People may adamantly stomp their feet and declare the need for a separation of *church and state,* or religion and politics, in truth however, that is impossible. Our ability to do so would be as unlikely as the ability to separate the body from the soul, or spirit. From the human point of view it makes sense that no specific religion should direct our decisions, laws and actions. And I agree. After all, we each treasure our freedom to worship as we please, or not to worship at all. On the spiritual level, we all live under Principle, or spiritual law, which cannot be broken. At some point, the two must be synchronized, to work together for the good of all creation.

Since their appearance on Earth, people have formed the world as we know it, both good and bad. We have left an indelible mark on the planet and our history as a people. Anthropologists have studied the development of our cultures, religions and governments. Religious communities have declared their own perspectives of creation and development. There are ongoing disputes over which is the *right* answer.

Both anthropology and religion have observed the need, or desire for leadership. We call this leadership *government,* and it operates through politics. As Americans, we have not only the right, but the responsibility to participate in our government. Many choose not to participate, for any number of reasons. This can result in leadership that does not reflect needs and requirements of a majority of the people.

Whether in government, or our own lives, where we are our own leader, Principle will dictate the outcome of the decisions we make and actions we take. Principle is omnipresent. The primary Principle is the Law of Cause and Effect, which works in both science and spirit. Outcomes are the result (effect) of our thoughts, feelings, words, decisions and actions (causes). Where politics come into play in this book, my intention is to point out how Principle is at work in a relatable way.

Because of the radical and explosive impact the results of the 2016 Presidential Election, I am going to begin there.

November 9, 2016, as dawn broke, a schism ripped through the United States of America. Half of the country was horrified, while the other half rejoiced. Everyone was in a state of shock. *How could this happen?* The questions would torment them in the days and months to come. While one side wondered how Donald Trump could possibly have become be President of the United States, the other side felt a shot of adrenaline at the win. From pure logic, we ask: How is it so many fell under the spell of this *Pied Piper of Politics?* How could so many accept the atrocious behaviors, cruelty, arrogance, and ignorance of diplomacy and politics?

A few religious organizations claimed the election results were the answer to their extensive and devout prayers. Throughout it all, there has been a nonstop circus of finger-pointing, lies, and blame as the dark side of the American mind emerged. We have all been pulled into it at one point or another, losing our ability to communicate and stand together regarding the things we all hold dear.

Unbeknownst to all, Pandora's Box was open, setting free minions of the false gods. It's not anyone's fault. We are a part of the cause. The election results are an effect. Humankind has been slipping into the shadows for decades. The Siren song of false gods—promised riches and pleasures that would never satisfy the soul, and justice that wasn't just. Over the past few decades, seduced into complacency, we let the government worry about governing. We abdicated our responsibility as citizens to be politically informed, vote, and hold politicians feet to the fire of their promises.

There was a method to the madness created by false gods. The divide brought us into, and held us captive in a prison of fear, anger and our darkest thoughts. The shadow of false gods fell across our lives, through daily dramas. It was not a matter of individual thoughts and beliefs, but groups, cultures, corporations, and county.

You might ask how more than half of America could grieve as more than half celebrated the victory of his opponent? It does not compute. But it does. Many folks didn't vote. Some, overconfident Trump's opponent Hillary Clinton would win, they didn't bother to vote. Others were too lazy or apathetic. Still others found both candidates unacceptable.

In early 2018, an ongoing investigation showed Russians had hacked into social media during the 2016 election. They manipulated the minds of Americans with inflammatory news stories that turned out to be fake. They exploited the people by instigating deep seated anger and resentment, which has bubbled up and exacerbated the breadth and depth of the divide. Violence, racism, debates, and disputes have driven the wedge deeper into the heart and soul of the country. Mass murders are now more frequent and tragic as millions reject responsible gun control. Americans are so divided and attached to their opinions that sensible gun regulation cannot be developed, and now children are being gunned down in their own schools as politicians stand silently by. I, personally, can no longer bear to speak the words *thoughts and prayers are with you,* much less listen to the hollow excuse for inaction.

This is a time of unprecedented disquietude in our history. If we step back far enough, the cause is easy to see. It won't be anything you heard on the news or declared by political pundits. This is a metaphysical interpretation.

On the day Trump was declared President, the United States of America became the Divided States of America. It had become split and splintered. Each day brings to those with eyes to see and ears to hear, new levels of shock and disbelief. In spite of countless lies, mean-spirited and outrageous tweets, speeches, and behaviors his base stands by him. In the face of factual information, fellow Republicans stand silent. Democrats struggle without the necessary representation to make a difference. Few from either side are able to bridge the gap and reconnect. Like the blade in Poe's *Pit and the Pendulum*, the sides each form part of a blade of potential doom—lies and disregard of amoral behavior whoosh toward the heart of the American people.

The divide happened on many levels, affecting communities, families and friendships. Visually, I imagine this would look like shattered safety glass. Facebook, once a great way to connect, became a battleground, littered with the corpses of the unfriended and blocked. Then came the greater blow, that we had all been used and manipulated by the capture of our Facebook information, which was used by unscrupulous people, primarily Russians, to further divide us.

There is good news in this, using the metaphor of safety glass: the glass is layered with plastic film that keeps it from falling apart completely. The safety layers can symbolize our oneness in God, or Spirit, that will keep us from likewise coming apart permanently.

It's important to understand how this happened, because failing to do so, locks us in the nightmare, and worse ones that follow.

False gods have lurked in the shadows, orchestrating us for eons. Over the ages false gods raised up, bringing unspeakable suffering. In response to the suffering of the people, God—Spirit by whatever name you wish—brought forth enlightened beings to awaken us from the spell. They appeared as Jesus, Buddha, Mohammed, Vishnu, etc. For a while it worked. Then people fell away from the Master's teachings. As the teachings of love, peace, and brotherhood faded, the door opened for the false gods to rise again.

If you are a Christian you might take offense because I mentioned other spiritual leaders with Jesus. Try to be okay with that as you read. It is possible to accept Jesus as Lord, without discrediting other great spiritual leaders. Nobody has a monopoly on God. To assume we do diminishes the power and presence of God. Many of us profess a particular faith, and will fight to the death—or to the loss of friends and family members, in defense of that faith. Innumerable people forgot what it means to practice their beliefs. We have let distraction from matters above, seduce and bind us to carnal appetites and concerns.

TRUE OR FALSE?

It's much more difficult these days to discern true from false. As I've said, we're inundated with fake news, false advertising, and an adulteration of our language. It makes one feel they're standing at the foot of the Tower of Babel. The more information, and misinformation available, the more confusion increases.

Fear not. Truth is, was, and ever will be. In this book, you will note that the word *truth* is sometimes capitalized and sometimes not. When it is not in caps, it refers to our common use of the word to mean *factual,* or an actual state of a mater. When capitalized, it refers to Truth as Principle: absolute, eternal and unchanging. In a quote, the word appears as written. Gravity is an example of a physical, or scientific Principle. It draws us to and keeps us pulled by its force, lest we float away. A scientist could explain it more clearly but that would not be me. The force of gravity is the manifestation of unbreakable physical or scientific law. While we can get in a rocket ship and force ourselves beyond the gravitational pull, it's still there. Spiritual, or Metaphysical law, lies behind the physical. We use the term *Principle* to define spiritual law. Principle is that which is absolute, eternal and unchanging.

"You will know the truth, and the truth will set you free." (John 8:32) Think of a time you heard something, and knew it was true. There was no question. You sensed it within you. In Jeremiah 31, we learn *"I will put my law within them, I will write it on their hearts."* (Jeremiah 31:33) In Biblical times the heart symbolized the joint thinking and feeling faculties. As you read on, stay focused on the sensations of your mind and body. You would not dispute that one and one is two. You know without a doubt. If I say, *one and one is three,* something inside says, *that's not right.* We can feel it in our bodies. That is what it is like when we encounter and discern the validity of information we have received.

Truth is truth whether or not we want to believe it. We knew this at birth. As we mature, the sensing faculty of mind can become jaded.

If we want to live more peaceful and productive lives, we can to work toward re-sensitizing our consciousness.

Here's a fun experiment: For the next month, watch only vintage television programs. You can find them on channels found on Roku or Amazon Prime Video, or other resources. Watch a variety of shows, but ONLY vintage programs, pre-1975. At first, you may find this difficult. The shows may seem too slow-moving or colorless at first. Well, many will be colorless since they are black and white. You will find everything was different. You won't find much graphic sex or violence. The good guy always won, parents were always right and police were always good.

Not everything is perfect. You will also find little diversity. In the face of that, however there is still little to no disrespect regarding people of color or different religions. If you give it a sincere try, you will find when you return to your regular programming it has lost some of the appeal it once had. At this point you will either change your viewing habits, or make conscious choices that support who you are and what kinds of things you want to have impressing your consciousness.

I also suggest spending time each day in prayer and meditation. Relax your mind and body. Let your breath be deep and peaceful…See yourself surrounded in the light of God's love, and say, *I am open and receptive to Your living spirit of Truth*. Let your mind move to your wisdom center, located right behind your navel. Repeat, *I am open and receptive to Your living spirit of Truth*. This will help to develop the faculties of sensitivity to Truth, or untruth.

Many people are uncomfortable with prayer and meditation, unsure of how to pray beyond rote prayers learned in Sunday school or Bible study. In the Resources section at the back of the book, I have listed a few suggestions. The trick is not to make it more complicated than it is. Prayer is talking to God, Meditation is listening for God. Prayer and meditation are not limited. There are as many ways to communicate with God as there are songs, written and unwritten, to sing.

FACT VS FAKE

At one time, fake news was a joke. The source was newspapers called *rags*. Their names include *The Star, National Enquirer*, or *Midnight*. Today fake news has found an avid following of armchair politicians. By that, I mean that they are influenced by the sensationalism. Fake news is propaganda. It can be addictive and plays on the emotions. Fear-or-anger based, they lure the reader or listener to believe what they want, whether or not it's the truth. The people we disagree with are not *bad,* they have been victimized. Recent news stories about Cambridge Analytica's use of our Facebook information to profile people. They would then *feed* people with particular profiles fake news specific to their political beliefs. This strongly indicates propaganda to be a primary influence in the outcome of the 2016 Presidential Election. I myself lost friends who refused to research the stories, continuing to believe the lies because of the promises made.

Through the Internet, disinformation spreads like wildfire. Words like *bots* and trolls have become a part of our everyday language. By its nature, propaganda pulls us like the force of gravity into our lower, carnal mind. This is the part of our mind that is concerned with the physical needs. It thrives on the appetites and emotions of the animal nature. In today's world, the domain of false gods, it's difficult to resist the call. What makes the deceit even worse, is when spreads through ignorance. There's an old saying, *"Oh what a tangled web we weave, when first we practice to deceive."* Thoughts are contagious as are the beliefs they embody. When we spread false information, it multiplies. Through the Law of Cause and Effect, it will come back bearing the adverse effects we shared, multiplied. We have to ask ourselves if we want to be a part of the solution, or part of the problem.

Why, you might wonder, would anyone want to buy lies? It would be like building a house on sand. Oh wait—Jesus already said:

"Everyone then who hears these words of mine and does them will be like a wise man who built his house on the rock. And the rain fell, and the floods came, and the winds blew and beat on that house, but it did not fall, because

*it was built on a rock. And everyone who hears these words of mine and does not do them will be like a foolish man who built his house on the sand. *²⁷*And the rain fell, and the floods came, and the winds blew and beat against that house, and it fell, and great was the fall of it."* (Matthew 7:24-27)

Life throws us enough curves. We have mental, emotional, spiritual, and many other problems. If we build our lives on lies, or believing what we want to be true, even though sounds dicey, challenges will follow. We will repeat our lessons until they are learned. The good news is that the lessons can be learned, and we can determine the pace. Research indicates that cheating on tests, and lying on resumes or job interviews is common today. That won't help with doing the work you are applying to do. If we don't have a grasp on the knowledge and skills required to succeed, we're doomed to fail. Even if we can fake it for a while, as my dad used to say, *"Cheatin' proves."*

We all have gifts, skills and talents. Some come naturally, others are developed through learning and practice. What did you want to be when you grew up? Is what you are doing now related in any way to that early desire, or do you spend your days working at job you have no passion for regardless of pay. We will find most success in following our dreams and desires. To think it's all about the paycheck, is error. Of course even applying for a job you have a desire for, without the necessary skills will not assure success. The good news is that you *can* own those skills with a little effort.

Wanting something to be true doesn't make it so. The irony is, we have to override our intelligence, common sense, and intuition to believe falsehood. I know this to be true because I've done it. I am sharing this example to help you recognize whether you are choosing fake for fact.

After my ordination, I was very excited to lead my first church. I interviewed for a position in a particular church. Something stirred in my gut—a mild warning I might make a mistake. But my yearning to lead a church caused me to ignore the warning and accept the position. By the end of my first thirty days, it had become obvious I'd made a big mistake. The philosophy and theology of the church were more aligned with the EST teachings of Werner Erhard, and Divine Science. While there is nothing specifically wrong with their theology, it clearly was not the teaching of Unity.

In my naiveté, I believed that since they loved what I taught, they would come around to the Unity teaching. I was wrong. I should have taken the clue that something was not right when I heard they had an argument about where they would hang the picture of Jesus that I brought with me as a gift for the church. I kept my agreement to be with the church for two years, but they were not easy years.

After deep reflection, I realized I'd done this with both of my unsuccessful marriages. I wanted to be married. I didn't want to wait for a good match and preferred the illusion in my mind to the Truth. I also had the belief that any two good people with some chemistry could make a successful marriage.

Whether it's at work, politics, relationships, or other aspects of our lives, the little time and effort it takes to seek the Truth is priceless. It will bring a happier life. When you hear something and get an uncomfortable sensation in your gut, research it. It takes so little time to research on the internet once you learn to identify reliable resources. I have developed many, and always check several. Good sources are reliable and have good reputations. One example is NPR.

Working these Principles on a larger scale, could even change the world! Always remember, *like attracts like*—Truth attracts Truth, falsehood attracts falsehood. As we live our lives focused on Truth and integrity we will discover an increased sensitivity, and ability to discern one from the other. Following the tragic massacre at the Marjory Stoneman Douglas High School in Parkland, FL, where 17 died, the surviving students banded together with a goal of stopping gun violence. They planned the March for Our Lives, which was held on March 24, 2018. Other schools joined them, then the energy spread. By March 24th, almost 800 other groups, tens of thousands of people young and old supported them. They have given us all hope for a better tomorrow: a safer world for everyone. The changes are coming slowly, but they are coming. While the White House is slow to commit to change, states across the country are making many changes. Every event, demonstration and speech is like a seed planted in the consciousness of the people. The seeds (causes) will sprout and grow into change (effects). I am proud to say I was a participant in our local march.

GOD, GODS, AND FALSE GODS
WHO OR WHAT IS GOD?

Most of us formed our impressions and beliefs about God through the Bible, belief systems of our parents, and the churches we have attended. The teachings are a mixture of positive, negative, and some so offensive we rejected them altogether. There are people who cling to God, fearing that to challenge the doctrine or dogma, will land them in a state of eternal damnation. Many see God as anthropomorphic, which means a person: *a guy in the sky*, always masculine, with human traits. If we're good, and follow the Commandments, we receive favor. If not, we will suffer. This anthropomorphic God is a great and harsh taskmaster placing burdens on us through his unbendable and fragile Commandments.

This is not the *version* of God I worship. Nor is it the God Jesus taught about. Before you declare me a heretic, let me tell you my belief and how I found it. From childhood, until my forties, I practiced the Catholic faith. It is important to note here, that I do not consider myself to be a *recovering Catholic,* which I see as a derogatory term. While I no longer consider Catholicism my primary path, many teachings it contains continue to enrich my life.

I left the Catholic Church, but not my relationship with God, who I believe in my heart is loving and righteous. I treasure Jesus' teachings and pray daily. The cornerstone of my personal beliefs, or credo, was laid when I was twelve years old. As I walked home from school reciting the Lord's Prayer, I had the lightning-bolt realization that Jesus said *our* father not *my* father. Rather than seeing Jesus as distant and out of my reach, I saw him as my brother, teacher, wayshower and savior, since His teachings showed me right living. Decades later I found Unity, which agreed with my theology and became my primary spiritual path.

Don't misunderstand me. My path may not be your path, but that doesn't mean one path is right and the other wrong. I believe we have many paths to choose from as we seek God. Each person has to find their own and follow it. This is your primary path. It can bear the name Catholic, Christian, Jewish, Buddhist, or any other of the countless names we use. We can look at what we hold in common with other paths, as a source of prayer, inspiration, and acknowledgment of our Oneness in God. In the core of my being, it doesn't matter to God what name we call to reach out, just that we reach out. The only wrong path is the one that takes you farther from God, and deeper into carnality and materialism.

My spiritual path is Unity. An early definition of the Unity philosophy states: *"Unity is a link in the great educational movement inaugurated by Jesus Christ; our aim is to discern the Truth in Christianity and prove it. The Truth that we teach is not new; neither do we claim special revelations or discovery of new religious Principles. Our purpose is to help and teach mankind to use and prove the eternal Truth taught by the Master."* Charles Fillmore, co-founder of Unity

I am a metaphysician. Metaphysics is the study of the unseen behind the physical. It is a study of ideas and their manifestation. Metaphysicians explore: *Who or what is God? Who or what am I? What is my connection with God? And what is my purpose?* We call ourselves Truth Seekers, and look at the deeper meaning of scriptures and holy books through the literal, moral and spiritual—symbolic meaning. Jesus is my way-shower, brother, and savior. Everything He taught, whether through parables or his life, showed us a way of living that brings happiness and a strong relationship to God.

Based on this premise, the nature of God is: love, law, truth, all-good. God is omnipotent: all-powerful, omniscient: all-knowing, and omnipresent: everywhere present. God is Principle: absolute eternal and unchanging. God is Spirit, not *a spirit* as the King James Bible translations reads. God is Divine Mind the creator of all ideas.

Within each of us is a spark of divinity we call Christ. It is the same spark of divinity in Jesus Christ, who embodied His divine potential, and taught us to do the same thing. This makes us all, I repeat ALL, children of God. We, as children of God, are a Divine Idea in the mind of God, in expression. God is present in all faith groups. Our purpose it to embody and express attributes inherent within each of us as God's creation.

All means all. This is one of the ways Unity differs from the traditional church. While the drunk down the street, the prostitute or abusive husband or wife may not be expressing their divinity, Jesus taught it is there. Even those who hung on crosses next to his were promised they would be in Paradise with him that very night. This neither excuses, nor makes acceptable their behaviors. It acknowledges that within them is a greater potential awaiting expression.

Son of Man ~ Son of God: In the Bible you will notice the terms *son of man,* and *Son of God.* They both are speaking of Jesus. We are sons of man by birth, and Children of God in Spirit. The part of us we call son of man, is the part being transformed. We have the ability to discern truth from falsehood, and the connection between sin and the suffering that comes from it. It is developed as we learn to attune to God. Through observation of our lives, we can choose the behaviors that will free us from our bondage to false gods (beliefs). The Son of God, which lives within each of us, is the Christ idea in the mind of God. It is what God intended for us at creation.

Our mind is our connecting link with God. We converse with God through prayer and meditation. An analogy I like, is that prayer is like talking to God, and meditation is like listening for God to talk back to us. Our mind is pivotal. We can change its focus from God, or Spirit, to what we call *the world,* or earthly life, and concerns. False gods are in the world where they can influence us. Self-focused prayers, are prayers to ourselves, not God. A friend of mine had a timer that would go off at random times. When the timer would *ding,* she would stop and ask herself where her mind was: whether she was thinking about concerns or problems in her life, or knowing that God is in charge.

God's Commandments are Spiritual Principles, with a foundational Principle called the Law of Mind Action: the thoughts we hold in mind manifest in and as our lives. It is to keep our mind focused, uplifted to Truth Principles.

WHO OR WHAT ARE FALSE GODS?

False gods are everything God is not. They are states of mind formed through error thought of humankind. God is all-good, false gods are misperceptions of good. In the Bible, we can find two primary false gods. One is Baal, the nature god. We worship, or give worth to this false god through our carnal or lower nature. It is idolatry and includes sex and senses. The other is Mammon, or materialism. This is the worship of money and things, material riches instead of inner riches of the mind, spiritual substance, life, and intelligence behind every outer manifestation.

Many people live an imitation of life, and never experience the abundant and fulfilling life we were created to have. They may live in a big, beautiful house that isn't really a home. They may have children who excel in school or sports but hunger for the attention of their parents. They may seek perfect relationships promised by perfume or mouthwash commercials, without finding relationships with depth and meaning.

While there's nothing inherently wicked about the self and possessions, when we give them more importance than God, or all-good, it's contrary to right living. Look at it this way, the word *evil* is *live* backward. Worship of false gods stunts our spiritual growth. It blocks the pathway that leads to our return to paradise—a high state of spiritual mastery. Through the development of our spiritual faculties we are able to cocreate the abundance, serenity, security and joy we hunger for.

To believe that money and power will make us better than anyone else is not true. We are all equal in God's eyes. We are all invaluable. In fact we are richer for sharing what we have with others than accumulating money and things. We are more powerful when we serve others than when we try to make others subservient to us.

For eons, false gods have arisen, wreaked havoc, death, and destruction. Wars have been fought in a hunger for power and wealth. People have been murdered by genocide because of the color of their skin or the faith they practiced. Women have been denied rights simply because of their gender. Sex, confused with power, has been used to abuse and control.

During the Holocaust, more than six million Jews were murdered. Once that was over, we would think that humankind had learned something. But we didn't. In 1994 the Tutsi genocide in South Africa was responsible for up to a million more people being murdered during a 100 day period.

After such things happen, people become outraged, pass laws, and say *never again*. While the effects of the works of false gods are addressed, the cause was not eliminated. They may have pushed the false gods back into the dark corners of the human psyche, but did not eliminate them. In order for that to happen, we have to bring the light of Truth to the darkness of ignorance, transforming it to light. Changes come through awareness. The good news is, they are not real because they were formed by humankind, not created by God. They are not eternal. The bad news is, they can, with our help, bring immeasurable pain and suffering.

FALSE GODS AND THE ANTICHRIST

Antichrist is a term originated by the Apostle John. In the Greek translation it would be pseudo messiah. Some Christian churches see the antichrist as a personal opponent of Christ, expected to appear before the end of the world. They say the antichrist will appear and reign over the world until the overturn at Christ's second coming. Antichrist is the energy of everything opposite of Christ. This perceived embodiment of evil is called the Prince of Darkness. Christ, is the Light of the World. Jesus affirmed that we are the light of the world, and not to hide our light.

The second coming of Christ, defined in metaphysics as the awakening—coming of the light—to the mind of the soul. It is the knowledge we have the same spark of divinity that Jesus had, and fully expresses. He called us to follow him and do as he did. We each have the spark of divinity within us, so we have the power to stand against the energy we call antichrist.

False gods are aspects of antichrist. Like the false gods, antichrist is not an entity. It is thoughts, feelings, and beliefs that try to block us from expressing our spiritual power. This energy has only the power we give it. We must remember antichrist is not Truth. It will be overcome as we develop spiritually and become empowered. It's up to us. It will take work but is possible. The light of Christ casts out darkness, or the concept of antichrist. Like switching on a light, standing up to false gods or antichrist is all it takes to eliminate it.

Many politicians today are not standing against things that are harming our environment, fellow Americans and immigrants, and international relationships because they fear loss of their job or standard of living. They do not want to risk losing votes, and fear the wrath of their bosses.

IF THEY ARE FALSE GODS WHERE DO THEY GET THEIR POWER?

To answer the question of where false gods get their power, we go back to Adam and Eve, and the story of the fall of man. I invite you to look at this story not as a true story as literal interpretations do. See it as a Truth story, because within it you will find kernels of Truth—spiritual principles that are eternal, absolute and unchanging. This is a simplified version.

Here is the short version, which will be followed by the metaphysical, or spiritual interpretation:

God created the world, and the Garden of Eden. He then created from the dust, a man named Adam to till and care for the garden. He told Adam he was free to eat from every plant in the garden except the two trees in the middle of the garden, the Tree of Life, and the Tree of Knowledge of Good and Evil. God told Adam that if he were to eat from those two trees he would surely die. Feeling Adam would be unhappy being alone, God created the animals, birds, and fish and brought them to Adam, who named them all. But none of them were sufficient to be a helper to Adam, so he created a woman, named Eve.

Adam and Eve were very happy in heaven until one day when a serpent came to Eve and told her she should eat from the Tree of the Knowledge of Good and Evil. Although she told the serpent they were forbidden from eating the fruit of that tree, with a little convincing she decided to try it. It tasted good, and she took the fruit to Adam. He reminded Eve that they were not supposed to eat the fruit, yet with him also, a little convincing was all it took for him to eat the fruit.

They suddenly realized they were naked and sewed fig leaves together to cover themselves. Then they heard God coming through the garden and hid. But God called out to Adam, who responded that they were hiding because they were naked. God became very angry and asked if they had eaten from the forbidden tree. Adam confessed, but blamed Eve, who blamed the serpent.

God cursed the serpent and expelled Adam and Eve from the garden. He gave them clothing of skins and told them they were on their own, that life would be very difficult and they would have to work very hard to get food. Next he sent a cherubim, angels that serve God, to guard the tree of life with flaming swords, to prevent Adam and Eve from getting to the Tree of Life and living forever.

This story tells the beginning of what we call original sin. It is what prevents us from living lives of ease and plenty. *But what does that mean to me,* you wonder? The story of Adam and Eve and the great fall helps us to understand our own human issues and problems. Within each of us is *Adam,* the part of our mind that thinks from a purely human level. Also within each of us is *Eve,* the part of us that is ruled by human emotions. Here is the metaphysical interpretation:

Adam is the generic man, humankind epitomized in an individual-man idea. Eve is the feminine aspect of generic man. We remember, this relates to states of mind. God created Adam and Eve, who lived in Paradise, a place of higher awareness. Everything was beautiful, every need met. God gave Adam dominion over everything in his world and let him name all the creatures. It was a good and happy life. There was just one rule. They were forbidden to eat fruit from tree of the knowledge of good and evil.

Enter the serpent. In this story, the serpent represents sense consciousness and ego. The serpent brings temptation, and tells Eve if they eat the fruit of the tree, they will become like God, knowing good and evil. This is where our separation from God began. Eve, enticed by the serpent, and intoxicated the thought of being like God, eats the fruit and then brings it to Adam, convincing him eat it.

As soon as they ate the fruit, they realized they were naked, and sewed fig leaves together to cover their nakedness. God came looking for them—they hid. But you can't hide from God. When discovered, they lied. Long story short, they are banished them from Paradise. God warns them their lives will be difficult, with much suffering. Cherubim and Seraphim ordered to guard the Tree of Life, lest Adam and Eve, eat its fruit, and live forever. Before they go, God provides *garments of skins* for clothes.

The story describes the change of awareness from wholeness in God, to separation from God. They had tried to be like God, without earning the right through experience, wisdom, and understanding. I'm sure you know someone with scholastic degrees, but no wisdom. Knowledge and wisdom are not the same. The animal skin garments they wore, represent the move from spiritual to carnal, or human. Adam and Eve now have to earn for themselves the wisdom of God.

And so, here we are—living in garments of skin—yet children of God. How can we get back home? The answer is simple but not easy. Our human self loves carnal pleasures while our spiritual self is homesick for heaven. Carnal, or sensual pleasures are not in and of themselves evil. In fact they are very pleasurable—so much so that we may be tempted to misuse them, and put our personal pleasure above God and all that is good.

Sex is a good thing. Without it, none of us would be here. Like all good things however, it's not what we've got, but what we do with it that matters. We are in a culture that has demoted God, and prompted false gods, i.e. money, stuff, ego, and sensuality. I say we are in denial concerning the reality of God while worshipping false gods, aware or unaware.

Emotions and thoughts of carnal mind fuel the false gods power. Their energy is activated through the survival instinct and ego. The ego, represented earlier in the story as the serpent, presents us with a never-ending stream of stimuli. It calls us to worship or give worth to false gods, or good. We can be seduced by a piece of chocolate cake, or a sex scene in a movie. Our spiritual resolve can be weakened by a friend who wants us to join them in sinful behavior, saying *everybody is doing* it, or by provocative lyrics to a song. (See lyrics exercise at end of book)

Distraction is a major tool of false gods, because it separates us from each other, Truth, and even our true self. The distraction can range from daydreaming to romantic obsession, or a lust for personal power and status. I have seen this all too frequently in the *Disney Kids,* children who starred in Disney programs or movies. Those who choose to stay in the entertainment industry often go through a difficult time including making the transition from child star to adult performer. Lindsey Lohan, Brittany Spears and Cory Feldman are three prime examples. Sometimes they are able to work through it, others they are not.

Addiction to technology is out of control. The addiction distracts us, absorbs our time, energy, and thoughts, preventing us from lifting our minds to God, our higher good. We get lost in video games, social media, mindless television, or worse, television programming that normalizes violence, hate, promiscuity, and self-indulgence. It is difficult to find a television program that does not curry favor to the carnal nature and materialism. If you doubt what I am saying, pick up a TV Guide and read the listings. Credit card companies woo us with a promise of 0% financing, and small print with rates and rules that can cause us to go broke.

Sixty years ago, communities were tighter. Everyone knew their neighbors and looked out for them. Church, Synagogue, or Temple was central to the lives of most families. The nuclear family was stronger, and virtues of integrity and honesty valued. In those days we had less *stuff* but more of what matters. I know this because I was there. It wearies me to hear people say, *oh, things aren't really different—you just hear more about it now because of technology.* My response? *"You do not understand what you are talking about."*

The past was not perfect, but better than our current state of affairs. Our lack of knowledge of Spiritual Principle stands in the way of fixing our issues. Not all change is bad, not all technology is bad. It's not what we've got but what we do with it that matters. Our mission, should we accept it, is to re-connect with our true selves, shift the paradigms of life and its meaning. We shift from what we formed in a false belief to what is in Truth. We can participate in and strengthen our communities. While it does not matter how young or old one is, those of us who knew the simpler, more secure life have much to share, we can lead through experience, inspired and encouraged by the brilliance of today's awakened youth.

A wonderful thing that emerged right behind the false gods is activism. More people are getting involved than ever before. We've marched together in the Woman's March and the March for Our Lives. Each one of us has a passion. This is one of the best gifts Spirit has given us. Follow your passion. Maybe it is for clean water or growing organic vegetables, or supporting those who do. Ask: *What would you have me do, God? Where would you have me go? What would you have me say?* When we earnestly ask, we will receive our answer.

Several years ago, I connected with a young man in The Gambia, West Africa. When he sent his first friend request I was very cautious. I did not want to wind up a victim of some Nigerian type scheme. We communicated for about four years, sharing stories of our lives, both ups and downs. From time to time I would send him a Unity book, or one time I sent him a Bible. I tucked $20 into the Bible. It was not requested. A year ago, I made the decision to help him complete a computer training program. I did not do this lightly or without much thought and prayer. It's important that you understand this is not something I could do without a degree of sacrifice. Because of the exchange rate, it was not outrageously expensive, either.

Sometimes, just reaching one person can make the world of difference. Whether you are helping a homeless person on the street, or someone across the globe, these are the things we were born do to as a part of our oneness in Spirit.

THE HIERARCHY OF FALSE GODS

A hierarchy is a group that controls an organization. It has levels, based on importance of role. Those in higher positions have more power than those below them. Ranking in a healthy hierarchy is determined by education, experience, the ability to set and achieve goals for the common good. Hierarchies are present in governments, businesses, and churches, and countless organizations, including families. Hierarchy can be positive or negative, depending on the awareness people involved. A positive hierarchy focuses on the highest good of the whole. This includes the organization, leadership, and people who take part.

Unity teaches, *life is consciousness.* Consciousness is a state of being—awareness of one's own existence, sensations, thoughts, surroundings, and circumstances. Through conscious awareness, we are able to discern Truth from illusion or falsehood. We can then live on purpose, aware of the consequences of our thoughts, words, and actions.

The hierarchy of the whole—the business, government, church, etc. expresses the collective state of mind of the members of the whole. Whatever the opinion or belief a majority of people hold, on the level of human awareness, predicts the outcome. This is called, *by right of consciousness.*

Does this mean we're helpless—doomed to the gravitational pull of carnal mind? Not at all. Divine Mind will overcome because it is Truth. First, we have to dethrone the false gods, and dissolve their power. This will take time, effort, and strength. It takes faith, and we already have that.

Our founding fathers vision for the United States was a government that worked for all people, who would share life, liberty, and the pursuit of happiness. To function, we must each participate. The vision has fallen by the wayside. Many people have abdicated their responsibility, relinquishing their power to elected officials. Without active participation by the people, elected officials become vulnerable to the power of false gods. Many politicians have traded the responsibility we entrusted them with for personal power and financial gain.

As discrepancies and questions emerge and negative consequences manifest, the grip of false gods has tightened. Fear of losing face or power is so intimidating, it causes moral paralysis for many elected officials.

To the delight of false gods, we are now teeter-tottering between anarchy and authoritarianism. The political relationships have degenerated from cooperative to adversarial. We are not the ideal government Lincoln spoke of in the Gettysburg Address, *a government of, by, and for the people.* This is our own doing. When we put self above the whole, we are living contrary to the Divine Plan of God, Spirit, The Great Spirit, Allah, or whatever name we call the higher power.

This is my take on how hierarchy functions in the typical Christian church: the hierarchy has, at the top, God/Jesus. Followed by the Pope/Monarchy, Bishops, Priests—which have their own ranking, and Deacons. Even the church can fall under the spell of false gods if ego and greed take control. Consider the Crusades, Inquisition, and the terrorism that plagues our world today. To terrorize in the name of God, is an ultimate separation contrary to the Truth of our unity. In the traditional church the hierarchy dictates behavior of the followers who blindly go along because of the leader's perceived authority. Therefore they don't mature spiritually. It's a matter of ignorance vs enlightenment. It was Jesus' intention to enlighten and empower all people to follow his example. Not only did he teach this, but that we could do even greater things.

This is my perception of the hierarchy of false gods:

Antichrist: The hierarchy of false gods has at the top, what we call the Antichrist. It is a core false idea composed of everything contrary to the inseparable connection to God and each other we are in Truth.

Ego: The false-self in its extreme form, or narcissism. It's a state of mind that sees self as a power unto itself, with no limits, rules, or consideration for others. It worships, or gives worth to the carnal man. The patron saints of ego are celebrities, which serve as idols to worshippers, on which they model their lives.

Faux Popes and Monarchs—Gurus of Self-Centered, Antichrist Dogma: These are voices of pseudo-authority. They tell us what we must have to be happy. For a price, they operate workshops and retreats of little substance. The claims and promises they make are lies. What they say or do may trouble us at first, but it's easy for them to seduce us with the lure of pleasure over happiness and self over others. The subtle ways and means they use can dull our sensitivity to its sinister nature. Spiritual Principle however, remains active. We stumble around, chasing the next emotional or physical high, insatiable, and miserable. I understand that these are strong words that may feel negative. But they are also a powerful wake-up call when we are in under the influence of false gods.

PROPHETS OF THE FALSE GODS

A prophet is one who speaks for God—Spirit, or by divine inspiration. In religions of the past, the prophets stood between the people and God. Today that's still true for many churches. It was through them that the people received their guidance. Today, people still seek gurus, prophets, etc. for guidance. As long as they develop their own relationship with God, this idea fine and can edify and inspire. But without uplifting their own consciousness they might fall prey to false prophets.

False prophets, or prophets of the false gods are deceptive thoughts built up by error, or selfish desires. They are the rationalizations—rational-lies we tell ourselves, or hear and decide to believe. They allow us to live under the illusion we can find a loophole in spiritual law. False prophets appeal to what we want to be true, not what is true. The Lord, or Principle, will not be fooled. We will reap what we sow. We, the citizens of the United States, are reaping the effects of our own mistakes. Yes, the false gods led us, but we let them.

Propaganda, lies of false prophets, permeated the 2016 Presidential Election. Disinformation and lies flooded news reports. Social media spread the lies, much of it coming from *bots:* fake accounts which claim to be real people, able to produce more than1000 fake posts a day. American people have been manipulated by this deception. Meanwhile, the deceivers and hackers declared factual items as fake. Many people chose to believe this rather than determine if it was true. The problem with this is it succeeded. People chose what they wanted to believe without question.

The Money Changers: The hunger for money, power, and ego support the hierarchy. Our money lines the pockets of Mammon and Baal. The money changers provide products, services, and pleasures that draw us deeper into self-absorption, further from our true self and connection with the whole. We no longer want to *keep up with the Joneses,* we want to surpass them. It's all an illusion. They promise us adoration and opulence, flattering our ego, if we buy what they have to sell. The providers are also under an illusion that this will make them rich, powerful and happy. It may make them wealthy, but it will never make them rich. Money changers have no interest in what the true needs of the people are. The levels of hierarchy are many, but the message is the same: Self is all that matters. What matters is: what *I* want, what *I* crave, what *I* wish *I* had regardless of consequences.

As I have been writing this book, there has been a need to revise almost daily to keep up with the hijinks and atrocities. Protections for clean water and air have been removed, including allowing mining companies to dump their waste into our waterways. Provisions to protect us from gun violence have been overturned, including open-carry allowances across state lines. Most recently a trade war that has brought the stock market crashing down. Unconscionable changes to our immigration programs are denying the human rights and protections that once truly did make America great. Add to that the fact that we are at increasing risk for nuclear war and one can see how many are escaping their fear and frustration with drugs and alcohol. We also have to question a general sense of hopelessness and apathy and the increasing suicide rate.

The true battle lies within each of us. We have the power to live under the rule of Spirit, or bow down to the false gods. To choose Spirit instead of demons, we enlist conscious awareness, as Unity teaches *life is consciousness.* This is the difference between rolling along with whatever happens or taking action. We have to ask ourselves with every thought, word and action: *what will be the fruit of this seed I am planting?* Learn to consider effects of the cause you are about to send forth—the action you are about to take.

Scripture tells us that the Truth is within us, and we will know the Truth, which will set us free. There is a moral compass inside of each of us. My mother would say a *niggling* feeling inside, which means an almost unnoticeable sensation. But it is there, if we pay attention. Next time you feel that little flutter of warning stop. Ask yourself if the thought, word, or action you are about to express is right. A favorite scripture of mine is: *"Put thou a guard before my lips, o God."* (PS 141) You can guess from that where my greatest problems lie.

A CONFESSION: I am opening my heart now, to expose a very painful part of my journey. It shows how false gods show up in our lives. For almost 40 years I lived under the influence of false gods. While I was both a spiritual and religious person who followed the rules, I also lived under the illusion I could manipulate my fate, or God. I was more of a beggar and deal maker who would not accept *no* as an answer. I started with begging prayer, and if that didn't work I'd take whatever action I could to get what I wanted on my own. This never works. It may seem to work for a while, but it doesn't—and it didn't for me!

Let me explain: I always wanted to be a wife and mother. That was my inner desire. I was under the delusion created by our cultural expectations and reinforced by romantic music and movies, if I did not marry I was flawed. My desire to marry and have a family comes from Spirit. My anxiety about not being married comes from ego. When God did not fulfill my desire in the (my) allotted time frame I took action. I married the first man who asked me. It took seventeen years of suffering to realize my error. I knew nothing I could do would change it. I worked diligently to be a good wife. I read every book, tried every magazine article and catered to his whims. Nothing worked. Nothing was good enough.

One of the most painful parts, was that every night without fail, I prayed for my marriage. This was my prayer: *"Heavenly Father up above, please protect our married love. Teach us to love and help us to stay happy and healthy together I pray."* One would think it should have worked, no? It didn't. It couldn't, because it was not a God-ordained marriage, but a human choice. In the beginning I was angry with God. After all, I had prayed every night.

It took two failed marriages and a number of unpleasant relationships for me to see that my own expectations and error thinking were drawing this to me, not as punishment, but opportunities to learn and grow. Which I did. Which took quite a long time because I tend to be stubborn. I surrender my errors more willingly now, and find I am stronger and happier for it.

What I didn't know back then, is that our prayers are not a means of changing God. Their purpose is to bring us closer to God. That may mean we need to change the way we think or act. Today, I may pray for a specific outcome, but always add, *this or something better,* because God knows what is right for me better than I do. As my relationship to God grows, I can clearly see that prayer is not about changing God, or getting my way. It is about asking God, and being willing to change if necessary.

In the past, I let the hierarchy of self-worth-ship determine my worth, based on the approval of others. As insane as that sounds, it was true for me. I threw myself into one unhealthy relationship after another, insecure and codependent. It took decades to learn I was wrong. My thoughts were Illusion and clinging to the illusion brought me nothing but pain. It took years to heal because of the grip the false gods held on my carnal mind. My illusions were supported by romantic movies, music, and a culture of romance.

Here's a *good news-bad news* tidbit. I consider myself to have a very strong mind. I have the ability to figure things out, solve puzzles, write great stories, counsel others, and such. I have great self-discipline, and heck…I belong to Mensa for crying out loud. *How,* I so often asked God, *could I make so many mistakes? Why can't I get past this?* The problem, it turns out, is the same as the gift. A strong mind can also be very resistant. This is where it is imperative to consciously determine whether I am being influenced by Principle, or personality.

An affirmation that helps me during these times is: *My mind is one with the all-knowing mind of God. I think clearly, and make right decisions.* The words alone are not what empower an affirmation. It is the combination of thought plus feeling. Say the words. Feel the words. Try it!

FALSE GODS ~ ARE YOU UNDER THE INFLUENCE?

Influence: power or effect something or someone has. The root of the word is in-flowing, like water. Speaking metaphysically, manifestation originates in mind, through thoughts and ideas. The quality of the thought determines the quality of the manifestation.

To Inspire, means to guide or control by the divine. In = within, spire = spirit, means: received by Spirit. Influence comes from carnal mind, Inspiration comes from God—Spirit. The word spirit means breath.

Review the diagram below:

THE FOUR QUADRANTS OF CONSCIOUSNESS

Spiritual	Spiritual
Higher Mind	Higher Mind
Intuitive	Sensing
Carnal	**Carnal**
Lower Mind	Lower Mind
Thinking - Thoughts	Feeling - Emotions

The top two boxes represent higher consciousness, which receives inspiration from Spirit, or Divine Mind. The bottom boxes represent lower consciousness, which is influenced by the world or human thoughts and emotions. Because of the pivotal nature of the mind, and free will, we choose to focus through higher or lower consciousness. Our awareness of this helps us to decide whether we are being inspired by Spirit or influenced by our mortal mind.

To achieve Spiritual Mastery, our goal is to live in higher consciousness at all times. While this is a major part of Jesus teaching, being in the world but not of it, this is easier said than done, because it requires time and effort as well as change. While we are all Children of God, i.e. Spiritual Beings, at the same time we are living in a physical body—in a manifest world. When we are operating in higher mind, we are expressing as a spiritual being having a human experience. When we are operating from the lower mind, we are a human being having a spiritual experience. Higher mind is serene, orderly, and placid, while sense mind is turbulent, discordant, and violent.

I like to look at this from the perspective of training a dog. The dog represents our animal nature. Yes, physically we are animals. We have many of the survival instincts of animals. It is the job of our spiritual self to train the animal self. Dogs are trained by the person who becomes the *Alpha*. It is the one they obey. In the Book of Revelation, Jesus says: *"I am the Alpha and the Omega,"* which means the beginning and the end. We can also look at this like the perfect working of both our human and spiritual natures.

To live under the guidance of higher mind does not mean our troubles will disappear. It does mean we will respond rather than react. Even in the worst of circumstances we will be able to connect to spiritual strength beyond the human level. When we make a practice of learning and practicing a God/Spirit/Principle-centered life it is like having a spiritual bank account to draw from that will carry us through life's challenges. This is the difference between being a victim, and a victor.

Thoughts and feelings are contagious. We can *catch* them from anyone or anything we see or hear. We respond to the vibration of their words. Our response depends on where our focus is. If we are operating from the lower, carnal quadrants we will react with emotion or feel threatened. When we come from the higher, spiritual quadrants, we respond with discernment. Ponder these words: react and respond. From higher mind, we respond to carnal thoughts with rejection. The lower vibrations will repel us.

Building relationships with people of like mind supports us. We should avoid those stuck in carnal mind. Some people call carnal mind the *mind of the flesh* because it seeks satisfaction of the senses and self above qualities such as integrity, Truth, commitment. Our intention is not to eliminate sense-consciousness, only to realize its place in our lives.

Consider gravity. Without it, we'd just float away. Yet if we see it through a metaphysical lens, attachment to earth—the manifest realm—gravity prevents us from rising to the spiritual. While we may come to the earthly realm with knowledge of a spiritual reality, over time we forget, due to a constant influx of mortal thoughts, feelings, and beliefs. Our goal is to overcome control by these errors, so they can serve us in living our spiritual reality.

There is an old saying, *"Angels can fly because they take themselves lightly."* By following Jesus' teaching to lift our spiritual eyes, the way we see things, we can shift from a lower to a higher state of mind, which impact the world. Jesus taught this when He said: *As I am lifted, I shall lift all others to me.* When we uplift our own minds and hearts, we inspire others to higher consciousness.

Mastery in any field takes time, work, and effort. The influence of lower mind can be compelling. This is true with spiritual mastery. To strive for excellence is inconvenient and uncomfortable. Self-discipline is not fun, but the rewards are invaluable. Imagine, manifesting the Kingdom of Heaven—all good right here on earth! We can do it, and live a life of peace, abundance, laughter and every good thing.

In your quest for Mastery, you will face, and overcome the illusion of antichrist energy. Have no fear. There is only One presence and One power in the universe, and in our lives, God—the good—Omnipotent. To face Antichrist consciousness, we must be able to recognize it. This is easy because it's everything unlike Christ.

A QUESTION OF EVIL

The word *evil* can strike terror in the heart. It brings images of a horned ugly demon wielding a pitchfork lurking in dark corners, ready to strike, tossing hapless souls into a hell of eternal damnation. We don't have to search very hard to find evil. False gods are thoughts and feelings contrary to goodness, and God. They don't have horns and pitchforks. Instead, they have a charismatic, magnetic draw. Instead of feeling fearful in the face of evil, we are drawn by an inviting façade.

Although Unity's cofounder, Charles Fillmore, had no problem with the word evil, based on a metaphysical understanding, many people in Unity today avoid the word, preferring to use *error*. As with the word *sin*, they take it personally, as if it defined them. This is putting personality before Principle. While we may have done wrong things, we are still Children of God, so inherently good. Evil is a parasite and a phantom. Evil is error, but using that definition in place of its true name, *evil* diminishes the impact it can have on our lives. It softens the image and downplays the need to address it.

It is irresponsible and unkind, to deny what is evil expressing. In Unity, we teach, and believe, that when we transform our mind, evil will disappear as darkness vanishes when exposed to light. We do not deny an experience of evil, but we do not give it power to wreck our lives. We strive to do the work to bring ourselves to a state of spiritual mastery.

When we enter a dark room, we turn on a light. Light fills the room. Where did the dark go? Dark does not exist, only the absence of light. When we expose ignorance to the light of Truth—knowledge and wisdom, the ignorance vanishes.

It is the fallen consciousness, the carnal/animal nature that formed the concept of evil. It is how we explain why we suffer. We place blame rather than consider we have any part in our suffering. The accusation can be placed on a perpetrator, the devil, or even God. We don't want to consider the possibility that our suffering results from our own erroneous thoughts, words, feelings, and actions. We call things evil, which are not. Dandelions for instance. To us, they're a nuisance and a weed. To bees, they are a wonderful source of food. We put poison on the dandelions. The poison kills the dandelions, eliminating a source of food for the bees, and even the bees themselves. Where can we place blame? We often name people from other faiths, races, or cultures evil, because we don't understand them.

Take a new look at the word evil, if we spell it backward, we have *live*. Evil is living backward. Likewise, the word *devil,* becomes *lived* when spelled backward. Instead of having any substance of its own, it's an effect, a symptom of being out of harmony with Principle. It is my intention to help you understand, not to diminish the size of suffering caused by evil. With a new understanding, fear surrounding evil is overcome. There's only one way to overcome evil. We overcome evil with good.

While some experiences of evil may have catastrophic consequences, others, like what we call a white lie, have little visible effect. But the evil there. Evil is evil. Candy coat it, but beneath the candy is still evil. To achieve spiritual mastery, we must overcome evil. To overcome, we must first acknowledge it. Many evil things are being normalized today. This is a very dangerous situation. Cause and effect are non-negotiable. When harmful behaviors become normalized in the minds of people, it does not exempt them. It only blinds us to the reality of the causes, which will grow.

Evil is present in our world, not as truth, but a current reality. Reality can change, truth is absolute, eternal and unchanging. Remember, everything God created is good. We, ourselves, brought about the effects of evil through seeing the manifest realm as our reality, seeking personal power, and falling under the control of false gods. Jesus said, *"I have said this to you, that in me you will have peace. In this world you will have tribulation, but be of good cheer, I have overcome the world."* (John. 16:33)

As I have observed the crisis of gun violence in the United States, and the ever increasing number of murders and mass murders happening, I have a grave concern. The concern is not just the unnecessary deaths, but our failure to address the crisis. Instead of addressing the cause, we have a knee-jerk reaction calling for more guns. Others cry out for the elimination of guns. Neither will solve the problem, because it is not about guns, it is about consciousness.

I have no use for guns. Yet I don't deny the right of others, like hunters, to have guns. Even those who believe a gun will bring them security. One does not need an arsenal, nor automatic, semi-automatic weapons, or bump stocks for self-protection. As gun lovers demand their so-called second-amendment rights, the death toll soars. It will continue to rise, until we address causes, and not effects.

Jesus taught the heart or understanding of the law. Before Jesus' teaching, people followed the letter of the law; as interpreted literally. The letter of the law is what, and the heart, why. The letter of the law says we must rest one day of the week. The heart of the law agrees, understanding that sometimes an immediate need arises. This is not a matter of either/or, but this/and. Jesus taught we are in the world but not of it. Refer back to the quadrants of consciousness. The lower quadrants represent in the world and of it, the upper quadrants, in the world not of it. Once we comprehend the spiritual meaning of the Commandments, the struggle will end.

THE CRUX OF THE MATTER

"Hence, there shall be such a oneness among you, that when one weeps the other will taste salt."
Old Jewish Saying

We are One. One with God, One with each other, One with the planet, One with creation, and I expect One with the many expressions of God in our unlimited universe. Anything contrary to our Oneness and that does not strive toward its expression works against God's plan for the creation of a literal heaven on earth. This is a radical idea for some. Yet it is absolutely true. The Divine Idea lives in our souls. Why, then can't we express it?

I know why. I am going to share the answer with you. You may find some of my comments offensive *if* you take them personally. If you find yourself of wanting to yell at me and tear up the book, please take a deep breath, and say to yourself: *It's Principle, not personal.* Please wait until after you've reached the end of the book to tear it up. You may find a little 'aha' here or there.

Our world today is in a state of crisis brought on by worship of false gods. We teeter-totter on the verge of oblivion as nuclear threats, global warming, and pollution threaten the planet. Mother Earth blesses us with food, clothing, shelter, and the air we breathe—yet she struggles more each day to provide these things, as she is depleted by our self-centered appetites.

Then there's the matter of gun violence, addiction, divorce, bullying, crime, I could go on, but for brevity's sake, will not. It's easy to just point the finger of blame at God, or *them,* whoever *they* may be, or we can blame it on big business, multinational corporations, globalization and the government. Blame will do nothing. One thing that will help is enlightenment. This is the attainment of wisdom through knowledge and understanding; it is the light that eliminates the shadows of all that is not true. Enlightenment comes through knowledge and application of Spiritual Principle in our lives.

Within each crisis in our lives, we will find both danger, and opportunity. If we see only danger, we will fight, flee, or freeze, and solve nothing. We must seek, instead, the opportunity to bring light to the situation. The light comes from knowledge, wisdom, and understanding of Spiritual Principle. The crisis is real. It is imbedded in our personal mind and the collective—the combined consciousness of all people. We must not drag our feet on this one.

Many declare Jesus is coming back; it's the second coming, as foretold in the Bible. Jesus did say *"I will come again and take you with me,"* (John 14) but what if he came back and took us with him? With our current state of mind, the beliefs we hold, and false gods we worship, what would happen next? We'd be in trouble in no time. This is why God expelled Adam and Eve from Paradise. We must transform ourselves, mind and heart, be redeemed, and break the grip false gods have on us. We must come to know our enemy, even if it is an illusion.

The *enemy* is the thoughts, feelings, beliefs, and actions that deny our Oneness. Instead of living as we were created, in God's image and likeness, we become our own gods, creating God in our image and likeness. Here in America, we love to celebrate Independence Day. While it's good to be free from the countries our forefathers fled, we still need each other. Our freedom does not make us better than anyone else, or they better than us. The perception of power is measured in weaponry, or money. These are not a measure of who we are. We have become arrogant while we claim to be patriotic. The false pride we tout, all the hoo-hah, is a lie because in Truth we are interdependent, we must depend on each other. Separation is death, Community is life. War will never bring peace. Violence breeds violence.

I feel I should note at this point, regarding violence and war. After a deadly shooting, we frequently hear that the shooter was suffering from PTSD. If that is not proof that people are not meant to make war, I don't know what is. This is another case of getting to root cause.

Separation or isolation is contrary to Divine Law. This does not mean being homogenized into an inconsequential glob. Oneness in diversity, is like the diversity of the organs of our physical body. Each organ expresses its individuality while supporting the whole body. Likewise, we are each individualized expressions of the allness of God. I have always loved Disney's *Small World* ride. As the boat floats through the ride, we see scenes from around the globe. Figures of people in cultural attire, smiling and singing as they go about their daily chores, waving. Walt Disney knew. He understood. Somewhere deep within each of us, I think we know. We know that we are connected by love, appreciation, and oneness in Spirit.

In America we have declared separation of church and state. This is a confusing and convoluted issue. The polar opposite has run through civilizations for thousands of years. Kings have been likened to gods, as have Pharaohs, and conquerors. One reason many people came to America was to seek religious freedom rather than being subject to a religion run by the ruler of the government. Likewise, the general population did not want a religious figure running the government.

To achieve a high level of spiritual understanding, we will have to comprehend the paradox. A paradox is: a self-contradictory proposition, or a person or thing exhibiting what appears as contradictory characteristics. Example: *The only thing that never changes, is change.* What we may see may not be as it appears. We tend to think *this or that*, about something, but it is really *this and that.* Everything is not a matter of black or white, it is a matter of black, gray, white. Jesus frequently addressed paradoxes. You may wonder, *how can two opposite things be true?*

Consider Jesus' teaching on the Sabbath. Religious leaders chastised His disciples because they were hungry and picked grain on the day of rest. This was illegal by Hebrew precept. Jesus challenged them, saying the Sabbath was made for man, not man for the Sabbath. On another occasion, Pharisees tried to catch him breaking the Law by healing a man on the Sabbath. In the second case he asked them, if their child or ox fell in a well on the Sabbath, would they rescue it? He taught them it is lawful to do good things on the Sabbath.

He did not negate the Law. We benefit when we rest, renew and focus on God one day a week. We become happier and healthier when we do this—more positive. There are also times we need to take action. Both statements are true. And, in Truth, we cannot separate church—or religion—and state, any more than we could separate our heart and body.

Many years ago, I was a participant in the Dale Carnegie Course. In the fifteen-week duration of the course, leaders give participants topics. Each participant prepares a two minute talk on that topic to present the following week. The first night I pigeon-holed every one of the other participants, categorizing them by ones I liked, ones I did not like, and such. This is a very human behavior. It is a part of our survival instinct. As we mature, it transforms from judgment to discernment. At the end of the course, we enjoyed a wine and cheese party following the last gathering. It was then I realized I'd fallen in love twenty-five times, because each week I learned a little more about my classmates. Through two minutes of sharing each week, l learned volumes. If we can learn about each other, and find what we agree on—common ground—or how we are alike, we will appreciate our Oneness. And our diversity.

I urge you to develop and expand relationships with others. Consider the possibility of starting a *Conversation Café* in your area, with the purpose of simply getting to know and understand others, making meaningful connections. For more information, check out: http://www.conversationcafe.org/

PART TWO ~ SIN

THE TRUTH ABOUT SIN

The Unity definition of sin is: *"Missing the mark, falling short of perfection. Sin is man's failure to express the attributes of Being: life, love, intelligence, wisdom, and the other God qualities." The Revealing Word* by Charles Fillmore

The word *sin,* comes with feelings of guilt, fear, and shame. It brings images of God's wrath, and condemnation to hell, suffering for eternity in a prison of fire and brimstone. A simple definition of the word, sin is *a transgression of God's Law.* Scripture is jam-packed with demands. We find more demands as we read. It may seem to be a good idea to stay in bed to avoid getting into trouble. Oh—wait, that would be the sin of laziness.

It's said, that there are six-hundred-thirteen laws in the Torah, the Hebrew Bible, alone. I have a theory about this, based on the average person's understanding. As God observed the people he created, he noticed that they were experiencing and causing much pain and suffering by not leading good lives. He realized, while He knew of the workings of Principle; they did not. So he called Moses to him, and sent him to the top of Mt. Sinai where he received the Law. He returned with the Ten Commandments. When he came back down, the people, who had given up on Moses returning, had melted their gold to make an idol, a golden calf which they worshiped. When Moses saw them, he then threw the tablets down in a rage, and they broke.

The people salvaged the tablets and committed to live according to the Commandments. Over time, they started nit-picking the words. They split hairs regarding what the words meant. They looked for loopholes. The phrase, *yeah but,* sums up what was happening. So the laws grew to include sub-laws and amendments, until one day there were six-hundred-thirteen.

Observing this, I'm sure God wondered: *What have they done? They've complicated everything. There must be a better way.* So he sent Jesus to simplify everything. Jesus brought us two Commandments: *"You shall love the Lord your God with all your heart, and with all your soul, and with all your mind. This is the first and great commandment. And the second is like it; you shall love your neighbor as yourself."* (Matthew 22:37)

Over time, as we humans do, we changed that simple teaching, expanding it to where the Bible has sixty-six books, chock-full of thou-shalts and thou-shalt-nots. Church leaders disagreed and other denominations emerged. Each with its own commandments and sins. Thou can hardly get out of thy bed in the morning without thee sinning!

Why? False gods were afoot. People questioned the laws; they looked for loopholes that would allow them to satisfy their own wants while remaining *holy* according to authorities. Others used the edicts to control the masses. One reason was their own quest for power, another under the belief they could control others to come into alignment with what they believed. Goodness, or holiness cannot be forced from the outside. It is an inside job. We are saved through transformation, not conversion.

Today, because of the negative feelings it brings, we don't want to discuss sin. The minister may preach on sin in church, but is what we hear the truth, the absolute truth, and nothing but the truth? Maybe, maybe not. If sin is a transgression of God's law, then it would behoove us to know which one we're breaking. That way we'd be able to understand it and not make the same mistake twice.

Consider this point of view: Moses brought the letter of the law. The people were to follow it. Understanding was not required.

Jesus brought the heart of the law, the understanding, removing the desire to break it. Divine Law cannot be broken. It's a matter of cause and effect. You send forth a cause; you receive an effect—eat a whole package of cookies (cause) and get a stomach ache (effect). Continue that behavior and you will become sick and could die. I find it interesting that eating sugar creates a craving for more, which makes it harder to stop eating.

Many people misunderstand sin, and believe God is punishing them, when the law is working as it should. When you eat a whole package of cookies, you are putting your health at risk. Your body is sending you signals when you get sick, so you can alter your behavior. There is no judgment although we do judge ourselves and others. This metaphor can apply to every known *sin*.

Unity teaches this about sin: Sin (error). It begins in mind, and is redeemed by a mental process, or by going into the silence. We bring our error into the light of Spirit and then transform it into a constructive force. Unity also teaches that sin is the negation of a Divine Idea. For example, love is a Divine Idea, a Principle, so if we try to negate love with judgment and hatred, it is a sin. But if we release our judgment and hatred, we are redeemed. The love never changed, only our experience changed.

SIN, SIN, AND MORE SIN!

In Unity, which is my primary spiritual path, many people don't like to use the word *sin*. Most likely it's because people have experienced condemnation from their religion of origin. The church told them they are sinners, worms of the dust, and unworthy. I believe to do that is wrong because it denies we are all children of God.

When we live in a way contrary to the Commandments, we sin—we make an error in judgement. We then face the consequences. Sin is evil, we think. We don't want to say we're sinners because it makes us feel shame and guilt, when all sin really is making an error. How could a child of God be bad? We were created by God, weren't we?

NAME THAT SIN

The word name means, nature of. There are many names for, or varieties of sin, but without exception, an adverse action will receive an adverse reaction in kind according to the Law of Cause and Effect. If the behavior does not change, the effects will get worse. This is through the Law of Increase. If we have a bank account and put money in it, the money will grow by accumulating interest. In our lives, we have a mental storehouse: whatever we put in it grows according to the interest (attention) it receives. Everything we send out comes back multiplied. It's just the way it works. This is something to consider before taking questionable actions, contrary to God's law.

Two ways to identify a sin are: 1. It causes useless and unnecessary suffering and 2. It negates a Divine Idea. Prosperity, is a Divine Idea. To take someone else's prosperity negates that Divine Idea.

THE BIG TEN
A look at the Ten Commandments

The following is a list of the commandments in their scriptural context. They are presented in abbreviated form. We will look at them from the literal and moral interpretation and a spiritual or metaphysical perception. This will bring a deeper, spiritual understanding to the literal, and moral law.

Earlier, I stated that Moses brought the letter of the law, and Jesus brought the heart. The letter is the written word, the law itself, and the heart is the spiritual understanding. We recall, the letter is the what, and the heart, the why. I will keep my explanation short and simple. Unity has many resources for Bible interpretation. There is a resource list at the back of this book for further exploration.

I AM the Lord your God, who brought you out of the land of Egypt, out of bondage. These Commandments are addressed to the Hebrew people, freed from bondage in Egypt. It applies to everyone because everyone is in bondage to something. The basic interpretation tells us that there is a power greater than our carnal (human) selves, who has the power to help us break free from bondage. Here is a metaphysical perspective:

I AM, is a statement of being. It refers both to God, and each of us as Children of God. While we are Children of God, we are not the all-ness of God. Just as our children are not the all-ness of us. I AM is the metaphysical name of the spiritual self as distinguished from the human self.

The Lord your God: shows that God is Lord, or Law, and our God, or good. In Unity we teach that there is only One presence and One power in the Universe and in our lives, God, the good, omnipotent. God is good as is the law. The laws, or Principles are intended for our good, to assure us good.

Who brought you out of the land of Egypt: The Israelites were in bondage in Egypt. They could not escape their bond-holders. In metaphysical interpretation, Egypt symbolizes mental bondage to sense thoughts and material consciousness, aka Mammon and Baal.

Out of bondage. It was the desire of the Israelites to break free of this bondage that caused them to turn to God. We can benefit by asking ourselves what we are in bondage to. It could be pride, wealth, power, sexual prowess, etc. Or it could be fear of failure, lack, or rejection. As we turn our focus to the Lord—Law, God—which is good, we can change the thoughts and feelings that bind us, and find our higher good.

You shall have no strange gods before me. You shall not make a graven image. We look to God alone for our good. The false gods may make us promises, but they are lies and deception.

You shall have no strange gods before me. A strange god is anything we think of as a god that is not godly, or in agreement with Principle. It would be a false good. Sometimes we make money our god, or sex, or power—variations of false good.

You shall not make a graven image: A graven image is a material, or mental idol, representing a false god, or sense of good. It could be a person, thought or thing we give false worth to. A celebrity could be a graven image, jewelry, or self-centered obsession with our own body. When we are busy worshipping, by giving worth to material and self-indulgent things, the Law of Mind Action is still engaged, and will draw to us the things we focus on. That includes fears, wrong relationships, and even illness. We worship only good.

You shall not take the name of the Lord, your God, in vain. The common interpretation of this, is that we should not cuss, using the name of God, or Jesus in the Christian faith. But it's much bigger than that.

You shall not take the name… In metaphysical interpretation, the word *name*, means *the nature of*. The nature of God is good, including attributes identified earlier. Therefore, reference to any connection of the word, name, or nature of God in a negative way, is erroneous, or sinful. The cause sent forth with our words, will bring negative effects. A common misuse of the name of God is saying *God damn you!* First, God will damn no one. Because Oneness is the truth of our being, if God damned someone, we would also be damned because we are all connected. It would be like blowing up your own foot due to an ingrown toenail.

In Vain… Word *vain*, means *falsely, or to no avail*. Because God is all-good, it would be useless to use God's name without thought to associate it with something not good. When Moses asked what God's name was, God responded, "I AM." The essence of God is Being—I AM. As Children of God, having the essence of God within us, to connect the I AM with something negative, is sinful. Our words, thoughts, and actions must align with good. We cannot go around saying, I AM a Child of God, while acting like the spawn of Satan. We must be accountable and consistent in connecting God, and our own essence in a positive way.

In our tendency to alter words and laws to our own liking, we have diminished the gravity of this error. It is common for people to letting it fly in written and spoken word as, *goddamnit*. But even if we try to beautify a pig with lipstick, it's still a pig, and a sin, is still a sin. When we blame God, or threaten others with fear of God, we are taking the name, the nature of God falsely.

Remember the Sabbath day, to keep it holy. Six days you shall labor and do all your work; but the seventh day is a Sabbath to the Lord your God, in it you shall not do any work

Remember the Sabbath day, to keep it holy. The word *Sabbath* means *rest,* and the word *Holy* means whole, in body, mind, and Spirit. We are required to take one day to rest, connect with God, and release our concerns.

Six days you shall labor and do all your work. We may not believe it, but we can get all of our work accomplished in six days. I know, that gets your hackles up, declaring this as an impossibility. To which I reply, If God can do it, so can we.

The seventh day is a Sabbath to the Lord, your God, in it you shall not do any work. I can't imagine everyone deciding to give an entire day to rest, reflection and relaxation, though I think we'd all benefit from it. Instead, let's consider another perspective of its meaning. We have become, especially in America, a nation of driven over-achievers, running nonstop, 24/7/365. We erroneously believe it's up to us to be, do, and have it all. Many parents are indoctrinating their children to this dogma of the false gods, believing there is never enough. How true the scripture is that the sins (errors) of the fathers are passed on to their children for four generations! The most important part of Sabbath is releasing everything to God. This is where we have faith we've done our part, and trust God for divine order, and our highest good to manifest.

The image many of us have regarding the Sabbath is one of kneeling in church for hours. Or listening to a minister drone on with a boring, depressing message about our sins. Instead, imagine a world where people practiced keeping the Sabbath. On one day a week, everyone would spend the day at ease, maybe resting and becoming renewed from the previous week, and for the coming week. There would be no pressure, but plenty of time for reflection, to connect with family, pray and give thanks. It provides time to mend fences and hearts. It would be a time to worship with like-minded others, receiving inspiration—a spiritual transfusion. Can you imagine it? Ask yourself what that would look like. Consider the possibility that not practicing the Sabbath keeps us in bondage to false gods. We chase our error beliefs where money and power represent good. Or we choose pleasure instead of happiness, not trusting the Principles we practice. Note the Sabbath exercise at the back of this book.

Honor your father and your mother that your days may be long in the land which the Lord your God gives you.

Honor your father and your mother: On the literal level we should honor our father and mother by treating them with respect. As children, our parents were gods to us. We saw them as wise, rich and powerful. As we grew, we see they are fallible human beings, just as we are. They did the best they could with what they had. But we are looking deeper.

On the metaphysical plane, *father* represents the inherited thinking faculty, and mother the inherited feeling faculty. It includes not what we learned from our parents alone, but what we brought with us at birth. To honor is to give regard for. Whether our parents were perfect, or imperfect, we look to see what we can learn from them. Some parents provide a role model of how to be a good parent, and others how not to parent. It is our duty to sort out and glean the lesson, so when we become a parent we're ready.

Likewise, we honor the thoughts and feelings we brought with us to this life because they, too, are an important part of our path.

That your days may be long, on the land the Lord has given you. The word *days* symbolizes degrees of unfoldment. Our life, lived with conscious awareness achieves growth. *Land* can symbolize earth—the earthly life the *Lord* or Law—has given us, to use for continued growth.

A father and mother come together to create a child. The creative process through which we shape and express our lives requires agreement of the thinking, male faculty, and the heart, feeling, female faculty. Thinking plus feeling equals manifestation. The quality of what we manifest will be the *child,* of our father *thought,* and mother, *feeling,* faculties. It is our awareness that will bring us to Spiritual Maturity, embodiment of Christ—just like Jesus.

You shall not kill. (some translations say murder)… In an effort to keep this brief, I will address only killing a human being. We did not create life and don't have the right to take it. Killing is not a solution to any problem. We may tell ourselves it is, but we're wrong. It is a complex issue because of the illusions that bring us to rationalize, justify and normalize killing each other. We hear the commandment, then comes the laundry list of *yeah-buts*: But what about war? What about self-defense? How about the death penalty? Do we believe *an eye for an eye?* If a person killed someone I love, could I kill them in return? I imagine God's response to our excuses would be, *"What part of shall not do you not get?"*

Believing killing is going fix anything is an illusion. It won't. If we declare all killing is wrong, we would be under the rule of another government by the end of the day. It's imperative we understand this, because spiritual law, is both individual and collective. Cain tells the Lord, when asked where his brother is, "Am I my brother's keeper?" God knew what had happened. The truth of the matter, is that we are our brother's keeper. We must always strive to be mutually accountable and collectively responsible for each other, always considering the common good—our Oneness.

Through the Law of Cause and Effect, something incited anger, and retaliation through utter destruction. This would be a negative cause. To react in kind, would create more negative energy. It escalates, until someone thinks they've won. Yet through Universal Principle, the effects will come, from channels expected, and unexpected.

Consider the feud between the Hatfields and McCoys. It started in 1865, when Asa Harmon McCoy, was shot and killed. Although there was no evidence or arrest, the McCoy family said it was a cousin of Anse Hatfield was to blame. In the years that followed, incidents and accusations flew in both directions. Battles over a stolen pig, and a romance between Roseanna McCoy and Johnson Hatfield, escalated the feud that cost two dozen people their lives, and injured many others. This happened, because no one would end it. In 1979 the feud ended with a handshake, and on June 14, 2003 Reo Hatfield and Bo McCoy signed an official termination of the feud. Killing is not the answer.

You shall not commit adultery... On the literal level, adultery is sexual activity with someone who is not your mate. Marriage is a commitment sealed by a vow. When a vow is broken both a marriage and family are at risk. Adultery causes suffering. The word *adultery* has nothing to do with being an adult. The Hebrew root, of adultery means a total or complete abandoning of one's Principles, and a Latin root means to corrupt.

There are several references to adultery, in the Bible, but the constant is being unfaithful. We can be unfaithful to God, or mate, or our personal values. Another definition is impurity. The word adultery means *add-other*. Whatever word we use, every time we adulterate, corrupt, or dilute Truth, we are committing adultery.

Consider this: You are putting fuel in your car. In order for the car to serve its purpose, it requires clean fuel. Putting water into your tank will not make the car run better, or increase the mileage you will get from the fuel. It will blow up the engine. Being unfaithful to God, ourselves, or another will corrupt our purity of mind. At the core of adultery, is putting our carnal appetite before God, worshiping Baal.

You Shall Not Steal… This is clear. Don't take what isn't yours. Most of us work hard for our money and use it to buy things we want or require. If someone steals what we have worked so hard for, and love, we suffer. If we cause someone else to suffer, sin.

Consider universal energy flowing as the blood that courses through our body. Any interruption to the flow, negatively affects the whole body. God has provided abundance for everyone. Taking what is not ours, interrupts the flow, and exposes an error belief in lack and limitation. This negates, in our mind, God's abundant provision. Because we are One, we cannot steal from another without stealing from ourselves.

Theft is insidious, wily, and easy to rationalize or justify. A thief comes from a *me first* mentality: what we want is more important than anything else. There is little support available to avoid conscious or unconscious theft. Think about the television commercials where lawyers suggest you can get huge sums of money from an illness or injury. We don't always see theft for what it is. Consider these forms of stealing: employee theft, taking things from the work place for personal use, tax fraud, claiming invalid deductions, etc. Others would be insurance fraud, buying pirated music and movies. It goes on and on.

The universe *will* claim its own. Every cause you send forth, will have an effect. It may not be obvious. Cheat on your taxes, your car breaks down, and the repairs cost exactly the amount of your refund. Maybe this could be *cosmic justice*? Victimless crime is a lie and illusion. Sometimes we are the victim. Stealing is one way we worship Mammon—giving worth to material things, instead of God.

You shall not bear false witness against your neighbor… To bear false witness, in the literal sense, would be to lie about another person. It could be about a personal experience, or gossip. It could be malicious, influenced by jealousy. It's difficult to live this commandment, since most of our words are the product of perceptions we have, whether factual or not. We all may be Children of God, yet know little about each other. We judge when all we see is the tip of the iceberg. This doesn't mean we have to spend our entire lives afraid to open our mouths. Sometimes it is necessary to acknowledge a wrong doing. This is when we can speak our truth with love, not fault finding. We have to do it in spite of being afraid.

The spoken word has great power. Our words are seeds we plant in another's mind. For the best results, before we speak, we can ask ourselves: is it true? Is it kind? Is it needful? Will it help? Observe your conversations. As you do, consider this: great minds talk about ideas, average minds talk about events, and small minds talk about people.

One last thing: it's important, not to bear false witness about ourselves. The minute we declare ourselves to be stupid, or mean, or such, we are bearing false witness. We don't want to put those thoughts into anyone else's mind, or to affirm them in our own. Remember, we are all children of God, making gods of ourselves worships Baal.

You shall not covet your neighbor's house; you shall not covet your neighbor's wife, or his man-servant, or his maid-servant, or his ox, or his ass, or anything that is your neighbor's… To covet, is to have a strong desire for something, to lust for it. This passage is telling us not to covet what belongs to another. In its worst form it's not just wanting the type of thing they have, it's wanting their good, and depriving them of it. It's not about keeping up with the Joneses, it's about *becoming* the Joneses instead of honoring who we are..

Through the creative process, the thoughts we hold in mind, connect with strong feelings about those thoughts. Then manifestation occurs. When we try to manifest what belongs to another, the outcome will never be good. An example would be alienation of affection, which is common today. It is easy to say, "It's just a little harmless flirting." There is no harmless flirting, because it plants seeds in mind that will sprout, and if fertilized with a little encouragement, can produce toxic fruit. Even if an affair does not ensue, a marriage, family, or relationship can be shattered. Coveting infers lack: someone has something we want, but don't have.

One definition of sin is *the negation of a Divine Idea.* God is our provider. A true desire, *de* (of) *sire* (the Father), is a Divine Idea planted within us. It is meant to be ours. When we focus our thought-power on what someone else has, with a belief in lack, we block our good. When we rejoice with them, holding thoughts of joy and anticipation for our own good, we open the doors of opportunity.

SINS OF COMMISSION AND SINS OF OMISSION

The word, *sin*, means missing the mark; falling short of divine perfection, which is the goal we strive for. It does not mean one is evil by nature. It means we made a mistake. *Sin,* or mistakes, start in mind as a possibility. Coupled with our feeling about that thought, we chose whether to take action. The action we take, or refrain from, determines whether we commit a sin. This a sin of commission.

It's easy to say, *Oops, I made a mistake* which is taking the error much too lightly. When we don't take the error seriously, we are likely to repeat it. When the effects of the sin appear, we wonder *why is this happening to me again?* Negative cause sent forth brings a negative effect. It's always a good idea to consider the effects of every thought, word or action we send forth.

Sins of omission happen when we don't do something we should. Telling a lie is a sin of commission. Saying nothing when we hear someone being falsely accused, or gossiped about is a sin of omission. It is a sin of omission to look away when a sin is being committed. Stealing cable TV is a sin of commission. To say nothing when someone else is stealing cable TV is a sin of omission. Evil can only exist when good people do nothing. A clear result of this is when everyone's rates go up!

CORPORATE, OR COLLECTIVE SIN

Every organ, cell, and tissue of our body serves the whole body. Likewise, every part of creation exists to assure the good of the whole. If a flower had free will, imagine the effect, if it withheld its fragrance, or pollen, or color from any other part of creation. If this happened, it would be dire and devastating for the whole. It would be a sin against nature and creation. But flowers don't have free will. Human beings do. Sin is committed whenever a human being intentionally uses their free will in a way that does not support the whole. This can get tricky when things like war and pollution cause harm to the whole. How can we be responsible for someone else's actions? Is it guilt by association? Can we be punished for someone else's sin? Punished, no. God does not punish. Suffer negative effects, *yes*. We are not exempt from the effects of a collective cause.

Shifting the lower consciousness of groups of people has many names, including mob mentality, herd mentality, and groupthink. This is how people are manipulated, to adopt certain behaviors and beliefs from outside sources, including friends, advertising, and emotion. The same influence that causes riots is responsible for shifts in cultural values and morals. It is important that we remember this is about the lower, collective carnal mind, once called race consciousness. Through misunderstanding—it referred to *human* race not the color of one's skin—the term race conscious is no longer acceptable. And that's how it works! This is Populism, and it is wreaking havoc on planet Earth today, to the delight of the false-god consciousness of lower human mind and materialism. An interesting theory about this comes from a study that resulted in the theory of the Hundredth Monkey. During the study of a troop of monkeys, one monkey started to wash the sweet potatoes thrown to them daily. She didn't like the gritty feel of the sand that stuck to them. She taught other monkeys, who taught other monkeys and soon everyone in the troop was washing their sweet potatoes. Then, according to the story, monkeys on remote islands far from these monkeys started washing their sweet potatoes, as though they learned telepathically.

Think that's a myth—or fake news? Possibly, but I don't see it as that surprising at all. If you go to the Orient, you can eat wontons and in the Ukraine, pierogi, and Italy, ravioli. It's all similar forms of stuffed pasta. How'd that happen? I'm sure there is an expert who will say, migrants spread the recipes. Maybe. Maybe not. There are too many examples of similar ideas sprouting up around the globe, with no logical explanation.

It makes sense in our current rash of crises on Earth. False news has exploded through hacking, leaked information, interference in other country's elections, and most concerning, a buildup of nuclear weaponry. This is not isolated to the United States. Nor is it a cultural problem. It's a human problem. Jesus taught we should be in the world, not of it. This means we must not get caught up in the web of fear, hate, and separation. Instead, we must become grounded in our truth, and speak it, with love.

When we open our minds to great possibilities, great things can happen. This is why it's critical we stay in a higher state of mind than lower. The higher state of consciousness cannot be compromised. Lower mind can be swayed by ego and the senses. Higher, or Christ consciousness is inspired, not influenced. As we maintain a high state of awareness, we will be guided to right action. People who are seeking what we have to say will be drawn to us. Speak our Truth with love and respect. Keep in mind we can't convert someone to our way of thinking. Enlightenment happens within, but if you live from Christ consciousness, everything you ever said or did in their presence will click, and you can provide real spiritual support.

"Do not find fault before you investigate; examine first, then criticize."
(Sirach 11:7)

I AM ONLY ONE:

By Cannon Farrah

I am only one, But I am one.

I cannot do everything, But I can do something.

And that which I can do, I ought to do.

And what I ought to do, By the Grace of God, I will do.

MORTAL VS VENIAL SINS

The Catholic Church, defines two types of sin: mortal, or deadly sin, and venial, or pardonable sin. This always confused me when I went to confession. I didn't have a long list of sins, but thought if I didn't have to confess the venial sins it would help. The priest listened and forgave our sins. As I think of mortal and venial sins today, my thought is that venial sins, or errors, are easier to *overcome*. An example would be *little white lies*. However they are still lies. Maybe we should call them *gateway lies?* Like the old saying goes, *"Oh what a tangled web we weave, when first we practice to deceive."* We may start with one little lie, then we need another lie to cover it up, and, well, I'm sure you've experienced this in your life. At some point, we have to stop the downward spiral.

THE SEVEN DEADLY SINS–PLAYGROUND OF THE FALSE GODS

(AND THEIR ANTIDOTES)

The seven deadly sins, are error ideas that block one's spiritual progress. They are deadly, because if we don't overcome them, we will remain earthbound and suffering from dis-ease *of the psyches*. When in their grip, it is very difficult to see the truth. While their lure is strong, we can overcome them with the antidote provided.

PRIDE (false): This is the belief we are better, prettier, richer, holier, etc. than others. It negates that God is our ultimate good, and we are all equal children of God. When we are in the false pride state of mind, false gods can manipulate by flattery.

Antidote: Look for the good in others. Know there's plenty for everyone. We are all equal children of God. See equality among all people. Narcissism, another definition of this behavior is reaching epidemic proportions. For more information, read *The Narcissism Epidemic: Living in the age of Entitlement*, by Jean Twenge and W. Keith Campbell.

ENVY: Is desire and jealousy regarding others possessions or achievements. This can include money, attractiveness, power, status, talent. It negates a Divine Idea because it assumes favoritism by God, and the error that someone else has everything you deserve.

Antidote: Count your blessings every day. Instead of looking at what others have, develop your own untapped potential.

WRATH (anger): A wrathful person is always angry and thrives on the adrenaline produced by their anger. At the core is a false belief that everyone has victimized them. It negates the Divine Ideas of love, harmony and peace and wholeness.

Antidote: When feelings of anger arise, we can take a deep breath and affirm, *nothing can disturb the calm peace of my soul*. Each time, relax your body. Repeat ten times. Find healthy outlets for your energy, like sports.

LUST: Is an inordinate craving for pleasures of the flesh, and the belief nothing is more important than physical pleasure. The person in the grip of lust will sacrifice marriage, family, career, and reputation to fulfill the craving.

Antidote: Connect with your higher self, reminding yourself that you are a beloved child of God, and your body is a temple of the living God. Develop a new paradigm for passion. Visit sacred places, churches, temples, etc. Attend a retreat. Learn to meditate.

AVARICE (greed): Is the desire for material wealth and gain, ignoring the realm of the spiritual. The perceived need for riches is voracious. There is never enough to feel happy. This sin negates God's unlimited provision. The Bible tells us, "The love of money is the root of all evil," this is because, it denies God's provision, and causes us to withhold from the Law of Circulation. It also puts material gain before what matters most for self and the whole.

Antidote: Begin each day giving thanks to God, the provider of every good thing. Circulation prevents stagnation, which blocks the flow of your prosperity. Try to find at least one good item you are not using, or money to give to someone who will appreciate it. Clean out your attic, closets, garage, etc. and give to a charitable organization. You will soon find you are engaging the Law of Circulation.

GLUTTONY: Is an inordinate desire to consume more than that which one requires. People suffering from gluttony always feel empty inside and eat to fill a void that food cannot satisfy.

Antidote: We can shift the quality of food we are eating, as we decrease amounts. Spend time in daily meditation, searching for the empty place you are trying to fill. Thank God for healing we require. Eat alone at least once a day, at the table, in silence. No distractions.

SLOTH: Is avoiding physical or spiritual work. This sin, as gluttony, is deadly, since failure to overcome it, can bring death.

Antidote: Commit to performing at least one physical activity every day. Add a spiritual component. The activity might be a walk, even if it's around the block. Walking is an opportunity to connect with Spirit. It could be prayer, or just making ourselves mindful, and present for God.

BUT WAIT–THERE'S MORE!

In what I believe was Jesus' effort to clarify the Commandments, He gave two more. The first: *You shall love the Lord your God with all your heart, and with all your soul, and with all your strength, and with all your mind; and love your neighbor as yourself.* (Luke 10:27)

And second: *A new commandment I give to you, that you love one another; even as I have loved you that you also love one another.* (John 13:34)

Then there is the Golden Rule: *Do unto others, as you would have them do unto you.* This is a part of spiritual practices worldwide.

Adhering to these teachings, can eliminate a need for any others. Beside the fact it makes sense on the level of love and compassion when we realize that we are all One. We are one with God, and one with each other. To sin against another is to sin against ourselves. It's like the old cliché to *cut off your nose to spite your face.* A perfect example is with ecology. We live on an interdependent biosphere. When we poison the air or water, we eventually poison ourselves. If we kill bees, there will be no pollination and we will experience famine.

The primary, doctrine of the false gods, is that we are separate. In every major religion, there is a version of *The Golden Rule: Do unto others, as you would have them do unto you.* In the doctrine of false gods the 'golden rule, is *the one with the gold, rules.'* Anything that reinforces separation or *us vs them*, is contrary to the truth of our interdependence, and will lead to suffering. False gods, or beliefs about God and ourselves, also negate the reality of a higher power, God. Through their wiles, they first instill the thought there is no higher being, then when there is a disaster, we blame God, or wonder where he is when we need him.

But the greatest, and deadliest sin of all is the sin of separation: not living the Truth that we are all One. We are One with God, One with each other, One with all creation, One with the earth. Failure to live this Truth will lead to certain hell. It is an unfortunate fact that this sin is common today, through racism, segregation, prejudice and our politics.

Here is where it gets tricky, because while we can change ourselves, how can we change others? If you've ever flown on a plane, you have witnessed the flight attendant's demonstration of the safety requirements, prior to takeoff. Attendants tell Parents, if the oxygen masks fall down, put your own on first, and then put on your child's. That's because you can be of no help to your child if you pass out. Likewise, work on your own enlightenment, and then when others are gasping for breath (spirit), you will be there to help them.

In Unity, we teach that there is no physical location called hell. At first glance, we might think: *Oh good, I don't have to follow those ridiculous Commandments. I can do whatever I want.* That's not the way it works. Just because there's no actual fire and brimstone, with a horned devil poking us with his pitchfork, doesn't mean we are free and clear. The consequences of our individual and collective thoughts, feelings and actions, can bring hellish results. Under the influence of false gods that lead us to believe we have absolute freedom, we think we are the exception to the rule—Spiritual Principle.

Spiritual Principle is absolute, eternal, and unchanging. We reap what we sow. Welcome to hell. *Is hell eternal damnation,* you ask? It is as eternal as we let it be, until we will surrender our self-centered, carnal, or animal nature to something higher–the spark of divinity within. Ego, from the lower quadrants of mind edge God out.

Here is an acronym: EGO = Edge God Out. There is no room for thoughts of God, church, Principles, only self. Then when something evil befalls us, we demand to know: *Where was God in this?* God was in the midst, as Principle, as God always is.

"All things are connected. Whatever befalls the earth befalls the sons of the earth. Man does not weave the web of life; he is merely a strand of it. Whatever he does to the web, he does to himself." Ted Perry, 1972

MONEY, SEX, AND POWER

Money, sex and power are earthly manifestations of Divine Ideas. In pure thought, money represents substance, sex, the creative force, and power is the ability to act or control. When expressed through the mind of spirit, money—divine substance—brings abundance for all. Sex releases creative energy that appears in fertile, creative forms through art, science and true intimacy in relationship. Spiritual power manifests through divine mind as unbending integrity and intention to complete whatever task is at hand.

The pivotal nature of mind, and our free will allow us to choose, what we focus on—where our mind goes—what we want to see. We can choose the spiritual, or mortal perspective. Operating through mortal mind, the focus shifts to satisfaction of sensual appetites. Money becomes greed, sex craves gratification of insatiable lust, and power is directed to control and overpower anything and everything the person wants, with no concern for others.

The mortal mind is not inherently evil. It operates from the animal nature, unaware of the unseen realm of beyond the physical. Even religion can operate through the mortal mind while spirituality comprehends the world of formless Truth. As the mortal mind becomes enlightened through our use of spiritual practices—learning and living Principle—it is transformed.

We all want others to love and accept us. That's a beautiful thing. In truth, not everyone we want to love us, will. We are not on the same wavelength. It's not personal, it's Principle. If we try to force the matter, we will only buy ourselves a boatload of hurt.

I Love Lucy, is the oldest sitcom still being broadcast in local syndication. What makes it funny is Lucy's human antics. Her crazy schemes to get her way or manipulate her husband Ricky have kept us watching for over 70 years! For Lucy, everything always worked out because of her husband's love and tolerance. It's such fun, we forget it's all an illusion and life doesn't work that way. It was all just a story—a funny story, still pure fiction. Behind the scenes, their happy marriage was an illusion.

The real Lucy, Lucille Ball, tried desperately to hold the marriage together. She loved her husband. She wanted her family to be whole despite her husband's infidelity, drinking, and fits of rage that could erupt without warning. Lucille feared what people would think. She didn't want to destroy her fan's treasured image of a healthy family. Then the camel's back broke. They divorced after almost 20 years of marriage.

What illusions are we living with in our own lives? There is no need to trouble ourselves over another person's opinion. Here's the truth I discovered one day. It changed my life forever: *What anyone else thinks of you is none of your business. What God thinks of you is your only business.* The same is true for everyone.

PART THREE – SPIRITUAL LAW
LAW OR GUIDELINES?

In the *Pirates of the Caribbean* movies, Elizabeth Swann challenges the pirate Barbossa, to honor *the Code*. Once a hard and fast code of conduct for pirates, over time it relaxed into, as Barbossa put it, to being *more like guidelines*. In our world today, the Ten Commandments, the Great Commandment, and even civil statutes have been reduced to watered-down guidelines. Like Barbossa, we rationalize them with rational-lies, to justify behavior that is contrary to the law. Whether or not we live under Principle, it is always active. We are wondering why we are in such a mess. Bad things are happening in increasing numbers and severity. Many have little regard for laws and few if any consequences.

Laws, both religious and civil, are for our protection and highest good. They provide safety, justice and order. In the beginning, we're taught the rules by elders with wisdom and experience. Through the process of growth and maturity, we have the potential to no longer require rules because we live Principle. Our children went from a crib, to a playpen, to free run of the house as they matured. The more we grow, the less we need a safety-net of external rules to be imposed. This would be spiritual maturity; when we learn from experience how Principle functions. We will have attained wisdom. Aware of and understanding the law, we embody it.

Behind religious and civil law, is spiritual law, also called Principle. Principle, is that which is absolute, eternal and unchanging. An example would be mathematical Principles. One plus One will always be two. It is something we can count on. Because we have free will from our creator, we have the choice to live in alignment with the law or not. We may be spiritual beings, but we are also having a human experience. Human nature often compels us to look for a loophole. When we live contrary to Spiritual Principle, we find our lives plagued with problems and suffering. This is not God punishing us. It's Principle, working as it should, not a personal affront.

The word, *Law,* translated by metaphysics, is Lord. There is one primary law, and that is the Law of Cause and Effect. It has many forms of expression: The Law of Sowing and Reaping, The Law of Giving and Receiving, etc., but behind it is always cause and effect. If we sow (cause) carrot seeds, we will reap (effect) carrots. It can't be any other way. If the seed packet had no label, we wouldn't even know what type of seeds we were planting. When we learn about God as Principle, we know that if we sow good things, we will reap good things, in abundance.

The mind is powerful, but it works only within the parameters of Principle. Imagine if you could plant carrot seeds and through the power of your mind, grow peaches! What would life be like? It would be chaotic at the least, I am sure. Through Principle, divine order manifests. Here's an interesting way law can work to get you the peaches you want: Plant the carrot seeds you have, nurture and care for them, water them, and see an abundant harvest of carrots—see the harvest of carrots now being bartered for some beautiful peaches. Through the Law of Mind Action, focused thought, you can attract peaches when you plant carrots! It's not magical, it's metaphysical.

"There are many planes of causation, but nothing escapes the law." The Kybalion

SPIRITUAL LAWS AND FALSE GODS

False gods come through the human (lower) mind, without knowledge or consideration of spiritual law, or Principle. The focus is on self—self-power, self-indulgence, self-centered and self-satisfied. There is no room for God. This is why the Ego can be defined by the acronym: Edging God Out. When presented with a spiritual law, the first thought of the ego, is a knee-jerk reaction that there might be someone trying to control it. The second thought, *how can I circumvent the law to my benefit?* Enter scheming, manipulating and conniving. A perfect example of this in the eternal antics of Wile E. Coyote and the Roadrunner. Our ego is like Wile E Coyote, chasing something we haven't a prayer of catching. Yet, like Wile E., we think of one trick or another, always provided through ACME. The false gods of material gain and ego power are the Roadrunner, zipping along and laughing at us. I think if Wile E. just stopped long enough to relax, he just might find there is plenty within reach, and so will we.

Failure to understand Principle and how it works brings frustration. It's like trying to assemble a piece of furniture without instructions. Learning and living by spiritual law does not confine, it supports us. A man needed $400.00. He was taught in a class about tithing, everything we give comes back multiplied. So he gave $40.00 *he did not have* to the church as a tithe. The check bounced. All he received was humiliation and an overdraft fee. He received AS he gave, from a belief in lack, with money he did not have. We do not give to receive, but because we already have received.

It's easy to minimize our behaviors with words like: *just,* or *only. It was just a little lie,* we tell ourselves, or *the IRS gets plenty from me as it is,* or a biggie, *just this once.* Then there's the cliché, *it's easier to beg forgiveness than ask permission.* This is rationalization; it is a phony excuse for one's behavior, not a valid reason. *"Do not find fault before you investigate: examine first, then criticize."* (Sirach 11:7)

What we don't realize is that a law, is a law, is a law. Spiritual law is unbreakable. *"Do not be deceived, the Lord cannot be mocked."* (Gal 6:7). It's not personal, it is Principle. The law is always engaged. If you touch a hot stove, you will get burned. The stove is not angry with you. It is not punishing you for touching it. If you touch it again, you will get burned again. It's that simple. Think about that the next time you say to yourself: *"Why is this happening to me again?"*

As far as mortal and venial goes, yes, there are little things we may do, like returning a library book through the night drop and not paying the fine. Then we go to the grocery store to discover the avocado we bought is spoiled inside. At one point, we will discover the universe will claim its own. If we lie, we will be lied to. If we cheat, will be cheated. It doesn't matter whether we get caught or not. The energy of Universal Principle is working. Through the Law of Increase, when we don't learn our lesson and change our error, the effects of future infringements will come back increased. We call this the *cosmic 2X4: If we don't get the point, the next time we will get whacked with the cosmic 4X8.* It's just the universe trying to get our attention.

We all make promises to ourselves, and break them as fast as we made them. Did you make New Year's resolutions? Did you keep them? Most people don't. And what was the effect of that cause you sent forth when you broke your promise to yourself? A lie is a lie, even if we lie to ourselves.

"No one can serve two masters, for either he will hate the one and love the other, or he will be devoted to the one and despise the other. You cannot serve God and mammon." (Matthew 6:24)

ONE GOD, MANY FACES ~ ONE LAW, MANY EXPRESSIONS

LAWS: Laws are Universal Principles through which manifestation occurs. The laws, or Principles lie behind all creation. The one primary law is the Law of Cause and Effect, the others are variations of it.

Confused? Look at it this way: While you may be one person, you have many expressions. You could be a homeowner, parent, child, in-law, employee, artist, writer, or fisherman. Each aspect, expresses a part of you—a many faceted diamond. Law, also has many expressions.

Let's explore a few of the laws, or Principles at work in our daily lives with or without our awareness:

The Law of Mind Action: Thoughts held in mind manifest in kind. Where the mind goes, energy flows, and manifestation follows. The word *mind* refers to the combined thinking and feeling faculties. If we *think* about a chocolate cake, and our *feelings* are stimulated—there is a biological response such as hunger, or salivation—and chances are we will soon eat chocolate cake. Thought, plus feeling, brings manifestation. Chocolate cake is a good thing providing we're not on a diet.

Law of Sowing and Reaping: When we plant a garden, we plant what we want to grow. I prefer to plant vegetables than flowers, and I know I will get vegetables to eat. If we want to reap love, we sow love. When we want to reap friendship, we sow friendship. If we want to reap Truth, sow Truth. Time and patience are required, from seed to harvest. Likewise time and patience are necessary for manifestation through the law. Many of us want instant results, and try to force outcomes, and grab what is available, rather than wait for something better. "By your endurance, you will gain your souls." (Luke 21:19)

Law of Giving and Receiving: The Bible states: As you give, so shall you receive. Paired with the Law of Mind Action, whatever thoughts we hold when we give will impact what we receive. If we give with a tight fist, and thoughts of depletion, we are not open to receive much. If we give with an open hand and heart, we open ourselves to a greater good. This is not about money as much as it is the thoughts and feelings we have regarding money and its purpose.

Law of Increase: Everything we send forth comes back multiplied. We can count the seeds in a tomato, but we can't count the tomatoes in a seed. God intends for all creation to *go forth and multiply*. Whether our return is positive, or negative, depends on what we are thinking and feeling as we release it.

The law, or Principle does not belong to any belief or religious organization. It functions at all times, in all circumstances, regardless of where you worship or whether you worship.

SPIRITUAL LAW AND THE LAW OF THE LAND

The law of the land refers to all the laws in force within a country or region. The difference between spiritual law and the law of the land is its expression. Spiritual law originates in Divine Mind. It is discerned and interpreted according to the consciousness of the receiver. Interpretation happens either through the filter of the higher, enlightened mind of perceiving and sensing, or the lower mind, of carnal thoughts and feelings. Spiritual law exists for the good of all. It cannot be broken, but not living under the law will bring adverse consequences.

We, as civilizations, created the law of the land, aka civil law, criminal law, etc. with the good of everyone in mind. They are based on human logic, experience and understanding. Laws regarding speed limits, have the purpose of keeping people safe. Because we construct the laws through the carnal mind however, many people see them as an attempt by the government to restrict or control them. The laws may appear to be broken, but people continue to die or suffer unnecessary physical injuries because they live outside the law.

Unless agnostic or atheist parents raised us, we learned about spiritual law at church. We learned more about the letter of the law than the heart, or understanding. We learned the *what,* without the *why*. What if we were to consider laws as safety nets, or as a way we show love and respect for each other?

Too often we see grieving parents or loved ones with news cameras shoved in their faces, as they urge people not to drink, or text, or speed while driving. Despite the law, tragedies continue to happen. The problem is, we cannot legislate intelligence, enlightenment and morality. We put laws in place to protect people. Obedience of the law is up to the people. Their decision to disregard laws is not sufficient reason to stop creating or enforcing them. In fact, it is all the more reason to help others understand what they are and why they exist.

Now, in 2018, truth, justice and integrity are being abused as never before. Those in the highest positions of the United States laugh at the laws, with total disregard. Diplomacy is nonexistent in the White House. Nobody knows where it is going. Once seen as a benevolent guiding light in the world, our beloved country is becoming a laughingstock. Even in the branches of government, and within its parties, there is no cooperation. January 25, 2017, *Fortune* magazine posted the declaration of the US moving from being a *full democracy* to a *flawed democracy*. This is an excerpt of the article:

While U.S. citizens could once claim to be part of the 9% of people in the world governed by a "full democracy," they are now part of the near 45% who live in a "flawed democracy." That's according to the Economist Intelligence Unit, which downgraded the U.S. in their 2016 Democracy Index published Wednesday. The move puts the U.S. in the same category as Poland, Mongolia, and Italy.

What are we to do? We are to keep on keeping on. I write these words coming from the belief in my heart and soul, that the Lord of my Being, God, has commissioned me to share my truth. Guided by Spirit I am committed to sharing a metaphysical perspective of the human condition. With the hope of enlightenment, I share what I have learned from Jesus, my brother, wayshower and savior, and other enlightened masters. I believe this is key to our salvation. In doing this, I pray to inspire others to join me, as I follow my Master Teacher in the name, and to the glory of Spirit—God—All that is good.

THE DOGMA AND DOCTRINE OF FALSE GODS

Both doctrine and dogma are teachings of a belief system. Dogma is considered infallible, having come directly from God, or Jesus. Dogma is not open to dispute. The dogma, or unchangeable aspect of the cult of false gods is self and separation. God has laws, false gods have lies. The allure of Mammon and Baal pulls us down, like the force of gravity, binding us to the earthly realm. This occurs on an individual and collective level, sometimes called the *herd affect,* which is when individuals do something because everyone else is doing it. Individual expression is compromised as people fall victim to *what's happening now.* False gods make what is unimportant, important, and what is important, unimportant.

An ego-craving in young people today is to be a celebrity. They don't realize real fame is earned, not given. Anybody can achieve infamy. Through television programs like *Keeping Up with the Kardashians*, *Sixteen and Pregnant,* or *My Super Sweet Sixteen,* a false image of success and personal worth is formed. This is a dangerous type of idol worship. Compounding the problem, is that many celebrities exhibit bad behavior they are not held accountable for, and there are few good, healthy role models.

As you read these lies of Mammon and Baal, it is important to understand that the law *is*. It doesn't matter whether you believe in the law, it *is,* and it is always in operation. The causes we sow, will reap a harvest in kind. Stop and ponder before you speak or act, what is the cause being sent forth, and what effect will it reap?

Below are some lies Mammon and Baal tell us through human awareness, or as I call it, *the collective perspective.* We receive these lies through many channels, including television programming, advertising, movies, charlatans that claim to be spiritual or religious, books, and our friends. If the intellect is impaired under the influence of stress, drugs or alcohol, it makes us more susceptible to false gods. The list is not complete, and I'm sure you could add to it with ease.

LIES OF FALSE GODS

The lies are shown here, in an order that will align them with the Ten Commandments.

Money and Power will make you happy. There is not enough to go around, so get what you can by any means. Exert your power regardless of fallout or consequences.

You are your own God. Everything centers on you, and what you want. Religion is the opiate of the masses. You are separate from, and better than everyone else. You make your own rules. Rules are made to break. The world and people in it are important to the degree they can serve you.

You are entitled. Your good is in this realm alone. You are free to consume, and live for the pleasures of the flesh. Money, power and pleasure are yours for the taking. Manipulating others is a means to getting what you want. Use people and love things. Money is everything. It must increase at all times, at any cost. You must have more stuff at cheaper prices.

You are entitled to everything and anything you want. How you get it is not your concern. Nobody is the boss of you. You exercise your personal power. Designer labels matter. You must have the best of everything.

There is no time to rest. You must have things, lots of things, better things, more things than anyone else. There is nothing more important than doing what you have to do to get more things. Rest is for sissies. Stop, or slow down and someone will get ahead of you. Acquire and Accumulate. Consume. Work now, make money and buy stuff now. You can spend time with your family later.

Being a stay at home parent is not possible, you need money and stuff. Money is a requirement for happiness.

You owe nothing to anybody. You did not ask to be born. It was your parents' choice. They are grownups, and responsible for themselves. You can't afford to take care of them, nor your sisters or brothers. It is none of anyone's business how you got where you are. What you had to do to get there is not important.

It's a dog-eat-dog world. You must protect your stuff and the people you love at any cost. An eye for an eye is a good rule to live by. Lives of others matter little. The poor and hungry did it to themselves. Shoot first, ask questions later. *People* from other countries are our enemies. They have stuff we want, like oil. Don't negotiate, go get it. The bigger the guns, bigger the bombs, the safer we are.

Marriage is like a car, if it isn't working, get out and get yourself another one. Vows are just words. If you see greener pastures, go for it. Better yet, why even bother getting married? Like they say, *why buy the cow when you can get the milk for free!* Get the best part of the deal if you get divorced. Kids are tough, they'll be fine. There are ways to make unwanted pregnancies go away. Cheating doesn't matter if you don't get caught.

It's not stealing to take home office supplies from work. The company can afford it. Insurance fraud is a victimless crime. The government has plenty of money, you can lie on your taxes, there's not much chance of getting audited. And if you do, you can just plead ignorance. Buying pirated movies and music is no big deal. The artists are swimming in money.

Impress others with that gossip you heard today. They'll think you're important and in the know. If you tell the boss your co-worker isn't doing their job right, maybe they'll get fired and you can get the position. You can make up information on your resume, employers rarely check them out. Honesty doesn't matter. If you say it often enough, loud enough, with conviction, people will believe anything. Oh, it's only a little white lie, for crying out loud! You can make a lot of money from that accident you had. You can make an accident happen and sue the innocent party.

What do false gods want? Because they are states of mind, and not entities, they can't want anything. Yet they can compel us through the power of thought in carnal mind. The attraction that appeals to our lower nature, can be irresistible. In Unity, we teach thoughts are things. False gods includes thoughts of denial of anything greater than the manifest realm. This thinking thrives on taking our money, our time, our full attention, and our life under the false belief it will make us happy. We work against false gods when we follow Jesus' teaching, *lift up our eyes,* which is to turn our focus from selfish concerns to Spirit—God.

TAP DANCING ON THE SLIPPERY SLOPE

Imagine you are tap dancing on the top of a hill. You dance at the edge of a drop-off. A slope covered with green slime is right by the tip of your toes. At the bottom of the slope, are jagged rocks sticking out of the slime, that could cause great harm, if not death, should you slip. Opposite you is another hill. Standing along the edge of that hill are people who are cheering you on to dance. The cheers and applause are intoxicating. You want to dance closer to the edge so the people can see you better and cheer your talent and bravery.

We may not have danced on that slippery slope, but most of us have danced on our own slippery slope in foolishness and ignorance. Cheered on by false gods and our own ego, we put ourselves in harm's way when we toy with temptation. Consider these examples:

Steroids are a temptation to an athlete who loves trophies, cheering crowds, and the possibility of a lucrative career. *Everyone does it,* he's told. Maybe he should ask himself if he is the one performing, or is it the steroids.

A producer propositions an actress, auditioning for a great part. Is the part worth compromising her values? Same issue, different situation, her boyfriend tells her if she loves him, she'll have sex with him.

Your mate leaves his/her wallet on the table. You want to see what's inside. Do you look?

We all want love and acceptance. But when we put these things above our own core beliefs and values, we negate the Divine Idea of who we are, and fall short of our potential. You will know you have integrity when your words and actions match what you believe.

The first time we attempt something is hardest. Each time we try it becomes easier. When we are striving for mastery, we always feel satisfied, encouraged when making and following through on a difficult task. When we waffle, or do something contrary to good, while we may suffer regret, with each repetition, the error is easier to repeat.

WHAT'S KARMA GOT TO DO WITH IT?

"Those who do not learn from history, are forced to repeat it." George Santayana

The word, karma, means fate or destiny. In Eastern religions, it refers to the requirement for reincarnation to pay for, or work out our past mistakes. In Unity, we look at it from a perspective of cause and effect, and the opportunity to learn lessons in this life, or perhaps another. Karma is like a flow—from cause, to effect, to cause, to effect. It flows all the way to wholeness. It is a vibrational flow of spiritual energy and enlightenment. The enlightenment will come. We determine how long it will take. If we want to stop the cycle of karma, it would look like this: cause to effect, analysis and learning—to new cause—to new effect, etc., and analysis and learning. As we progress, there will be fewer incidences of adverse effects, because we won't be doing the things that bring them on. In my personal experience, I have noticed that the time between cause and effect shortens, kind of like *instant karma*. This is likely due to increased awareness.

There is another type of karma, called collective karma. This results from groups of people, with a shared mentality, like they're on the same wave-length or frequency. The law works as it does with individual karma. The vibration thought-energy sent out attracts in kind. People are drawn to groups with the same frequency, which Fillmore defines as *nucleating*. The energy nucleated will lead to manifestation.

In karmic relationships, with one other person or a group, we draw either what appears to be a perfect match, or the opposite of where we are in consciousness. The truth of the matter is we are attracting what we need to learn. There are many resources available to explore karma in depth, but for now, let's keep our focus on the reason it's included here: the role it plays in healing our lives and current human condition.

There are hard questions that require answers. As an individual creates through ideas, so do groups. Here's an example: as long as we refuse to find a means of sensible gun control, innocent people will continue to die in increasing numbers. This falls under the Law of Increase. Now, in this *land of the free and home of the brave,* since the 2017 mass murder in Las Vegas, many are no longer as brave about going to events where they feel vulnerable.

Until and unless we will address this issue, the deadly effects will increase. Our experience, in the United States anyway, has been cause-effect-no lesson learned-cause-effect-no lesson learned-increased cause-increased effect-no lesson learned. We must seek to learn the lesson so we can change the cause. It's not just the guns. It's about the consciousness of support for unregulated gun ownership. Yes, we have freedom, but with freedom comes responsibility. To change our thoughts, we need to learn the lessons that will change our minds. A traditional church word for this is *repent*. It means to rethink—to look at, consider, and choose a better thought. Karma. Cause. Effect. It's simple, but difficult. This Principle works in every aspect of our individual and collective lives.

Experiment: Think about some issues we are facing in the world such as poverty, war, climate, disease, broken families, racism, and gang issues. See if you can perceive causes, effects, and lessons learned. This is great for a group discussion, or class activity.

IS OUR CURRENT WORLD CRISIS KARMIC?

When we look back at the horror of the Holocaust, we may think we are past that; we think it will never happen again. But did we learn *how* to never let it happen again? Hold that thought in mind as you read the following. Consider each question carefully, and ask yourself if there is validity, and what we can do about each consideration.

EARLY WARNING SIGNS OF FACISM
From a display in the United States Holocaust Museum

Powerful and continuing nationalism

Disdain for human rights.

Identification of enemies as a unifying cause

Supremacy of the military

Rampant sexism

Controlled mass media

Obsession with national security

Religion and government intertwined

Corporate power protected

Labor power suppressed

Disdain for intellectuals and the arts

Obsession with crime and punishment

Rampant cronyism and corruption

Fraudulent elections

Good news: Times may be tough, but history will reveal tough times bring out the best in people, while easy times make us lazy, entitled, weak and selfish. Through enlightenment we will overcome both the mental and emotional distress of tough times, and the illusion of invincibility in the good times. Life is a journey, not a destination. The more enlightened we are, the more pleasant the journey.

PART FOUR–AWAKENING

HOW DID WE GET HERE?

Our current problems in the government or our lives didn't begin on November 9th. It started decades ago. I speak of the decline of our cultural consciousness, morals and standards as I have observed it. As stated earlier, I'm not an expert, but a witness—and knowing, or unknowing participant. The information I am providing here is in its simplest form for brevity's sake. What we have learned so far, just skims the surface.

In past conversations about this, I've often been told nothing is different, we just hear about it more. My response to that is: *"I was there. And I can prove it with statistics."* A simple and painful example when I was younger: we didn't lock our doors and there were no problems. A web page named Safewise, an independent review site, posted an article stating *in the US, every 18 seconds there is a burglary, which adds up to 4800 a day!* Now everybody locks their doors. This is another form of separation.

It wasn't a big bang, but a slow, steady erosion of consciousness—Truth decay—that has brought us to the current crises. While my observations come from the life I lived here in post-WWII America. I think similar things happened worldwide, because we all face the same journey as human beings.

We are more alike than we are different. The tide swells, crashes and recedes again and again. The changes to the shoreline are imperceptible, yet they are real. I was born in 1945, as WWII was ending. People worldwide were optimistic, seeing a great future. The nuclear family was the norm. Church was central to our lives in our behaviors, relationships, rites, rituals and celebrations. The people had shared virtues and values. Church attendance was the norm. It didn't matter which church your friend attended (although we were told by our clergy ours was the one true church and our friends and their families were going to hell). Lines were clearly defined, and we knew if we crossed that line, there would be consequences. We were content, unaware of the challenges the hard-fought freedom we enjoyed, would bring. Something was missing in the freedom equation—responsibility. With great freedom, comes great responsibility.

In those days, the United States was a producer of goods sold all over the planet, and we enjoyed many products imported from other countries. We could buy French wine, cheeses from Denmark, cars from Germany, the list goes on and on. Americans made it through the Great Depression and thrived again. Not everything was as peachy-keen as it looked at first glance. We still had racism and inequality. Today, while this should be a non-issue, it's not. The false gods that separate rather than unite, still slither in the weeds of mortal mind, and rears its head all too often.

On the surface of the nineteen-fifties and sixties, to my younger self, we stood on a firm foundation. We expected our future would unfold predictably. Men and women would marry, have children, and live happily ever after. Idealistic, perhaps, but a worthy—and contrary to what some folks would say—attainable goal. It was what my parents did, and their parents, and their friends. I, and many of my friends, married and started families, expected our happily-ever-after, and then it all crumbled.

Starting in the late forties, through the sixties, the Beat Generation emerged. They were soul-searching poets, writers and musicians who questioned the mainstream culture and politics. They were anti-war, and rejected materialism, militarism, consumerism and conformity; they were in favor of individual freedom and spontaneity, and rejected the establishment. Their music of choice was jazz, and many used drugs. Eastern religion was a fascination. Beatniks, as they were called, encouraged young people to practice spiritual and sociopolitical action.

Soon, the more superficial aspects of the Beatnik culture became a stereotype, exploited through marketing. Mammon and Baal had wriggled their way in, undermining the original values. Individual freedom and spontaneity corrupted the vision, which became freedom without responsibility. Presence of the Eastern religious philosophies clouded people's own beliefs. In subsequent years, church attendance declined, as it continues to do today.

Following the Beatniks were the Hippies, an amplification of the beat culture. They were a liberal, non-conformist subculture, rejecting conventional values. They held altruism, mysticism, honesty, joy and non-violence as values, promoting peace, music and free love. The free love they valued was pretty much promiscuous. Hallucinogenic drugs were a part of this culture. Timothy O'Leary a prominent leader of the movement, suggested LSD would expand your mind, help you experience ecstasy, and revelation. With their alternative lifestyle, many Hippies created communes, where everyone would share all they had, including partners. They rejected any form of authority. Then there were Yippies—Youth International Party—the Hippies political wing.

NBC News produced a documentary in 1978, titled, *I Want It All Now!* It was about Marin County, CA, which appears to be the springboard of the current rise of the false gods. The wealthy, devoted to self and accumulation, flocked to the area. According to a New York Times article on the documentary, the area had a natural beauty, and everything else a materialistic society considers essential to happiness. It said narcissism and the irrational reigned supreme as the insatiable, unfulfilled hoards rushed to assorted gurus and disciplines devoted to the frantic search for self. In the words of the article, they found the pot at the end of their overachieving rainbow contained little more than the next fad promising total happiness. *Note: Produced and directed by Joseph DeCola, Written by Joseph DeCola, Edwin Newman, and Jean Sprain Wilson Associate Producer.*

As this movement spread, those involved were first called Yuppies, which became an insult by 1985, although the lifestyle continued to flourish. At the end of the documentary, the commentator Edwin Newman says, "As we bid farewell to marvelous Marin County of the 70's, we may be saying hello to the USA of the 80's."

The following is my opinion, based on life experience and research. I don't ask that you accept it, only that you read it with a mind open enough to consider it as a valid possibility:

It was during the late seventies through the eighties the sexual revolution began. Values and standards from that time to the present have become increasingly lax. Premarital sex, cohabiting prior to marriage, and acceptance of sex without commitment are now commonplace. Today our fascination with sex has, for many, become an obsession exacerbated by the internet, especially the availability of pornography and hookup websites. I can assure you I am no prude. In fact, like I always say, sex is one of God's better ideas, and without it none of us would be here! Yet sex, like anything else, can be misused, or abused. On one hand it can be like mortar that holds together the foundation of a family or relationship. On the other hand, it can be self-indulgent and harmful to relationships, partners and yourself, physically, mentally and emotionally. Like my dad always said, *"It's not what you've got, but what you do with it that counts."*

Like a runaway snowball, gathering girth as it rolls, the decline of consciousness increases in size. It runs off the road of Truth, as it heads toward the black abyss of oblivion, or perhaps the primordial ooze, from which we emerged. We must stop and extract ourselves from impending disaster, to begin again our journey toward the good life. The biggest problem, that allowed all of this to happen, is complacency. Over time we became distracted by personal pursuits and technology. The very prosperity that could do so much good for everyone, everywhere, instead created a culture of self-indulgence and entitlement.

Fifty years ago, life was very different. Those born after 1970 have lived in a world unlike the previous generation. In the nineteen-sixties, most women were wives and homemakers. This does not necessarily mean women were un-fulfilled and miserable—kept *barefoot and pregnant*—as the old saying goes. Because we had the luxury of living—modestly—on one paycheck, we had time to truly enjoy motherhood, making a home, and the company of other women. I believe the *coffee klatch* is one of the greatest losses to the lives of women today. There were many avenues for personal development, ongoing education and creative expression.

The negative side of life in the 60's included male dominance in the household, chauvinism and inequality in the workplace. For example in the 60's and 70's a single woman could not get a credit card, and a married woman could only get one if it had her husband's name on it. Women could not keep their job while pregnant, complain about sexual harassment, or refuse their husband sex. Until 1973 women could not serve on a jury. They could not be astronauts until 1978. Women could not participate in ski jumping in the Olympics until 2014, and even now, paid maternity leave is not a requirement for employers.

Keep in mind this is not a matter of *this OR that*, it is *this AND that*. In the late 70's and 80's homemaking was looked down on, and many were embarrassed to say that they were *just* a homemaker. The reality is, while homemaking and raising children is both rewarding and challenging, it is not required. As Jesus taught: "You will know them by their fruits."

One of the most critical things we need to discern, is whether we are dealing with personality—ego-self, or Principle. We have come to the point of personality reigning over Principle. Instead of doing the right thing, we do whatever we want, then justify it. Imagine, what would happen if we put Principle before personality regarding ecology. Huge numbers of products in our stores thumb their noses at environmental concerns. But we can't put all the blame on the manufacturers, because we are the ones buying the products.

A perfect example are disposable, but not recyclable, coffee pods sold by companies such as Keurig, and Dunkin' Donut. An article from the New York Times dated April 17, 2016 says Keurig sells more than 9,000,000,000 pods every year. That would be enough plastic in the environment to wrap around the globe *ten times*. And that's only for one year! And it's just one of many companies selling the pods. Do you use one of these coffee makers? Would you be willing to get rid of it and use something more earth-friendly? The NYT report also states that while there are reusable pods available people do not want to use them because they are not as convenient as the disposable ones. This is a perfect example of the false god Baal at work through laziness and narcissism. And we all pay the price.

How long will it be until we wake up and start living in harmony with nature? Will it be too late to start over again? How big does that cosmic 2x4 of enlightenment have to get before we wake up?

A SEARCH FOR TRUTH

Charles Fillmore, cofounder of Unity, defines Truth in this way in *"The Absolute; is that which accords with God as the divine Principle; which is, has been, and ever will be. Truth is Principle. Consider the Principles of mathematics or music. While we can rearrange the numbers in countless ways, they still are added, divided, multiplied and subtracted the same way and get the same results. With music, you can play different notes. The notes themselves remain the same or the music won't work. Truth is something you can count on. Truth, Principle and law all have the same basic meaning."* The Revealing Word

The words *Lord* and *Law* are related. In everyday use, the word *Lord* is a person of authority, ownership and power. They make and enforce laws. In religion, the word *Lord* refers to God, the ultimate authority, and the Ten Commandments the ultimate law. Remember, laws are Principles. They exist with a meaning and expression. This is expanded later, under the topic Spiritual Law.

But where can we find Truth in our lives? There are several versions of an old story where the Lord God (different names for different cultures) wanted to hide a precious Truth from humans, because they were not ready for it. First, he thought of burying it in the ground, but knew the humans would dig for it. Then he thought about the bottom of the oceans, but he knew they would dive deep to get it. Even the top of the highest mountain wouldn't work because humans would climb the mountain to get it. Then the Lord God found the perfect place. He put it within humans because they'd never think to look there.

It is not surprising, in the Bible, God says: *"I will put my law within them. I will write it on their hearts"* (Jeremiah 31:33), and Jesus said, *"For behold, the Kingdom is within you."* (Luke 17:21) Both are true statements. Each of us can sense Truth. When I was under two years old, I told my first lie. I will never forget it. I can still see myself standing on the front porch. My mother, very unhappy to see her dusting powder spilled all over—and all over me, I would imagine—asked me *"Did you spill my powder?"* I thought about it for a minute and said, *"No."* But my gut wrenched, because I knew it was a lie. Sure, it was a survival instinct, but the guilt I felt showed I was aware what I did was not right.

The truth about Truth is: Truth is true. Whether we like it. Whether we want it to be true. Truth does not care. Truth *is*. It is absolute, eternal and unchanging. We cannot change or manipulate Truth. We can ignore it, but it's still there. Truth is not negotiable, and cannot be based on what we *want to be true*. Living in a way that runs contrary to Truth and Spiritual Principle, cannot have positive results. The consequences may not be immediate but they *will* manifest.

CAN YOU HANDLE THE TRUTH?

Our human nature is inclined to overrule and ignore the twinges that warn us we're out of integrity. They're uncomfortable. As a result we become desensitized to the warnings of conscience and guilt. This goes beyond the individual. On a larger scale, as the collective consciousness, dulls by normalizing bad behavior, aka sin, suffering increases. Call it good vs evil if you wish, but the bottom line is that when we send forth errant vibrations, we will reap in kind. The effects may not be immediate. We may feel as if we slipped through a loophole, but trust me, we will reap what we have sown.

Even if we've become jaded to the workings of Spirit within us, we can re-sensitize our mind. We can go back to our spiritual education, where we memorized the foundational teachings, the Commandments and teachings of Jesus, or the spiritual leaders of our faith community.

The more we work to develop our spiritual awareness, the greater sensitivity we will have to Truth Principles. We do the work through prayer, meditation, reading uplifting spiritual works, taking classes on spiritual growth, and practicing what we are learning.

It's difficult to hold on to truth in these days of lies, illusions, smoke screens and fabrication. There is much I call *truth decay*. What can we do to prevent truth decay? The same thing we do for tooth decay. We keep our teeth (mind) clean, by brushing and flossing away untruths and false beliefs. Get regular checkups with the dentist (a professional)—go to church regularly, and occasionally, schedule an appointment for spiritual counseling, or go to a retreat center.

It's very important that we realize the magnitude of this, if we want to stop suffering in our lives and around the globe. It is also crucial that we realize our own power for change as we apply the Principle in our lives, and share them with others.

We look around and wonder why it never ends: Why can we not live in peace? Why do people kill each other? Why can't we heal? Why is there poverty? Consider the possibility these things exist because we refuse to change. We refuse to live in alignment with spiritual Principle, civil, and religious codes. The term *As above, so below,* references higher laws—Principles—are showing us the way to live the good life. Yet we see ourselves as an exception to the rule, slipping through loopholes. We see it every day—exceeding the speed limit, texting while driving, taking supplies home from work, not putting in a full day, flirting when we are not available, fibbing, or telling flat-out lies.

Everything we want to change, starts with a change of mind and heart. We can change our thoughts, watch our words, and assure that the actions we take will have positive results. We have the power, but it takes commitment and strength to overcome the temptations and pull of the lower nature. Everything starts in thought. When we find ourselves in the grip of temptation, we must catch it as soon as we can, and shift our thoughts.

THERE WILL BE SIGNS

From the shadows, false gods emerge, seducing us with thoughts of personal power and pleasure. Their influence increasing as long-held virtues deteriorate. Like the biblical little foxes that spoil the flowering vine in Solomon's vineyard, promises of a harvest are wiped out. Solomon represents wisdom and understanding. These were the gifts he asked God for and received. The *little foxes* are ideas of doubt, fear, and ignorance, and the actions we take based on them. The vine symbolizes our growing knowledge and wisdom of Truth. We cannot let the *little foxes* of doubt and fear damage the vine.

Think about this—if you had a lovely vineyard, and discovered little foxes coming in and gnawing at the grapevines, you would have to eliminate them. To chase them away. What doubts and fears are gnawing away at your mind and heart? What *little white lies* have you told? Weakening your spiritual strength? Jesus said, *"I am the branch, you are the vine."* (Jn 15:3) He is speaking of the vine as growing from the branch of His teaching. The vine is nourished and made strong and fruitful by the branch. The *little foxes* even have names, like: Only-Yeah But-Just, etc. Beware of them.

One of my least-favorite scriptures is: *"There will be signs in the sun, moon and stars. On the earth, nations will be in anguish and perplexity at the roaring and tossing of the sea."* (Luke 21:25) It always scared the daylights out of me. I have a different perspective, now. I know how to look for the signs.

SIGNS OF FALSE GODS AT WORK

The presence of false gods, is exposed as we learn to discern the signs that are everywhere when we look. If we notice a focus on self and money, or stuff, that's a sign the false gods are behind it. Importance of church, and God has diminished. Churches are empty, but parking lots at the mall, the Temple of Mammon, are full, that is a sign. The Hartford Institute of Religious Research shows while 40% of Americans attend church, the true figure is more like 20%. As they say, *there's your sign.*

Attendance at the church, temple, mosque, etc. of our choice, provides spiritual guidance, and a support system of kindred spirits to share our journey. When we come together to worship, which means to give worth to, God—all good, we are strengthened. Not taking part in a spiritual community leaves us more vulnerable to our own ego or false gods.

Prayer and holiday pageants are no longer allowed in schools, and religious symbols in government offices are banned. Some communities do not allow religious holiday displays. While it is error to remove all forms of religious expression, equally erroneous to make everyone conform to one expression. Spirit did not intend for us all to be one religion. We're all free to practice the religion of our choice. Religious tolerance and understanding, let us explore and share each other's holidays, which can deepen our relationship with God.

Celebrities have replaced our Heroes. Once, heroes and role models were abundant. There are a few today, but not like before. Years ago we had sports figures, astronauts, talented actors and actresses performing in family-friendly entertainment, scientists and unscathed political figures. These were people with bona fide accomplishments who served as inspiration for people, young and old. They were also held to standards of behavior. Anti-heroes are more common today, for many they are preferred.

Team loyalty is outmoded, as free-agent athletes, go with the highest bidder. No longer does a child yearn to grow up and play for the Yankees, or Dodgers, but for the deals.

Athlete and celebrity paychecks are ludicrously high, while vital jobs such as a teacher, or CNA or many other necessary worker's paychecks are far below what they should be. The high wages of celebrities drive up the ticket prices, feeding Mammon as we work longer hours to continue pay them with our ticket money.

Big businesses have bought naming rights for stadiums, arenas, and conference centers that now advertise their businesses instead of bearing names that honor famous people. The name of stadium on the marquis, makes them shrines to Mammon and Baal.

Technology is replacing one-on-one, face-to-face relationships and communication. The impact is already felt in decreased communication and vocabulary skills. Popularity is measured in social media likes. We communicate more and say less. Teens live vicariously with video games and virtual reality. While there is no concise agreement, some studies indicate the games encourage violence and anti-social behavior. This fosters separation rather than connection and community. (Source: videogames.procon.org) From the perspective of the Law of Mind Action, it is more likely causative factors include not only the games, but movies, music, and peers.

Unacceptable, rude behavior is common. The President of the United States exhibits the behaviors of a petulant adolescent, with name-calling and a never-ending stream of unfounded lies and accusations. Violence, vulgarity and disrespect thrive in the entertainment industry. Unacceptable behaviors abound in the entertainment that comes to us. Rather than being inspired to raise the bar in our lives (which would bless us), we are being seduced by our carnal nature.

We are in an epidemic of narcissism. Craving for celebrity tempts us to spend thousands on unnecessary plastic surgery. When narcissism wins, compassion loses. Narcissism separates us, community binds us together.

The *selfie* obsession, a compulsive impulse to take countless pictures of oneself, posting them on social media, keeps the focus on self, rather than community, and the life that is happening all around us. It has reached epidemic proportions. The word, selfie, encapsulates the problem: focus on self, resulting on a false sense of worth based on the opinions or attention of others. Or as a Meme I saw the other day said: *"They call it a selfie because narcissist is too hard to spell."*

The ultimate sign of false gods at work in seen in disrespect and destruction of life itself. I would prefer to not even have to mention killing. It is so painful. We hear about murders every day, without a chance to catch our breath before the next report. Death and destruction of lives and our planet are now a part of our everyday lives. While it seems to be what we have come to, it was not always this way, and it can change. First we need to examine the problem from the metaphysical perspective.

We start with facts (remember there is a difference between fact and truth): Overall the crime and murder rate declined during the 1980's. A short while ago it was at a low not seen since the nineteen-sixties. In 1994 an assault weapons ban was put in place. The intention was to reduce the frequency and lethality of mass shootings. In 2004 the ban expired. According to a MIC Network article by Alison Durkee published February 28, 2018, since that time the mass shootings increased over 239%. In February 2017 Trump rolled back an Obama era restriction that would prevent gun sales to individuals with mental disorders, and in December 2017 the House passed legislation to allow concealed carry across state lines.

The current leadership flatly refuses to consider putting restrictions on assault weapons, or even outlawing bump stocks, which turn a semi-automatic weapon into an automatic weapon, capable of firing quickly and repeatedly. It's not just the speed and number of bullets, but the damage the bullets are designed to do to a human body. In fact, these guns can't be used for hunting because it would ruin the meat. This allowed one man to kill 59 people and injure 500!

We can no longer go to a movie, concert, church or even school, confident we will not be shot and killed. We appear to be in a losing battle, since the National Rifle Association (NRA) and gun manufacturers are in cahoots with politicians. By the way, these folks love it when gun control issues come up, because the fanatics run out and get more guns. They keep the rumor mill grinding away.

Without throwing up our hands in dismay, it is more important than ever to learn, live and share the Universal Principles of truth that will put an end to the bloodshed and insanity.

Now, let's look at the metaphysics. What is behind the appearance? All manifestation begins in mind. The nature of the manifestation depends on the state of mind that holds the thought. Also where and how Mammon and Baal are influencing mind. We can't look at the problem while we are in the middle of it. We have to rise above it.

Below is a process for evaluating. Using any of the examples above, answer these questions:

Where and how is money involved?

Where and how is ego involved?

How does this separate us?

What will the ultimate impact on the individual be?

What will the ultimate impact on the whole be?

In which quadrant of consciousness did the action take root?

What can we do to initiate change?

An interpretation: Gun Control–Why won't politicians support what the majority wants?

Where and how is money involved? (Mammon)

Politicians receive money from lobbyists and manufacturers of guns. In exchange for favoring the agenda of the organizations and lobbyists.

Politicians need the money for their campaigns and personal use.

Where and how is ego involved? (Baal)

Politicians want to retain their positions. They like the lifestyle it affords them, as well as perceived power.

They do not want to challenge the providers of funds or voters who align with their agenda for fear they will lose votes.

How does this separate us?

Politicians choose sides based on money and power, estranging those they are supposed to represent. Truth, or facts are irrelevant, propaganda is spread with funds and lobbying.

What will the ultimate impact on the individual be?

Individual citizens are at increased risk of gun violence. This has been statistically proven. Through the Law of Increase, the number of guns and gun violence will increase until and unless the pain becomes unbearable. (source: gunviolencearchive.org)

What will the ultimate impact on the whole be?

The divisions among the people who make up the whole will be expanded. There will be increased anger and separation. We will become weaker as a country.

In which quadrant of consciousness did the problem take root?

It is my belief that fear is at the root, and then engaged power. Fearing they would lose their freedom to gun access, anything—true or false—that might threaten them is considered a valid threat and they will do anything in their power to prevent change.

What can we do to initiate change?

What we can't do is allow our mind to drop into the lower quadrants. We cannot come from a place of fear and force change through power. Do our homework. Research issues and prepare to address challenges. Speak your truth with peace and love. Invite conversation without conflict. Don't accuse. Don't fight. Don't give up.

Psalm 124:8 Our help is in the name of the Lord, who has made heaven and earth.

This scripture is telling us to trust the Lord—law—Principle, through which everything we see has been made. We can do this by striving to stay in the upper quadrants: intuitive and sensing, where we find strength and guidance. I would say that we would be wiser yet to meditate daily opening our minds to Superconscious, or Divine Mind, God/Spirit.

This process can be a tool to understand and work with everyday problems in our lives and the world. Look for the good in people, places and organizations.

Not all signs are negative. There are good signs we can focus on. Considering the Law of Mind Action: *"Where the mind goes, energy flows, and manifestation follows"*, we have to ask ourselves what it is we want to manifest, and spend more time focusing on that than anything negative.

HIJACKED HOLIDAYS

The word holiday, comes from the word holy day. Holy days are days set aside for commemoration and celebration. Along with holy days, the Bible includes festivals. We have religious and secular holidays, each one with a specific meaning or purpose. Holidays are a time to commemorate people and events. It's a time to ponder God's grace and love, or sacrifices made by others so we can have a better life. When we celebrate holidays in the spirit intended, it keeps alive the memory of God's power and presence in our lives.

Our celebrations tell stories of events that underscore God's presence in our everyday lives. The repetition affirms, or makes firm, the Principles demonstrated, which then strengthen our faith and serve us in creating good. Ego-fed false gods, want everything to be about me, my, mine, and more stuff!

Think about it. For every holiday, there's a holiday sale. Thanksgiving, the day we have set aside to thank God for our abundance, thousands, driven by an insatiable craving, or fear of lack, pour into stores, aka the temple of Mammon. They stand in line, and sometimes trample each other for a perceived bargain. More importance is given to getting more than spending time with family giving thanks for what they have.

Black Friday, which stores sell us as an opportunity for folks to shop early for Christmas, is actually an opportunity for retailers, who may have been in the red all year, to get their books in the black, or making a profit. There's nothing wrong with that, until greed comes in. In the black wasn't good enough. Stores, again compelled by fear, lack, or greed moved up their Black Friday sales to Thanksgiving Day. A perceived competition among businesses to get to customers first ensued.

It would be one thing if that was the end of the holiday shopping, but then we've got Small Business Saturday and Cyber Monday, and so it goes through the year. Shopping occludes any other holiday experience.

Consider this holiday experiment: it could be Christmas, Hanukkah or other religious gift giving holiday. Based on the Biblical telling of the story of Jesus' birth, he received three gifts. One from each of the wise men. Could that be enough? Three gifts, purchased with love, for a reasonable price. Your ego will balk. Family members may have hissy fits. That will only happen the first year. I know this is true. My sister's family has gift exchange. One gift for the person whose name they have drawn, and a stocking. They have been doing it for several years now, and it works for everyone. Decades ago I simplified my Christmas giving. I would give one gift to each of my children as a family gift. I started this for financial reasons. My church was small, and so was my paycheck. But to my surprise, the lack of gifts did not take away my holiday joy. There is no need to curtail gift giving, just don't let that outshine the real meaning of a holiday.

Remember what the holiday is about. For me, as a Christian, it is about celebrating the greatest gift, Jesus, who taught us Universal Principles of Truth and love that bless us every day. Reminder: It's not YOUR birthday. How strange it is that Christmas is the celebration Jesus' birthday, but we get the gifts? Yes, we do like to give—because we want to behold the Christ, or Divine Spirit in each other. We just want to keep gift giving in perspective.

Christmas is not the only hijacked holiday. The false gods don't miss an opportunity to tempt us to self-indulgence and spending money. We've got Washington's Birthday sales, President's Day sales, New Year's Day sales, Mother's Day, Father's Day, Grandparent's Day, Valentine's Day and two that bother me the most, Veteran's Day and Memorial Day sales. Ask yourself, seriously, *what is it about these holidays that require a sale?*

A recent trend is *Easter Extravagance.* Merchandisers tempt shoppers with high-priced items that rival the greatest birthday or Christmas gifts. This worldly focus of the false gods, is attempting to overtake the core of the Christian celebration, Jesus' resurrection. This is insidious because it takes the focus away from the most powerful teaching of the Christian faith. The Christian faith would not exist without its powerful teaching of eternal life and Jesus leading the way by overcoming death.

Holiday sales are not about gaining stuff, it's about distracting us from the good we already have. When we take our eyes from what is meaningful to something that takes up space and we have to dust, we miss the true riches. It's about putting money in the merchants' pockets. It's about greed, not need.

In the Catholic Church, some holidays are called *Holy Days of Obligation.* Church doctrine requires followers to attend church, to commemorate the person or event and how it has blessed others. I see them as *Holy Days, or Whole-ing Days of Opportunity, a time* when we can reconnect with God, and the meaning of our relationship with Spirit. We can all benefit from this teaching. On the next holiday, take time to observe the event yourself. You can do it in your place of worship, or home.

Learn about the holidays and practices of other faiths. What is the message in their rites and rituals? Could it apply in your own life? How? Ask yourself what the universal meaning of the rites or rituals is. See how they express Spiritual Principle. We may find it can bring us closer to God and each other. Consider this: both the

Chinese culture and Jewish faith have New Year holidays, a great opportunity to start over, again and again. Who doesn't want to start over again?

Regarding secular holidays, we have to ask ourselves, what it is we're celebrating on Memorial Day, or Veteran's day. We can plan holidays to be more than a picnic, putting our focus on the meaning of the holiday. It can include family discussion, attending a parade, a visit to a military cemetery, or a gathering honoring veterans.

Many of the holiday traditions we practice today, came from other faith groups. This includes Easter eggs and Halloween. When early church leaders observed the religious practices of the converts they were making, they would often translate those practices into a Christian format.

We reclaim our holidays by understanding both the *what*, and the *why*, of the holiday. I can tell you from personal experience, not only can this happen, but it will enrich your experience, while it supports what matters most about the holiday.

SOMETIMES THE DRAGON WINS

Sometimes the good guy gets the short end of the stick. They could be a victim of circumstance. That's what a great number of Americans felt on November 9th 2016. As the months went by fears of many people were realized and multiplied. For them, everything got worse and worse. Countries that once admired America have become disenchanted. Blatant lies Trump told to the Prime Minister of Canada, were seen by him as acceptable. He joked about it. We have now been estranged from our International allies, while Trump curries favor with and praises a murderous dictator. Overlooking the sound reasons on the part of six other nations for removing Russia from the *G7* meetings, Trump requests readmission. While the errors of this man are public and clear, his base continues to worship him. They sing his praises, even in the face of disaster in the country. This is a matter of concern, because the offensive actions, and words can be factually verified, along with likely negative outcomes. Yes, it certainly appears that sometimes the dragon wins.

Everyone has had the occasion to feel the dragon won. We've either experienced financial disaster, divorce, war, or natural disaster. It's very important to remember our experiences are effects that followed causes. Our response—or reaction—to the experience will generate new causes. We cannot change the causes, but we can change the effects by sending forth different causes. We have the opportunity to change.

When Jesus and his disciples were at sea, a great storm kicked up as Jesus snoozed. His disciples, terrified, awakened him. He calmed the storm and then said: *"Why are you so afraid? Do you still have no faith?"* (Mark 4:40) Each one of us can ask ourselves where our faith is when we read the scary headlines, rumors of wars, personal crises, and frustrating commentaries of politicians and news reporters.

False gods shift our expression of faith from God, to outer things—to self, or force and coercion—or believe we are the director of the universe, trying to pull God's strings. We discover that isn't true. When we hurt enough to let go of our fear and need to control, we are ready to trust a Higher Power. When we're knocked to your knees, an old sage taught, we're in a perfect position to pray. This is a kernel of truth.

In Unity, we teach the power of the Law of Mind Action. Because it is law, it is absolute, eternal and unchanging. But it can only work if we work it, and how we work it. We may hold thoughts with diligence, visioning what we want. Or make treasure maps, spend time in focused prayer, practically demanding God provide fulfillment of our wish. If we have forgotten a critical component, working with Principle, this plan is doomed to fail. Either we will not get the thing or circumstance we desire, or we will get it, to find we regret it. Confused?

The old saying, *be careful what you pray for* is a valid warning. The more we listen to ego—our little self—the more we convince ourselves what we want, is what God wants for us. This is metaphysical malpractice, and that's not the way it works. We cannot make our will God's will. Instead, we yield our stubborn will to the will of Spirit, which always works for good. Instead of saying to God, *Thy will be done,* we usually declare MY will be done. This is yet another sign of false gods at work. Our mind is operating at the lower, carnal level.

When I worked in the Silent Unity Prayer Room, many callers requested prayer generated by the carnal mind. Some requested I pray their abusive, alcoholic mate would return. Or they would ask for a financial blessing as if God was Santa Claus. I could not and would not hold that prayer. Instead, I would pray with them, affirming that God's blessings were coming to them; the Spirit of peace would enfold them, good would come to them through channels expected and unexpected. I was in fact praying for their highest good. The years I worked for Silent Unity immersed me in affirmative prayer, affirming (making firm) Truth, not begging or magical thinking.

Unless we put faith in Spirit—Universal Principle—as our primary prayer, the dragon will continue to win. This doesn't deny the use of meditation, treasure maps, visualization, etc. to maintain our focus as long as we remember two essential components. The first is asking God's will be done. The second is including, *this, or something better.* We have to acknowledge we don't always know what's in our best interest.

Keeping in mind the Law of Increase, it's counterproductive to obsess over negative circumstances. That can overwhelm us. What do we want to increase? That is where we put our focus. Once we have prayed, we keep our eyes open for changes. When we do things right, but they still go wrong, it's an opportunity for growth. Spiritual growth can be painful.

BEWARE OF THE WOLVES

False gods operate the same way wolves, which are skilled predators do. We can learn much from the hunting techniques of wolves, to protect ourselves from the wiles of false gods.

Wolves position themselves near a flock of sheep, being sure to stay downwind, so the sheep won't notice their presence. Likewise, false gods lurk all around us, waiting for the opportunity to pounce. Emotions such as anger can attack even on a beautiful day when everything in our world seems perfect. As committed as we might be to being a peaceful, loving, spiritual person, that person with 15 items in the 12 item checkout lane can bring out the worst in us. Our good intention evaporates. The dragon wins. To avoid the sneak attack of emotions and thoughts contrary to our good, it is important to stay alert, and practice responding, not reacting in these circumstances.

Wolves seek the young and weak at the edge of the flock. A wolf will bite a lamb on the back, wounding and weakening it, then wait for when it can be cut from the flock, when he can kill it without encountering the rest of the flock. In our lives, it is important to stay strong, and not wander away from the *flock*. This can be interpreted two ways. The first, is to surround ourselves with strong, experienced kindred spirits—people who share our beliefs. This helps us to stay grounded in the teaching. The second is to be in a constant state of learning, living, and sharing Truth Principles. This will keep us strong.

Wolves have abundant strength and stamina and can run all night long. They fatigue the prey then go in for the kill. False gods run us down with a constant barrage of thoughts and feelings, maybe fear, anger, anxiety, one after another until we weaken. The greater impact the thought has on our emotions, generates more negative energy. In time, we will make a mistake. This is how credit cards get maxed out, diets get blown, and words are said we regret. We know right from wrong, but we still have to stay strong. We have to break the chain of thought before it breaks us. Whenever we are under stress it is critical to take care of ourselves. Eating right, getting enough rest and exercise, and of course taking time for prayer and meditation helps.

RELIGION AND SPIRITUALITY

It's common today to hear folks saying, *I'm spiritual, not religious*. When I hear this, I wonder if they know the difference. Do you consider yourself to be spiritual, or religious? In truth, we are both. Let's begin with the definition:

Religion: A formalized, or institutionalized set of beliefs concerning the cause, nature, and purpose of the universe or Supreme Being, or beings, containing a moral code governing the conduct of human affairs.

Spirituality: The true essence of every being, the spark of divinity that relates us to God, the Creator. It's our awareness of something greater than self and our relationship to it, and all of creation. It is a quality of being dedicated to God, religion or spiritual things or values, as contrasted with material or temporal ones.

Our spiritual nature expresses through the moral code written in our deepest parts. This our Credo. It is the *what*, and religion is the *how*, or the manner in which we express our spirituality. Religion without spirituality would be like an empty house. Spirituality without religion, is like a tumbleweed, blown hither and yon by the wind, with no direction of its own.

Many of the folks who say they're spiritual not religious were required to attend or take part in a religion they didn't believe at the core of their being—their inner-knowing. When they became adolescents, and would either rebel, and say they are atheist, declaring all religion is a lie, or they may choose spirituality over religion. Even if they didn't know what it meant. Many other people attend the church of their parents, adhering to the rules and rituals. This is a missed opportunity because Spirit is not being fed and reaching spiritual maturity would be compromised.

Another common reason those who have drifted away from church say they are spiritual rather than religious, is because it's easier than getting out of bed, going to church. It's easier than examining their own behavior, exercising self-discipline, or asking hard questions. Those who have been fortunate enough, as I have, found the perfect fit of a religion that aligns with their inner belief system, or credo. Whether it is a church, temple or mosque, if it feeds our soul, it's the perfect place. The mode is not as important as the match. God doesn't care where we go, only that we go.

Here is how I found my path: Realizing that I didn't agree with some teachings of my religion of origin I stopped going to church. This was after over 40 years of regular attendance. After six months, the yearning for my connection to God was like a great hunger. I began a search for something that resonated with what I believed in my heart and soul.

To this day, I feel weak in the knees when I recall finding my religious/spiritual path in Unity. My spirit cried out, *You're home! You're home! You're home!* Everything I heard made sense. Within me, my soul agreed with the teachings. I would listen and say to myself *that's true*. I saw all religion in a new light. What I learned did not invalidate, but harmonized with the teachings of most other faiths. While there were differences in different religions, I could see the common thread weaving through all of them. It was Oneness in diversity—one God, many paths. I could now see we are more alike than we are different.

As stated earlier, what I experienced was not a matter of conversion. It was confirmation of what I somehow knew was true in my heart and soul. In the Bible we read earlier: "I will put my law within them, I will write it on their hearts." (Jeremiah 31:33) One meaning of the word *heart* in the Bible, is the combined thinking and feeling faculties. This is the intuitive part of us. It knows right from wrong, without being taught. It was a part of us at birth.

Religion serves as a framework through which we express our spiritual beliefs. I believe religion evolved from an inner desire to connect, or re-connect with the Divine—with that something greater than all we know. Charles Fillmore, cofounder of Unity, called desire the *onward impulse of the ever-evolving soul.*

Definitions of *impulse* include: a psychic drive or instinctual urge, and the scientific definition, a sudden flow of electrical current in one direction. Scientists claim all is energy—everything we see—which can explain the impulse to express our spirituality.

We are all in different stages of spiritual evolution or transformation. As seekers, we will find we're drawn to different religions or spiritual paths. We emanate a vibrational energy that draws to us the path that will fulfill our needs. The axiom, *like attracts like,* is proven, if we allow it. It took decades for me to consider the possibility I was not on the right path for me. While I remained in the religion I'd followed all of my life, there was the constant feeling inside that something was missing.

When I found the spiritual path that was right for me, Unity, I realized from the moment I read the Daily Word it was what I'd always been looking for. I did not jump in with two feet for several months as I explored the teaching.

Religions emerge from the spiritual experience of an individual, like Jesus, Buddha, and Mohammed. The individual shares their experience, teaching the wisdom gleaned, developing a group of followers who resonate with the message. Jesus commissioned

His apostles and disciples who were committed to sharing the teaching. This evolved into Christianity. In religious history, a common occurrence is, after the death of the inspired teacher, the message becomes either adulterated, or expanded by the leaders as they interject their interpretation. The core teaching can get lost.

We can see this happening today. The lines around core teachings have become fuzzy. Long-held values in all faith groups are being watered down or adulterated. A common cause of this is an attempt to keep numbers in attendance. Churches have fallen victim to people pleasing and providing entertainment instead of firm, spiritual teaching.

There are times this is a good thing, and others not so much. If a false teaching or belief is discovered and eliminated, that makes the church stronger. If people come to church to be entertained, the church becomes impotent.

The core mission of religion is to provide people a means of expressing their beliefs, of knowing, loving and serving God, to worship, or give worth to (worth-ship) to all that matters most. It's about acknowledging something greater than ourselves. This is not what false gods want. False gods, thoughts in carnal mind, want more focus on being god than having a relationship with God.

False gods, our lower nature—materialism and carnality, want the manifest world to be our god—our perceived source of good. They appeal to our flaws of narcissism and laziness. Doing the right thing—subscribing to a moral code, striving to grow and become, refusing to bow down to materialism and carnality, is inconvenient and uncomfortable. It is the road less traveled. Going with the flow of human thought is easy. It requires little to nothing, as the human eye can see, yet the real price, the hidden agenda of the false gods is your bondage to them, and the power we give them in our lives.

Finding our own spiritual/religious match strengthens our relationship with God. We become part of a spiritual support system of like-minded others, and live happier, healthier lives. Our spirit is fed as we expand, express and practice our faith, then share it with others. If you are fed and inspired in your church, it's a clear sign you're in the right place. If you don't, I suggest you find a church that resonates with your inner-knowing. One of the most wonderful parts of this, is that rather than creating divisions, through practicing our own faith we learn to love and respect others. From this place in consciousness we live our Truth, of Oneness in Diversity.

Jesus said he was in the world, not of it. While this would be a great state to aspire to, and sounds simple to achieve, it's difficult. We each have both a spiritual and human nature. Jesus lived from the spiritual and called us to follow him. Most of us live from the human nature. Why? It is all around us. A second reason is, to achieve spiritual mastery, we must overcome the human, or carnal nature.

EVIL AS A CONTAGIOUS DIS-EASE

To be holy is to be whole, healthy, complete—having integrity in all aspects of mind, body and soul. It's something to aspire to. If holiness is not our current state of being, but we know of our need to grow, every step we take toward holiness feels great and calls us onward. However, if we find our lives troubled, and filled with challenges, pain and suffering, every day brings more of the same. Beneath it is a restlessness, a sense that something isn't right. In Unity we call this *divine discontent*. It's a sense that there must be a better way and compels us toward it.

To be progressing on our spiritual path brings a sense of comfort, when we are not progressing—when we stall or worse, regress, we experience discomfort. If we look at forward motion as ease that would make reverse motion dis-ease. Even if we are in reverse, we are not bad. We are living backward—contrary to our good. Remember: *evil* is *live* spelled backward.

We may not have a clue how we wound up going backward. A common cause is the collective consciousness we are immersed in every day. The dis-ease of evil is highly contagious. We can catch it anywhere. It might be commercials that tell us what we must rush to the store to get whatever they are pushing to put money in their pocket. Or, it could be the declaration *it's cold and flu season*, and next thing you know, you're sneezing and hacking. Then there's the ever-popular, *everybody's doing it*.

Personality drives the mortal mind, not Principle. Opinions have more value than facts. Ego, emotions, money and stuff are more sought after than community. Integrity, and self, come before the whole. Popularity is Prince. Yet there is an underlying, insatiable hunger for something else.

With integrity, it's all or nothing. We all have it within us as potential. Either we use it or we don't. With integrity, we are the same person in all circumstances. There is no such thing as a little truthful or a little lie. We can't justify erroneous behaviors. The good news is, we have symptoms of our errors to help us change the trajectory of our lives. We can shift gears and move forward again. If you've ever driven a car with a standard transmission—a rare experience these days—you'll recall you had to disengage the gears with the clutch, move the shift lever to engage first gear, and release the clutch to move forward. As your speed increased, you need to shift gears to keep your ride smooth.

We often have to disengage from people, places and things that keep us in a negative state of mind. We have to stop the constant stream of ego or fear-based thoughts that keep tugging at us. Consider some negative people you associate with, places that inhibit spiritual growth, and maybe long-established habits that need breaking. To keep yourself in a state free of dis-ease, let go. How do we deal with germs? We avoid them and stay clean. This is also true with germs of consciousness. Having integrity may mean making new friends. Turn off the news and stop watching violent or provocative movies.

They say *God hates a void,* so fill the void you are creating with positive things. Read good books, listen to uplifting music, join a club or find a church that has a positive message that inspires and encourages you. If you do not fill the void, believe me when I tell you, the negative energies will be back in a heartbeat.

Sometimes the *dragon* that wins is within us. We may catch ourselves in a sin—a rant of rage, gossip or a lie. As we become more attuned to Spirit, we become more sensitive to these errors. They threaten to shatter any progress we have made on our path of transformation. The decrease of faith in our own self can lead to further sins—errors. Consider the story about Jesus rescuing the woman caught in adultery, who was about to be stoned. He first said to the accusers, who were ready to stone her, "Let he who is without sin cast the first stone." Incidentally, Edgar Cayce, known as *The Sleeping Prophet* claimed it is a mistranslation, and should have read: *"Let he who has not slept with her cast the first stone."* One by one, the stones dropped. As the last accuser skulked away, Jesus asked the woman where her accusers were. When she replied that there were none, He said to her: *"Neither do I condemn you. Go forth, and sin no more."* (John 8:11)

If the woman had continued to condemn herself, she would have been holding thoughts of herself as a sinner, which would manifest. It's spiritual law. Jesus, telling her to go forth and sin no more, was like putting the period on the end of a sentence. We must each do this. If we've made a mistake, we acknowledge it, understand why it is an error, and then change that behavior. In doing this, we can bring our conscious mind back to the higher state.

THE PIT AND THE PENDULUM–IMMORALITY VS RIGID RELIGIOSITY

There is a widening chasm in the collective carnal mind on planet Earth. The chasm is between rigid religiosity and the anarchy of amorality. Confusion reigns as we struggle to discern right from wrong. In one hand, we have i-dotting—t-crossing fundamentalism, and in the other no moral compass, leading to a lawless freewheeling lifestyle.

While some warn of the wrath of God soon to come upon us, others claim there is no reality in the concepts of right and wrong—it is what it is. This, they believe, gives them license to do whatever they want, anything goes, based on free will.

In the Edgar Allan Poe story, *The Pit and the Pendulum*, the main character finds himself strapped down, at the hands of the inquisition, watching as a large pendulum with a huge steel blade at its end swings above him. With each swing—right—to left—to right—the blade descends. It comes ever closer to the man's body, as it glides with menacing terror. The man struggles to find a way to escape his inevitable fate. He realizes that the blade will cut him in half and will slice straight through his heart. When he struggles, the blade descends faster.

You can read the whole story on your own to discover how things turned out. For now, it's more important to recognize our own struggle. From both the individual and collective perspective, in rigid religiosity we are only puppets, tied to the strings of some perceived authority. With amorality there are no guidelines or blueprints, so we wander without direction, and experience a never-ending discontent, and the continued adverse effects of mistakes.

As we struggle with the issues of rigid religiosity and amorality, we keep the pendulum in motion. The way to stop a pendulum is by friction and gravity—by resisting the struggle, coming to center, and peace through understanding. Many of us have broken free from overbearing churches teaching concepts we couldn't embrace. At first, the newfound freedom was great, but it left us without a foundation to build on. Structure gives us a sense of security and stability. It's something we can stand on and for. It is my prayer that through considering the Principles presented in this book, and their application in your life, you find that peace at the center of your being that will stop the pendulum of struggle.

Overcoming years of false beliefs takes time. Misconceptions and lies need to be realized and erased. Patience is a virtue. I have seen many people come to Unity, often having great demonstrations right away. Then, when the result is not immediate, they give up.

We don't get the perfect physique with one visit to the gym. If we go every day, but continue to live an unhealthy lifestyle, we won't see the results we want. To achieve spiritual mastery, we must be all-in. The Principles must be engaged, and when mastered, shared with others. There may be times when it appears the Principles are not working. This is the most important time to affirm God's work is being done.

Keep in mind this problem is both individual and collective. It is the responsibility of each of us to live according to our beliefs, from a state of mind that knows of our inextricable union. Learn the Principles. Live the Principles. Share the Principles, always sharing your truth with love and not judgment. Even on the collective level the friction and gravity (understanding) we provide will help stop the pendulum's cutting blade.

An old cliché states, *there's nothing worse than a convert.* In terms of enlightenment once we *see the light* it's only natural we'd want to share it with everyone we know. When we try to share it though, we may find few who are open to change. Our friends from traditional, fundamentalist churches look at metaphysical teachings with disapproval, and our unchurched or de-churched friends look at our revelations with skepticism.

What can we do? Jesus told us we are the light of the world, and to put our light on a lamp stand, not under a basket, meaning to share the light we are. Keep in mind, it will be easier to open the eyes of others with a 30 watt glow than a 200 watt glare. What we can do is live according to our beliefs and wait for an opportunity to share it with others.

As stated earlier, *life is consciousness.* Ignorance is not bliss although enlightenment can bring bliss. What we don't know *can* hurt us. Enlightenment is knowledge and understanding of Spiritual Principle. Once we comprehend how the Principles work, we'll find that our lives transform. Rather than having bad experiences and thinking we are a victim, we can look to cause so we can change the effect. Instead of thinking God is punishing us, or you're just unlucky in a random world, we can look for the part we have played, if any.

The *pit and pendulum* of carnal mind shows up in the government, and right now we are not seeing the big picture. The Republicans would represent the rigid ideology, and Democrats the liberal state of mind. If the pendulum is in full swing, we have the alt-right and alt-left, both of which propel the menacing blade toward slicing through the heart of America.

The Independent party is more centered than the other two, but not big enough to make the impact that would lead to change. Some people claim we should eliminate the two-party system. I'm not so sure we are ready for that. What I know for sure is that the way of separation and division is not working. It never has, never will. We must stand for the roots of tradition, and the wings of freedom, to work for bi-partisan cooperation. We require both the letter and the heart of the law, the intuitive and sensing nature for everything to work together for good.

When either party runs a partisan agenda, everyone suffers. When we elect one-dimensional people to work in the government, we cannot meet the needs of the population. We would benefit by looking at candidates, and asking ourselves which quadrant of consciousness are they speaking to, and are they inclusive? Most of all, vote for candidates who mirror our values and what matters most for the good of all.

VERSUS ~ SORTING IT OUT

Recognizing false gods and their works, will help us understand and get past them. Consider the following word-pairs for a deeper understanding of concepts easy to misunderstand.

SELF-INDULGENCE VS SELF-DISCIPLINE: In the present stage of development in human consciousness, there's not much support for self-discipline, and much temptation for self-indulgence. The problem is every time we say, think, or do something self-centered, we stunt our spiritual growth. We are not living our Oneness. This is true if our self-indulgence is not in the best interest of the greater whole. One example is creating unnecessary waste and pollution, or littering. We do what we want although it's not healthy or respecting the environment that provides food, clothing, shelter, water, and the nurture of nature. When we practice self-discipline, we grow, help others, and feel better about ourselves.

INFLUENCE VS INSPIRATION: As our mind is our connecting link to God, it is also our connecting link to each other. Because the mind is pivotal it can shift its focus from heavenly, or spiritual things, to earthly, material—carnal things. We make ourselves vulnerable to influence when we turn our mind to our lower nature, or mind of the flesh. Consider the term, *under the influence.* If we de-construct these two words, in-fluence (to flow in), and in-spire (to breathe into, also spire as the highest point), we see that our lower mind is subject to the flow of race consciousness—the collective perspective, and realm of false gods. To be inspired is to look to the highest point, and let Spirit breathe into us. Everyday life is like living in a sea of thought, often with waves crashing across headlines or screens. To achieve inspiration, we must train ourselves to open to God's inspiration, not the influence of others.

LUCK VS DIVINE ORDER: The casinos overflow with people—glazed eyes pumping coins into machines, and laying down plastic chips that represent the money paid for them, hoping to get lucky. My research indicated that seventy percent of lottery winners are broke in a few years. Fifty percent of marriages end in divorce. There are many people who push their luck. They text, drink and drive, and cheat on their taxes, hoping they will get lucky. Some folks think they are unlucky. Others seem to win every time they buy a raffle ticket or enter a contest. What's up with that?

I have a friend who always wins! Whether it's a raffle or game, she wins. I have observed, at the campground my sister and her husband own, children win bingo games more often than adults. I believe this is because they expect to win. Through the Principle of mind action, we get what we expect; we draw our circumstances to us.

Overall, we live by the Law, which is always in effect. When one lives the law, they may win an unexpected windfall, and call it luck. It's more likely the residual effect of long-term positive thought. This is Divine Order—when positive thoughts, feelings and actions are consistent in mind, good will come. What we believe about luck determines outcomes. If we don't think we're lucky, we won't be. False gods tempt and torment us to take a chance, to get something for nothing. If we win, without doing the work in consciousness, the winnings will soon disappear. If it is not ours by right of consciousness, it is not ours. Our mind, our thoughts and feelings, must align with divine law and not the error belief in luck.

LOVE VS HATE: Love is Principle, not personal. It is not an emotion, although we express love through our emotions. Hate is an effort to negate the Divine Idea of love, so it is a sin. Because we are all One, in truth, love binds us together while hate is an attempt to separate, and good will never come of it. Hate comes from fear and ignorance.

SELF-ESTEEM VS ARROGANCE: We should all strive to have self-esteem, because we are all God's children. We are each gifted, regardless of age, social standing, or education. Some people have a mistaken belief that self-esteem is pride, which makes it a bad thing. Pride is not a bad thing unless it is an over-inflated sense of self. That would be arrogance. Low self-esteem creates a mindset of not measuring up, and often attracts arrogant people who will validate their false belief about themselves. Every day we can remind ourselves of the good things we do and acknowledge our goodness. Life is meant be good. For everyone. Arrogance can appear in ourselves, and the government. We may stand and shout *"We're number one,"* while in truth we are just one part of a greater whole or we are nothing. If the arrogance in our country does not cease, we may find we are not number one, but lonely—and unsupported by those who once looked up to us. Evidence of this could be seen in the outcome of the 2018 G7 Meetings, where our allies were alienated.

PLEASURE VS HAPPINESS: We can confuse pleasure and happiness. For clarity I would like to present this concept: Pleasure is enjoyment or satisfaction derived from what is of one's liking, which includes carnal, frivolous enjoyment. Pleasure comes and goes while Happiness is a state of mind. Daily pleasures may come and go, and we may have instances that bring temporary unhappiness. However, if we practice living in a state of happiness, life will be richer and fuller. We can practice happiness by keeping and reviewing a gratitude journal. A very helpful affirmation is: All we praise, bless, and give thanks for multiplies! As we practice using that affirmation, keep in mind, through the Law of Mind Action, all we moan, groan and complain about multiplies. What do you want to multiply? Pleasure is not a bad thing under the right circumstances. How could we *not* want to experience pleasure? However when we seek pleasure for pleasure itself, it is sin. It has no reality in truth, and will never satisfy long term.

FAULT VS CAUSE: It's easy to point a finger of blame when something goes wrong. Often, that finger of blame is pointing at ourselves. And it hurts. We shrink with guilt and shame. This hurts our self-esteem and causes more pain and suffering in our lives. Failure may bring fear of trying again because our last experience was so painful. We can see this from another perspective. Instead of seeing mistakes or failures as a fault, we can look at them as a cause. Follow the effect back, to see if what happened was intentional. My granddaughter once taped over a photo-greeting message that all of my grandchildren had made as a gift for me. When she realized what she had done, she regretted it in horror. Did she do that on purpose, aware that it was irreversible? No. She was seven years old. While she caused it to happen, she did not intend the outcome. When there is a fender-bender accident, people involved often get out of their cars and yell at each other, claiming it's their fault. One or both may have caused the accident, but was that their intention? That's why it's called an accident not an attack. When we look for cause without judgment, rather than blame through fault, we soon recover and harmony returns. When the ego goes wild and screams blame and fault, false gods are at work.

This is very true when it comes to drug addiction, where fault and judgment are freely poured out on those who suffer, under the assumption they were irresponsible and simply wanted the next high. As Jesus taught, we must not judge by appearances. We repeatedly hear stories from people addicted to drugs, stating they never thought it could happen to them.

Countless others became inadvertently addicted when medications were over-prescribed with the blessing of Big Pharma companies who offered incentives to prescribe their products. A CNN exclusive report published March 12, 2018 examined the problem at depth. The title of the article is: "CNN Exclusive: The more opioids doctors prescribe, the more money they make." It's available online and well worth the time to read. This problem must be addressed from the perspective of cause, not fault, in order to stop the tragic loss of life and destruction of families that has invaded Americans and others around the world.

On the other hand, sometimes actions are intentional, in which there still might be a hidden cause in the subconscious, yet because the person taking the action consciously knows it would be hurtful or harmful, it is fault. In this case we do not want to compound the problem by striking back because that would connect ourselves to negative cause and we don't want to go there. As the old saying goes, *two wrongs don't make a right.*

IGNORANCE VS IGNORE-ANCE: Ignorance is a lack of knowledge or awareness. Some say ignorance is bliss, but in reality ignorance makes us vulnerable, dependent on others, and disempowered. Knowledge is power. That makes ignore-ance a sin. To know what is right or true, and make a conscious choice to ignore it in favor of doing what one wants, is contrary to spiritual law, and will bring adverse effects.

PERSONALITY VS INDIVIDUALITY: Actors wear a mask, creating a *persona,* or personality. We all have a *mask* we present to the world. It's how people see us, or how we want them to. We change our mask, aka personality, according to where we are and who we are speaking with. But what's not visible, is our individuality—the divine spark of uniqueness within. It's our God Spark. As we mature, the mask of personality fades as the individuality emerges.

PATRIARCHAL VS MATRIARCHAL: The greatest error thinking which prevails in human consciousness is a black-and-white—this-or-that thinking of the carnal mind. We have an ongoing issue called the *battle of the sexes*. It is a reality of life. We've been living in a patriarchal culture for thousands of years. Women have had to fight for equality, including the right to vote and equal pay. There is inequality in the corporate world, and lack of respect for those who choose the critical and difficult role of homemaker. Many women believe it is time to shift the paradigm to matriarchy. While that satisfies the lower, long-suffering female soul, it is again an error. A functioning whole, must have a balance of both male and female energies. There must be a new standard established. We require both the protecting and providing qualities of the masculine nature balance with the loving and nurturing qualities of feminine.

LIBERAL VS CONSERVATIVE: Liberal means to be open to progress or reform, as in political or religious affairs. A Conservative is more traditional, disposed to preserving existing conditions, and limiting change. Most people believe they are one or the other. The United States is experiencing painful division between the liberal and conservative camps. Both are missing the point. We require both. We need both to work together for the common good. Liberal and Conservative, whether we are speaking of religion or politics, there are two essential parts. It's like wings on a bird. Both wings flap together for a bird to fly. If they don't work together, the bird can't get off the ground. Conservative and Liberal working together are like roots and blossoms of a flower. Roots stabilize and the bud reaches for the heavens. Both roots and blossoms are necessary for the development of the flower. Both serve the greater whole—not a select few with perceived power. There is grave danger in either taking over. The doctrine of false gods sees all creation from an egocentric perspective whether that is personal power or financial wealth. If the far-left took over, anarchy could result. If the far-right took over, freedom would die, and hierarchy would claim absolute power.

Ask yourself, *was Jesus a liberal or conservative?* (PAUSE and ponder for a minute) Unless you said both, you are incorrect. Jesus, brought the heart to the letter of the law. He brought understanding. The Law has a *what* component, and a *why* component. Jesus' teaching often repeats this concept. He said, *I have not come to destroy the law, but to fulfill it.* He fulfilled it by showing the teaching in the way he lived. The law, as taught by Jesus, may seem like a chameleon, changing by circumstance. Yet behind each circumstance there is the ultimate outcome which must be the good of the individual and the whole. Universal health and wholeness IS the law.

MATERIAL WEALTH VS RICHES: Wealth finds its value in dollars and possessions. Riches are immeasurable. Wealth is financial; Riches are spiritual. We can run out of wealth, but we can never run out of riches. Riches include knowledge of God as source, integrity, generosity, faith, love and joy. Wealth tries to store up money and things, riches circulate. Through the Law of Circulation, riches increase and bless the one who gives. Stored up wealth is subject to loss, thieves, or deterioration. Riches continue to circulate.

PRIDE, PREJUDICE, POPULISM, AND POLARIZATION

Many say the world has gone mad. Most days I'm inclined to agree with them. Yet, as a lifelong student of Truth, I remind myself, as the Bible says, "it came to pass," not to stay. Some people, feeling overwhelmed, are tossing in the towel, frustrated and apathetic. But there are others. Seekers. People who understand Principle and are seeking the cause behind our current painful effects of pride, prejudice, populism and polarization. In creation, there is a positive and negative side to everything. When we look with a spiritual eye, we are able to discern which is which.

PRIDE: false pride - an exaggerated sense of self-esteem and worth. The other side of pride is the feeling we get when we are living in integrity—in alignment with goodness. False pride, by its very nature, is its own worst enemy. When caught in its clutches we make many bad decisions and then suffer the consequences. Its effects are underscored when the ego will not let one admit he or she was wrong. The consequences are worse.

PREJUDICE: a preconceived idea, opinion or feeling, either favorable or unfavorable. The idea could be formed through false information, association with a previous experience, or an inner feeling. Prejudice based on gossip, misinformation, disinformation, or holding one group accountable for a single person's action, is an error. On the other side, we may sense something that comes to us without support or validation. Here, instead of taking action on the feeling, we can first explore and examine the feeling or information for confirmation of its validity. This would then become discernment.

POPULISM: The dictionary defines this as: *"a political strategy based on a calculated appeal to the interests or prejudices of ordinary people."* (Dictionary.com)

Its presence and power, however goes far beyond politics, reaching into religion and business. As with pride and prejudice, populism can be positive or negative, depending on its validity in a particular circumstance or situation. In the 2016 election, many were deceived and swayed by fake news stories. This brought out the worst in people in the grips of pride and prejudice because it blocked the avenues to factual information. In 2017, Pope Francis warned of the dangers of populism: "In times of crisis, we lack judgment, and that is a constant reference for me."

Populism is anti-establishment, yet populists have little workable knowledge of what is involved in how the establishment works. We have been dumbed down to the point we know little about government. In the past 40 years at least, we have become increasingly ignorant, and opinionated. While some are overwhelmed beyond fact, others, apathetic, turn their back, shrug their shoulders, and say, *"Whatever."*

Many good things have come through the efforts of populism, but when self-interests of populists supersede the best interests for all, and based on lies, we can expect effects that reflect it. How do we know the difference? *"We will know them by their fruits."* (Matthew 7:20) Our experiences will always be the fruit - result - of our past thoughts, feelings and actions. If we want change, we must be the change we desire. Change your thoughts, change your actions; change the world.

POLARIZATION: is what happens when people become divided into contrasting groups. The groups separate through the prejudice and pride of populism. The missing components that would dissolve the barriers that separate us are education, truth, and understanding. Many people are so attached to their personal opinions, they can't see the possibility of a world that works for everyone. Yet we do have the power. Together we can do it! The challenge is ours as individuals and groups.

In the first Star Wars movie, Obi Wan Kenobi is talking to Princess Leia. He moves, as if jostled, and says: *There's a disturbance in the force.* This mirrors what we experience every day that hate, war, and evil events occur. *The Force,* represents spiritual energy. When we come to where the positive energy of Spirit freely flows, we will not have to fear the future, or each other.

BUDDHIST PRAYER OF LOVINGKINDNESS

May all beings be peaceful.
May all beings be happy.
May all beings be safe.
May all beings awaken to
the light of their true nature.
May all beings be free.

HEAVEN, HELL, AND HOLLYWOOD

On the earthly plane, from a metaphorical perspective, we find Heaven above, Hell below, and ourselves caught in the middle of a spiritual tug-of-war. Through the pivotal ability of the mind, we can choose where to focus our attention. It is by far easier to surrender to the law of gravity, than to pull against the earthly world to come up higher, reaching toward what we call the heavens. Yet the rewards of coming up higher promise happiness beyond measure where our dreams come true and life is perfect every day.

When we consider the concepts of Heaven and Hell, we can shift our perspective so Heaven represents the highest state of being, and Hell, the lowest. Rather than geographical locations, we can see them as states of consciousness. In 1999 Pope John Paul II said: *"More than a physical place, hell is the state of those who freely and definitively separate themselves from God."* He added: *"The images with which hell is presented to us by Sacred Scripture must be correctly interpreted. They demonstrate the complete frustration and emptiness of a life without God."* At the same time the pope dismissed the notion of heaven as a *physical place among the clouds, adorned by pearly gates and harps* (Source: The [Nashville] Tennessean, Aug. 1, 1999). This has been a part of the Unity teaching for over one hundred years.

Hollywood, or the entertainment industry, is influential. It has the ability to manipulate thoughts, feelings and beliefs. Through the Law of Mind Action, as stated earlier, the thoughts we hold in mind manifest in kind. It's an interesting paradox—to have the power to inspire or influence through what it produces. The messages presented reflect the human condition, while projecting ideas into the collective, like broadcasting seed. These ideas appeal to either the lower or higher consciousness, sometimes both. We must keep in mind with great power comes great responsibility.

What makes media so powerful is that it engages both the thinking and feeling natures, both components of creative process. The influence it has depends on the emotional impact we experience. Love begets love, violence begets violence. While a persistent watcher of violent movies may not kill someone, studies show they have less compassion, or desire to help others. (MSNBC article 2012) When this topic arises, the common response I receive, is: *"That's ridiculous. It's only a movie, or game, or song."*

Nothing could be further from the truth. A Psychology Today article published January 8, 2018 notes a study Bandura, Ross & Ross back in 1963 that demonstrated the impact of exposure to violent programs and movies had on children, who not only imitated but expanded the violence in play after the exposure. Another study by Dillon & Bushman in 2017 supported the results of the previous study. The bottom line of the study, is that children exposed to violent games and entertainment tend to be more violent. This is not true of all children, but the ones who already have a leaning to it, in other words a hot temper or the like. This is a very enlightening article, which I encourage you to read. I have added a web address in the resources section at the end of the book.

When we see a movie, play or television program we like, we think about the parts that most impressed us, or watch it over and over. We reinforce messages each time we see the movie, talk about it, or recall it. The same thing is true in music, video games and the books we read. We want to emulate the characters that impress us. We see the celebrities as heroes and role models and want to be like them. Young people are most susceptible. They may start to dress, act, and live the way they imagine their idols do.

The entertainment industry itself faces a Catch-22 because on one hand is the desire to create—to produce stories, music and art. On the other, their stories, music and art must make money so they can continue to create. Their work must appeal to their customers, people who go to the movies, read the books, listen to the music, and play the games. It is an unpleasant truth that gratuitous sex sells. So does violence. These both appeal to the carnal nature, and temptation is compelling and unrelenting.

We have made the idols of false gods our role models. It's easy to understand. Wouldn't anyone want to live the life of the entitled, rich and famous?

Mammon and Baal permeate the industry through manipulation of the ego—the personality, or lower mind. It's an easy target for three reasons. One is because the industry is ego-driven. It's glamorous, seductive, and gives a sense of personal power to those who make the movies, music and entertainment. The second is because we let down our guard when we turn on the TV, etc. We relax into a fantasy world when we turn up the tunes, and tune out of our daily lives. The third is just plain greed. It sells.

Dreamers and awakened souls continue to produce meaningful works. They call us to raise the bar of our own behaviors and provide family-friendly humor to lift our hearts and souls. There are inspiring stories of true heroes, and chances are they were not box office hits, even if they win awards. It's up to us to engage our free will to make choices that nurture our souls and call us to come up higher.

How do we know? As we just learned: by their fruits. How do we usurp the perceived power of false gods? We counter them with our power of discernment. Every time we purchase a ticket, every time we use a product advertised on television, radio or other media, we vote for more of the same with our dollars. We should no more let the seduction of false gods enter our mind than we would put sugar in the gas tank of the car. If it is a movie, go back to the box office and demand your money back or a ticket to a different show. If it is a television program, make yourself heard by the advertisers. Call or email them to express your concern. We can be victors, not victims in this battle.

You can take what I say, or leave it. It's up to you. Just consider the possibility it is true. We will never bring higher integrity and lower violence into the world if we keep on as we have been. *"Insanity is doing the same thing the same way, over and over, expecting a different result."* (Source undetermined)

WORDS, WORDS, WORDS

"For by your words, you will be justified, and by your words you will be condemned." (Matthew 12:37)

My mother had her take on the subject: "Always keep your words soft and sweet, because you never know when you may need to eat them." (My mom, Muriel Parda)

Words are vehicles of manifestation with great power. Behind each word is an idea—the original, primary, or unlimited pattern behind everything. Even a scripture begins with, "In the beginning was the word…" (John 1:1) We receive an idea in mind. We wrap it in images and feelings formed through words and express them. Words we receive, whether heard or read, make an impression in the mind of the receiver. The impression made is shaped by the unseen vibrational frequency they were sent from as well as vibrational frequency of the recipient's current state of mind.

Words are either creative or formative. Creative words express ideas of Divine Mind, and Truth. Formative words express the same ideas of Divine Mind, but through the lower, or mortal mind. They do not produce lasting results since they come from ego and not Spirit. Words have the power to hurt. Words have the power to heal. The difference is in how we use them. Words are like tools. They can inform and enlighten or manipulate.

The spoken word, through the vibration of sound, carries the added impact of emotion—energy in motion—through inflection. You can experience this through a simple experiment with a partner. Using only the words, *I love you,* speak them to your partner with the following inflections: 1. Sincerity, 2. Disdain, 3. Doubt. Now discuss the impact the words had on the recipient.

False gods use emotion as a tool of manipulation. Words that instill fear, incite anger, or stimulate lust or greed engage our lower, carnal nature. They will bring negative results. Words grounded in Truth inspire, uplift, and empower. It is imperative we learn to test the words we hear, and pay attention to the words we speak, conscious of the effect they may have.

How do we handle moments when our emotions are swirling like a whirlwind and we need to vent? Can we do it without engaging the law? There is. Put all of your angst and frustration, fear, whatever in writing. Then burn what you have written. What has happened is you have released the energy without doing harm. Once it has turned to ashes, you can't go back and read it, thus stimulating the toxins all over again.

In face-to-face or phone communication, we receive the message through the words and inflection of the speaker. To remove the inflection, which is the emotion, takes away the message behind the words. It's not real communication. This happens with texting or email. Studies have shown the texting culture of our younger people is resulting in a loss of compassion and ability to communicate. Many words go out but the spoken part, the emotion, is missing.

Frequent repetition of words can embed their message, true or false, in our minds, making them appear true, even if they're not. Consider the impact of song lyrics. Many people claim they're just words and have no power. However, going back to the Law of Mind Action, thoughts and words held in mind, produce after their kind. We need go no further than to observe the lyrics top-selling songs over the past fifty years for verification. This is also true in sales and marketing industries; the *rule of seven* claims the average prospective buyer has to see or hear a promotion seven times before they will purchase the product. Repetition has the power of influence.

In the churches of many denominations, the service ends with the *Let There Be Peace Song* by Jill Jackson-Miller and Sy Miller. Yet, when sung with a group of people from different denominations, the flow of the song becomes dissonant because frequently the words have been changed. People who did not like the words, instead of accepting them as is or singing a different song, change the words to make them more comfortable. This alters the meaning intended by the writer. It also breaks copyright law. For example, somewhere along the line, in the lyrics of the song, somebody did not like the use of the word *solemn,* preceding *vow,* and changed it to *joyous,* which you will now hear in many Unity churches. Rather than change their understanding the word solemn, which means serious, they changed the lyrics. They confused solemn with somber. To make a solemn vow means to show strength and commitment.

Somewhere in the 1980's, a phenomenon called *Political Correctness,* or *PC,* emerged. The original intention was a means of avoiding speech or terms perceived to exclude, marginalize or insult the disadvantaged or people being discriminated against. Now, through ego-centered lower consciousness it has gone to extremes. We now find ourselves tap dancing around our words lest we offend someone. Under the spell of false gods, people are becoming thin-skinned. This creates an adversarial state of mind that separates us and prevents us from encouraging others to come up higher. I often find myself walking on eggshells lest I make someone angry or hurt their feelings. Think of the last time you had to describe someone. Would we dare say *black*, or *overweight*, or *Jewish*, etc.? That is one example of many. Even though someone may be chronically late, or rude, we're more inclined to overlook it than confront it.

The damage done under the guise of political correctness goes far deeper. The Bible has become more difficult to interpret because of efforts to make it gender-neutral. With metaphysical interpretation, removing: *he* and *she,* or *brothers* and *sisters,* and replacing them with words like *people* or *friends,* stymie interpretation. In Metaphysical interpretation, the male represents the thinking faculty, and female the feeling faculty. Therefore a crippled man would represent flawed thinking, and an adulteress, tainted emotions.

Wonder why God is always referred to as *He?* The first, and simple answer is that the Bible was written in a patriarchal culture. Hebrew is a gendered language, with nouns being either male or female. Grammatical gender, according to a BBC article is very different from biological sex. (source: bbc.com/news/world-europe-42073148) The second is my metaphysical perspective: since the male represents the thinking faculty and is in fact called Divine Mind, *he* would make sense. *Ruach* which is feminine is associated with Spirit, or the Holy Spirit. It is very helpful to not look at biological gender, but energy—assertive or passive, thought or feeling, etc.

When we change words because they are uncomfortable, we miss the opportunity to discover the intent of the message. The word *sin* is a very unpopular word, as is the word *wretch*, because we do not want people to think we are wretched sinners. Instead we candy coat the words to make them palatable. In the song *Amazing*

Grace, by John Newton, the lyrics were changed, calling sin error, and wretch, soul. Yes, sin is error, and so, error is sin. A wretch is someone who is hopeless and miserable. To change the word *wretch* to *soul* is avoidance. If you've ever felt forlorn and pitiful, that would be wretched. Rainbows and unicorns cannot do the work of transformation. Name it. Claim it. Fix it.

If you find a particular word bothers you, ask yourself, *why am I having this reaction? Is it in me? Is it valid; or is it a miscommunication?* When we explore these things, we can overcome them, find our healing, and never have to deal with them again. Likewise, if someone tells us we have offended them, we can consider if there is validity in what they said. Then we can ask: *what is it in you that finds this offensive?* Offended? Probably. Why? Because it puts us in a position where we have to consider the possibility it's more about us than them. It's all good though, because every opportunity for growth is good in the end.

Sometimes the power of the word is in *not* speaking it. In the words of the Psalmist: "Set a guard over my mouth, O LORD, keep watch over the door of my lips!" (PS 141:3) When we use our words, consider how we're using them. Before letting loose the power of the word, the power to hurt, or heal, be sure you're coming from your true self, and not speaking at the command of false gods.

PART FIVE–HOMEWARD BOUND
WAKE UP AND BE VIGILANT

As stated earlier, the challenges we face today happened over time, not overnight. They are the products of apathy, avoidance, denial, and abdication of our responsibilities as citizens of the United States of America via non-participation. We can't blame the government, because we are a part of it. We vote. When we do not vote, or we vote by a party because it's easy, or in absolute ignorance, it's on us.

In her book, *The Revelation, Our Crisis is a Birth*, futurist Barbara Marx Hubbard tells us we are in a great birthing process. The birth will either be a Lamaze type birth, or a painful breech-type birth which is both excruciating and dangerous. The choice is ours to make, based on whether or not we come to understand that we are all One. We must stop seeing ourselves as independent individuals, and face the fact we are interdependent beings, each an inseparable part of a greater whole. If we fail to realize this, our *rugged individual* persona, fueled by pride, will be the end of us. Stand in a mirror and look at your body. Imagine how it would work with only one organ missing? This Truth appears in the Bible:

> "For the body does not *consist of* one member but of many. If the foot should say, 'Because I am not a hand, I do not belong to the body,' that would not make it any less a part of the body. And if the ear should say, 'Because I am not an eye, I do not belong to the body,' that would not make it any less a part of the body. If the whole body were an eye where would be the hearing? If the whole body were an ear where would be the sense of smell? But

> as it is, God arranged the organs in the body, each one of them, as he chose. If all were a single organ where would the body be? As it is, there are many parts, yet one body. The eye cannot say to the hand, 'I have no need of you,' nor again the head to the feet, 'I have no need of you.' On the contrary, the parts of the body which seem to be weaker are indispensable"
>
> *(1 Corinthians 12 RSV)*

If we understood this, we would no more drop a bomb on another country's citizens than blow up our own foot. As I write these words, the Trump administration has taken more than 2,000 children from their parents and put them in detention centers. The only crime was trying to get to a place where the family could have a better, safer life for their family. Workers who watch over the children are not even allowed to show the children compassion. Kirstjen Nielsen, secretary of Homeland Security, claimed the children are being well taken care of, but I ask you, how would it feel if you were a child and you were taken away from your parents? Toys, crayons and videos are not a substitute for the presence of a parent, and wouldn't touch the pain of their loss. How would you feel as a parent if someone took your child away from you? Meanwhile Trump refuses to stop the suffering, while last week he praised North Korea's dictator Kim Jong Un, who has had many of his own people murdered, for being *tough*.

We are one with the planet, but laws to protect it have been reversed. The environment is being poisoned, which will ultimately poison us all. Our national parks are opened to the rape of mining. We are one with the animal kingdom, while endangered species are losing their protection.

In the midst of this, a recent poll said Trump's approval rating is the highest it has ever been. Why? Because the stock market is up, the jobless rate is down, and a shameless bully is telling everyone how great America is becoming, thanks to him. A sense of personal power is overshadowing the Truth that we are all connected. We may be gaining financially, but as far as being a functioning part of a greater whole, morally, we are beyond bankrupt. Mammon and Baal—materialism and ego—are puffed up and strutting. It would appear that we are in for an excruciating breech birth. Is there anything we can do?

There is. And it's simple. But it's not easy. First we need to learn and practice Spiritual Principle. We need to live the Principles, and then share them with others. These are our marching orders. The other thing we need to do is focus on keeping our mind and heart, our thinking and feeling faculties in the upper quadrants. That can seem like a monumental task as news gets bleaker by the day. But either we believe in a higher good, or we don't. I do. Anyone can *speak* the teaching, but it takes great strength to embody and live it. A great affirmation to hold in mind and heart when facing difficult times is:

"I place my life, and all my affairs (or our world crisis, or marriage, etc.), *lovingly in the hands of the Father, with a childlike trust, knowing God's will for me is good, and God's will is done."*

Every time I feel like I am getting tangled in fear and anxiety, I just keep repeating this. As I said, it is simple but not easy, and because it is not easy the rewards will be great. Look at it like this, strong affirmations that we hold in thoughts and feelings can build spiritual strength equal to a strenuous workout at the gym.

> *"...for God did not give us a spirit of timidity but a spirit of power and love and self-control."*
>
> *2 Timothy 1:7*

IT'S ALL IN YOUR MIND

Okay! This is where it gets personal! It's time to look at our own lives and ask ourselves if our thoughts, words and actions align with what we believe. Everything begins in mind. God, Divine Mind, is the creator of all ideas. Divine Mind generates the ideas we receive. We interpret them according to our current awareness, and manifest based on our translation. The term *mind* applies to both the thinking and feeling natures, so the state of mind, on reception of an idea, determines the nature of the manifestation. This is one reason prayer and meditation are so important. They help us stay connected to God's Divine Mind.

Things we think, feel, or believe don't change Truth, but they impact our life experience. A perception created through mind can appear to be true even if it isn't. This is where false gods can move to manipulate, and why Jesus taught that we must not judge by appearances. The Law of Mind Action states: The thoughts we hold in mind, manifest in and as our lives. This applies to both individual and collective awareness. An example would be wishful thinking, where we create a false reality based on personal wants, and not a higher desire based on the will of God—all good. A key here is the difference between a want and a desire. Our human nature may want any number of things, it is in the lower consciousness. If we break the word *desire* down: de sire, we see *de=of* and *sire=father*. For this example, consider a *want* as something from our human nature, and *desire* as something from God. The best part, is that God gives us an interest in and attraction to that which he desires us to be, do, or have.

If we want our world to change, we must first change our mind. Wisdom comes through experience. An idea progresses from theory, or knowledge, to wisdom—absolute knowing—through experience. Flexibility and an open mind, make us teachable. We want to keep an open mind, but not so open our brain falls out! Both our hearts and minds must be open to receive a new paradigm. The starting place for this is asking ourselves a difficult question: What do you know, without a doubt, to be true? How about 1+1=2? Now, a quantum physicist or mathematician can toss out some kind of theory to challenge that, but in all honesty, if I have an apple and I give you an apple, there are two apples, unless you want to count the potential apples in each seed, which is impossible. Again, ask yourself the question about everything you see or read: What do I *know*?

When learning to drive a car, students attend classes. First comes book study, followed by practical application. When the student completes the book lessons, he or she knows *about* driving a car, but they don't have practical experience. They know about driving, but they are not drivers. Once they have some experience to add to their book learning, they have to make the critical decision whether to abide by the rules of the road learned in driving school, or to follow the coaxing of peers and push beyond the limits of the law.

To not know the law is ignorance. To know, but pay no attention to the law is ignore-ance. Every day smart people make foolish choices. Here's an experiment for you: Take a 30 minute drive. Be sure to drive at the speed limit or the accepted 5mph over the limit. Watch how many people pass at excessive speed, pass in a no-passing zone, honk their horn, etc. Everyone knows the speed limit is a requirement, not a suggestion, but many choose not to abide by it.

There is another aspect of learning, or knowledge, called osmosis. This is when information or concepts come to a person with no conscious effort. This can be positive or negative, depending on whether the source is an influence or inspiration. For example, we pick up an accent when immersed in a culture where the accent is common. We learn by association with people or groups. Is this a mystery? I don't think so. I see it as the absorption or harmonizing with the vibration that surrounds us. People who are awakened to Principle strive to live their beliefs and become a living example for those who desire enlightenment. We must be cautious regarding who comes into their orb of influence—or close enough to be influential.

While there are many who have awakened, many others have not. Until all are awake, we cannot experience the joy of wholeness. Once we have become awakened, it is our responsibility to help others, not through coercion or force, but by learning, living and sharing Universal Principles of Truth. This should be a snap! But it's not. Even though Jesus taught all we have to do is love God, love others, and love ourselves, Mammon and Baal try to control us with laziness, narcissism and the lie of separation. Transformation is not mysterious. It is metaphysical, and worth every effort. First…WAKE UP!

WHERE THERE IS NO VISION

Several times in the Bible, it talks to us about sight and vision. I believe this is one of the most important things we have as a guide today.

> "*Where there is no vision, the people perish: but he that keepeth the law, happy is he.*
> *(Proverbs 29:18)*
>
> *"Hear now this, O foolish people, and without understanding; which have eyes and see not; which have ears and hear not."*
>
> *(Jeremiah 5:21)*
>
> *"Write the vision; make it plain upon tablets, so he may run who reads it."*
> *(Habakkuk 2:2)*

Under the influence of false gods, our eyes may see only gloom and adversity. For all rights and purposes, life on planet earth is in grave peril right now. Many crises surround us. Nuclear war threatens us because of decisions made by a few people in power. Millions more face the danger of losing health insurance and prescription drug coverage. The planet is being ravaged and buried in the waste of rampant consumerism, **and in dire risk of extreme global warming to the extent that many regions will become uninhabitable.** In America today, truth and integrity have taken a back seat to lies and deception.

As our sensitivity and sensibility plummet with bad news, day after day—sometimes hour after hour—we have to expand our vision from what we see with our human eyes, perceive with our human understanding, and hear with our human ears, to a bigger picture. We need to look at the *what* as we discern the *why* and *how*. If everything around us is an effect of the working of Spiritual

Principle, we will find answers when we widen our scope of vision to solve the problem.

It's difficult to be positive in the new *dark ages*. If we are to overcome, positive thinking is required. We are in crisis. Yet every crisis contains both danger and opportunity. The danger is a warning; the opportunity is to create change. The thought of changing this mess may seem overwhelming, but it's not. The activity of Principle, unnoticed by us, manifested it. Conscious application of the same Principle can change it! How? Through the creative process which we will learn about next.

Imagine you want to build a birdhouse. It would seem logical that you would get the wood, cut the pieces, nail them together, and voila! A birdhouse appears. Did you notice something missing there? There was no blueprint. No plan. No vision of the desired result. The project would be more complex if two people were involved. Imagine what it would be like with millions? An old cliché defines a camel as a horse built by a committee. To get the birdhouse you want, you would need a vision, and with a group, a shared vision. And a plan.

The same thing is true for all of us. The vision, must be big enough to consider all factors and implications. In a family, community, country, or world community there are many types of people, personalities, lifestyle, socio-economic and other factors to consider. A world that works must respect and protect all inhabitants, including natural resources. We are a part of an ecosystem on a biosphere, spinning through an immeasurable universe. As much as our egos would like to see us as independent, we are interdependent.

Whether we are building a birdhouse, a relationship, or a government, behind it is an idea. Everything that has ever come to be has its origin as a Divine Idea in the mind of God. Our mind is our connecting link with God, so we receive ideas through that connection. We attract ideas through a need or desire.

Once we receive the Divine Idea, it's filtered through our current state of awareness and formed by our vision with the help of our faculty of imagination. If we are to move forward, it's necessary to conceive a greater vision. The challenge is those who, for whatever reasons, cannot or will not perceive the vision. They fall deaf to the message and consciously choose to chase self-satisfaction, money and power. Therefore, people will continue to perish in vain.

What are we to do? Einstein spoke truth when he said we can't solve a problem at the same level we created it. The scripture noted: *but he that keepeth the law, happy is he*. That is something we all can do. We can live every day aligned with Principle, setting forth causes with the faith they will bring desired effects. We follow the call to lift up our eyes, open our minds, hearts, and ears to hear the voice of Spirit. God is both immanent, and transcendent. We can lift mind from the lower, carnal level of thoughts and emotions to the higher, spiritual, intuitive and sensing level where visions appear.

A great source of enlightenment, for me, is movies. As I watch a movie, I sometimes pick up Principles of Truth woven into them. A favorite of mine is Close Encounters of a Third Kind. In this movie, a number of people have a close encounter with an alien vessel passing over their area. The experience changes each of them. One of the commonalities of the people's experiences is a vision they struggle to express. Some people draw them, some search for them, some sculpt them with clay, and the lead character fills his living room with mud that he tries to shape into the vision. One day a picture of the vision is on television. It is Devil's Tower Monument. The affected people are all drawn to the tower, where the spaceship appears, and offers to take anyone who wants to go with them.

Within each of us is a vision of what we may call the *Kingdom of Heaven*, or *Home*. It is a vision of a place of all-good, peace, security, and plenty. We each go through our lives trying to find, or create it. We cannot manifest this vision with money or power. We manifest it by living in integrity and alignment with Spiritual Principle. It's not so much about religion, but spirituality and our interconnectedness.

THE CREATIVE PROCESS

Manifestation occurs through the Creative Process: the process through which unformed substance, or what seems to be nothing, takes form. The manifestation takes form through the Law of Correspondence. The Creative Process is: Mind + Idea = Expression. God creates, we take part. This is co-creation.

As stated earlier, our mind is our connecting link to God—Divine Mind, creator of all ideas. We call Divine Mind first cause. We connect with God through our mind. The connection is active at all times, even though at sometimes we know of it, other times we don't. The quality of the connection depends on our focus. If we have a radio, we plug it in. There is a connection, but the radio has to be on. When we turn it on, we may have music, we may have talk-radio, or we may have static, in which case we must turn the tuning dial to find the station we want. This is how prayer works. We plug in and tune in. We can tune in to God through prayer and meditation. One Unity teacher wrote a song whose lyrics pretty much explain it. As you read the lyrics, ask yourself what thoughts you've been praying:

OUR THOUGHTS ARE PRAYERS

Words and Music by Lucille Olson

Our thoughts are prayers, and we are always praying

Our thoughts are prayers, take charge of what you're saying

Seek a higher consciousness, a state of peacefulness

And, know that God is always there and every thought becomes a prayer

Charles Fillmore's definition of the creative process uses the term *holy trinity of creation*. This is, mind, idea, expression. Through our mind we receive the Divine Idea which we then press into manifestation, or express. He said: *"Fix your mind powerfully on the consummation of a certain idea until the idea nucleates a certain amount of thought substance. This is followed by a spiritual quickening, or the outpouring of the Holy Spirit, third in the Trinity."* (Keep A True Lent – Charles Fillmore)

We may wonder then, if God is the creator of all ideas, and we are cocreators in manifestation, where does evil come from? Is poverty an idea in the mind of God? How about divorce and disease? Is war an idea in the mind of God? Murder? The answer is no. While we do receive ideas from God, they come filtered through our current state of mind, or consciousness. Things like poverty, divorce, disease, war, crime and murder are aberrations of Divine Ideas.

We apply the Principles of the Creative Process to prevent what we don't want to manifest. Where do we stop it? The best place to intercept the process is at its inception: the first thought. To *nip it in the bud* before it blooms into something toxic. It's best if we don't allow the idea to take root in our minds where it can nucleate like thoughts and feelings which will manifest. The minute we find we've connected with an adverse thought or feeling, we must release it. A great affirmation for this is: *Cancel and erase. Love, love, love,* or *"This (person, situation, etc.) has no power over me!"*

Let's say you are driving to work and running late. Somebody swoops in front of you from a side street and is going 10mph below the speed limit. Step 1: Breathe. When we take deep and slow breaths, we can't think. This breaks the connection between thinking and feeling. Step 2. Affirm: All is in Divine Order, I am at peace." Step 3. Consider the possibility that Spirit put that car there for a reason. It could be to teach a lesson about leaving earlier, not being impatient, or staying grounded in the face of adversity.

This is why it's very important to develop a practice of daily prayer, taking time to bring your mind to a higher state of being. It's difficult at first, but becomes easier and more enjoyable. We find that lifting the mind and heart gets easier, and you will stay in an uplifted state well past your prayer time. It will also make it easier to shift to your higher mind in an unpleasant situation.

On the collective level there is increased difficulty. This is because many people hold a common error thought. For example, in a magic show, the audience—collective—may believe an elephant disappeared. That does not mean an elephant actually disappeared. Yet to try to convince audience it is just an illusion is not always that easy. Nobody wants to be wrong, and many want to believe in magic. Yet the Principles work the same. Therefore, error thoughts become error causes, and will manifest error effects. This is where our work lies.

One thing that helps is to realize that we are not alone. A dark sky lights up with billions of stars. Likewise the collective mind shines with the spiritual light of kindred spirits, who also aspire to cocreating a world of all-good. It's even greater than that, since all is one with the mind of God. We can start by cultivating a circle of positive, enlightened friends if we want to experience positive outcomes.

If we're in the lunch room at school or work, and gossip starts, we can redirect or shift the conversation. Make a positive observation, or in some other way, diffuse the adverse energy and stop the process in its tracks. We can expect that we may not get the immediate result we wanted. We may not get the response you wanted. We may find ourselves rejected or persecuted. We can't let that set off a negative creative process. Let it go. It helps to try to always speak our truth with love, not blame or fault. This is all about Principle. It is not personal.

Another way to be a part of uplifting the collective consciousness is to establish relationships with real or perceived adversaries. As we get to know them better, we may come to understand issues they have, or that we have misunderstood the completely! We may find as we get to know them, we can share our way of thinking. One day we may even inspire them. The best way to get rid of an enemy, is to make them a friend. There is the possibility the adverse energy between ourselves or a group, is such that it's not healthy to be around them. In that case, we can release them with love.

CREATIVE VS FORMATIVE

While it may surprise you, just about everything around us started out as a Divine Idea created by God, then made manifest through us. Or, I should say cocreated by individual and/or collective consciousness. God created our body. In spite of what we may think about it, it was created perfectly for our life experience: each is unique. As an old poster from the 60's said, *"God Don't Make Junk."* Even if we see our body as flawed, we trust God's plan for our life. On the other hand, we cocreate how our body looks and performs according to our beliefs about it. Many people who were born with what the human mind may see as deformities or handicaps have lives deeper and richer than the *flawless beauties* we see on magazine covers.

The trick to having life in a kingdom of heaven on earth is to stay conscious. Be awake every moment. Appreciate every aspect of your life and your body. One of the things Myrtle Fillmore, cofounder of Unity did as a healing treatment for a terminal illness, was to bless every cell of her body, even the ones affected by the disease. She treated her condition with prayer for a period of two years, and she received her healing. What does that mean, to us? It demonstrates that we each have a power beyond *what eyes can see and ears can hear,* that we can use to heal our lives and the world.

Every strife, every danger we are facing in our lives and the world today comes from error thoughts or beliefs. The experiences, relationships and circumstances of our individual and collective lives appear through thought. Thought can be creative or formative. Creative thought comes from God. Formative thought is Divine Ideas translated by self or ego. To cocreate good, we must keep our mind, functioning in the upper quadrants of consciousness, i.e. intuitive and sensing rather than thoughts and feelings, which belong to carnal mind.

The Divine Idea may be perfect, but the form it takes is the product our state of mind. It's a little overwhelming to know manifestation begins in thought. Many studies reveal the average person has 70,000 thoughts each day! Most come and go, or are attended to, such as adding an item to the grocery list. The difference between a thought coming and going or staying, resulting in manifestation, depends on our real or perceived needs, and a connection made between thinking and feeling faculties. What that manifestation would look like depends on where in the quadrants of consciousness they are focused: lower, carnal mid or higher, spiritual awareness.

The things Divine Mind creates are like the creator, absolute eternal and unchanging. Things the mind forms in mortal mind are temporal, earthly, limited and transitory. If we don't like what we have manifested, we can examine the thoughts and feelings that created it, aka *what the hell was I thinking,* following backward from effect to cause, etc. Once we understand what happened, we can have the opportunity to cocreate something new. It is that simple. But it's not easy.

When we look at the suffering and what can only be called insanity in the world today, it would be possible to assume God is either dead or has gone insane. But God did not create war, hatred, and prejudice. In the creation story in the Bible, with each thing created, God said it was good—it was very good. And then when mankind was created, we were given free will. As you recall, in the story of Original Sin, Adam and Eve were expelled because they wanted the knowledge of good and evil without working to earn it. Here, on earth, they would have to learn all about good and evil through personal experience. By observing the law in action, we can learn to make the choices and earn the wisdom of God.

TRUTH OR CONSEQUENCES

I'm sure we've all had moments of temptation, when we told ourselves, *"Just this once,"* or *"It's just a white lie,"* or whatever excuse we could come up with to ignore the truth. Like a boomerang, what we throw out, will return. It's like the game of *Truth of Consequences.* Under the influence of false gods, rather than accepting the truth, we find it restricting and cumbersome. In the unenlightened mind truth is relative to what we want.

During the 2016 elections, the term *fake news* followed disparaging stories planted by Russians in a plan to disrupt the elections. Voters took sides without researching the claims. Now we are experiencing the consequences. As stated earlier, we are all a part of it because we are all connected. Did that upset you? It upset me to write it, but I know it's true through research, experience, and knowledge of Spiritual Principle.

We have to ask ourselves, *Can I handle the Truth?* A more appropriate question would be, *Can I handle the consequences?* We may deny Truth, but that doesn't make it less true. Every thought, word, or action contrary to Truth, will have consequences. However, as a part of a greater whole, the whole will feel the effects of the consequences. Each life affects the whole. This includes our actions or refusal to act. This isn't punishment, it is effect. It's like symptoms that come up for healing. If your mouth ingests poison, the whole body is affected.

"Do not be deceived: God cannot be mocked. A man reaps what he sows." (Galatians 6:7) Women do too…and children. Because the consequences may not appear immediately, we may think we've evaded the law. The immutable law is unbreakable. It is Principle: absolute, eternal and unchanging. Too often, we find out too late the magnitude of the effects.

Newton said, *"For every action, there is an equal and opposite reaction."* However that's not how it works in the spiritual realm. Fillmore explained the Principle we call the Law of Increase, operates as everything we send forth comes back multiplied. It comes back in like kind. For example, if we sent forth a tithe with a clenched fist, coming from a belief in lack, we may expect an increase of what we sent forth. But what *did* we send? Was it lack, or resentment? The laws operate first in mind, then they manifest. I like to put it this way: Everything we send forth comes back blessed and multiplied; or if you send forth evil (thoughts or actions contrary to all that is good), then it comes back cursed and multiplied. This is because the Law of Increase works through mind—thoughts and feelings.

This isn't personal, it's Principle. It's the way the law works. Some people would say God is punishing us for our sins when bad things happen. God is love, and would not punish us. We are not punished *for* our sins. We are punished *by* our sins. The unpleasant experience is the effect of a previous cause. It's important to keep in mind, this works on both the individual level, and collective.

Rev. Eric Butterworth said we can't break the law, but we can break ourselves against it. This is called suffering. For example, if you exaggerated on your resume, then got fired because you really did not have the skills you claimed, it becomes really clear why we are told not to lie. Hopefully we learned from the suffering and that type of thing won't be repeated. He also said we must break it open, to see how it functions. Then, we will achieve spiritual mastery. First identify the cause behind suffering, aka: effects. Once we can do that, we can banish the false gods at the root of our problems, and cocreate with God, heaven on earth: As above, so below.

We hear questions every day, from many sources, regarding how it is possible the members of the current administration can accept the dangerous and unsound agenda. Also, how can they follow a leader who reflects none of the values we hold as Americans? There is a simple answer. They believe they are protecting their positions and money, under the illusion they are immune to the Law of Cause and Effect.

When under the influence of false gods we cling to a false belief in personal power and financial wealth equaling riches. We can see this happening in the administration, as the White House is confirmed to be in chaos. These are effects of deceptions. We may normalize lying but that won't neutralize spiritual law.

If America does not soon stand up, we will all reap the toxic crop from fields we did not sow. Education and enlightenment are our most powerful weapons. Even if everyone in the world is clinging to lies, it will benefit us to stand on Truth. It takes courage to stand for what you know is right and true. One of the people who has earned my sincere respect and admiration for his commitment to standing for what he knows to be true is John McCain. Even in the face of a debilitating terminal illness he manages to stand up and speak out for what is right.

As we increase our awareness of Universal Principle, we take on a greater responsibility to live what we have learned. To do that, we will need to un-learn habits and beliefs we have held for decades. Change is uncomfortable, and we don't like discomfort. I have a friend whose favorite saying was, *"Don't should on yourself."* She had the best intentions of removing unnecessary guilt, or taking on responsibilities. However, people who did not want to change used it as an excuse. Her saying, rightly used is a good thing. Manipulating the words to avoid the work we need to do just keeps us stuck. Whether we should do something is situational. The key is discernment through meditation and critical thinking.

GETTING TO CAUSE

If we want to stop pain and suffering, which are effects, we *should* identify and change the cause. Getting to cause is often like trying to untangle a ball of yarn the cat had its way with. We have to twist and turn, from effect to cause, to previous effect and that cause. As daunting as this process may seem, as soon as we get the *Aha* moment of understanding, we've completed the task. The problem disappears as if by magic. This is what repentance means: to see and comprehend error so we can stop the pain and suffering of our carnal nature, and not repeat the error. Once we achieve this, our next step is to share what we have learned with others.

Here is an example of how it worked in my life: For years, my former husband and I would play the card game Pinochle with friends. I didn't care for the game, and for some unknown reason, I could not comprehend the process of bidding. My husband would say, *"I'm playing three against one,"* which made matters worse. Blame helps nothing, it makes it worse. We must look to cause, not fault. One evening as we played, I had a sudden flash of awareness and understood how bidding works. As strange as it may seem, after that night, for no particular reason, we never played Pinochle again.

Likewise, in our lives, when we *get it,* when we comprehend the Principle, the hamster wheel of useless and unnecessary suffering stops turning and we can jump off.

As stated in the previous chapter, it's all in our mind. Knowledge and understanding have great power. When we experience that flash of realization, we've learned that lesson. Failure to learn our lesson will bring more lessons, in an escalated form.

We are experiencing massive effects of something first spotted back in the 1970s. I was a homemaker and mother then. This was the norm. Most of my friends were married. My parent's marriage lasted almost 63 years in this life, and I do not doubt continues in the next. You could see their love, right up to the end. My grandparents, aunts and uncles, with one exception were successful as well. Divorce was rare. The great majority of families were intact. I don't doubt there were unhappy marriages, but I did not experience many. When marriage and vows are taken seriously, and the family is put before self, everyone benefits.

DISCLAIMER: *As you read the following, you may find it offensive. That is okay. Read it. Consider the possibility there are valid points made. If you don't agree, let it go. Keep putting it in the perspective of Principle before personality.*

Here we go: A huge cultural shift began in the early 1970s. Women moved from homemaking to jobs or careers. The original intent was a more comfortable lifestyle. Within twenty years, women working outside the home went from being an option to being perceived as a necessity in many instances. Note that I said *perceived*. Most people could have a single-income home if they were willing to release the luxuries we've come to see as essential. On the other hand, I do acknowledge it was not a choice for some. The fabric of the family began to unravel.

At the same time, the sexual revolution emerged and infidelity spread like wildfire. The divorce rate soared, and families fell apart. Broken families and the blended families followed, and traditions a part of our cultural and religious or spiritual foundations, got lost in the shuffle. Financial burdens of split families now paying for two households brought a wave of hardship. This added second jobs and latchkey children. Children and adults lost the sense of security found in a family. Not surprisingly psychiatrists and psychologists businesses were booming.

What happened? Mammon and Baal, materialism and carnality, seeped into our lives, infusing them with lies and false beliefs, including a *me first* attitude. Our foundations cracked, compromising our stability. Good people under stress of broken dreams made bad choices. Our wholeness (holiness) became fragmented. The structure of the intact, nuclear family no longer exists for many people. Home-fires are no longer being tended. Full-time homemakers rare.

Was the past perfect? Absolutely not. Was life better than it is today? I believe in countless ways it was. While we have made great strides with technology, allowing people to live longer and healthier lives, to provide countless opportunities for creative expression, and the potential for a better world for all, that potential is being compromised by false gods. I'm not suggesting we return to the past, but to mine the past for the treasure we left behind when we became mesmerized by self.

AUTOPSY ON THE ELECTION

An autopsy, in the physical sense, is examination of a body after death to determine its cause. A pathologist performs autopsies. Concerning life events, it's examining the event after the fact. As stated earlier, I am not an expert in the political realm, however, I would like to share my interpretation from a metaphysical perspective. I have studied, practiced and taught metaphysics for almost thirty years.

A pathologist performing an autopsy must be impartial, doing the work with no preconceived assumptions. Metaphysicians also need to be impartial in their examination. The pathologist must know what evidence they need to determine cause. The metaphysician looks for evidence, signs, and potential causes, to verify effects.

The primary Principle of metaphysics states everything has its origin in mind. Metaphysical interpretation works in two directions: from cause to effect, or from effect backward to the possible cause. In the case of the current state of affairs for America, we'd need to go back to Adam and Eve. This was the start of the self-before-whole consciousness. The more we focus on our personal wants and perceived needs, the less we are able to consider what others need.

If you haven't yet read the Constitution and Bill of Rights, I encourage you to. It's inspiring. Looking at the self-interests and partisanship in the 2016 election, which is proving to be divisive and tainted, it would appear that we have drifted far from those of our founding fathers. As all-white land owners, they may not have reflected the people, and were not perfect, but presented a positive plan including life, liberty, and happiness as unalienable rights for all people, given to them by their creator.

As these words are being written, those exact ideals are in jeopardy. Usually, we fight for the expansion of our rights. Today we are fighting to maintain them.

NOTE: Okay—this is another place where it might get dicey for some of you. I've said before, I don't claim to be an expert in politics, but I am well-versed in metaphysics. I have done my very best to research all claims, yet without a doubt my opinions, fueled by my passion will emerge. YOU MAY NOT AGREE with my opinions. They're here for consideration, not debate. I pray you will read through, even though you don't agree. Consider the possibility there is merit in my words. Most importantly, I invite you to research the things you do not agree with. With the internet, well-sourced information is readily and quickly available.

Confirmation of Russian interference to influence the election did not break until February 2018, too late to cry *foul*. The minds of Voters had been manipulated, the election tainted. Negative emotions stirred up with inflammatory news and Facebook posts during the campaigns permeated minds and could not be extracted. The toxins were planted by human *trolls:* individuals making false and inflammatory posts, and bots, robotic programs that spread them. There appears to be a question as of this date, whether there was collaboration from American candidates and their staff. Evidence uncovered so far, does appear to point to that. The result of interference influenced the outcome of the election through mental manipulation and Cyber warfare.

What was the utter failure of our electoral process? I see it as a poisoning of consciousness. The toxic cocktail of deceit, disinformation, and malevolence, under clandestine Cyber-attacks by Russian operatives continues to eat away the fiber of our freedom. The election of 2016 died from poisoning, but the toxins continue to spread, as the 2018 midterm elections and 2020 elections are at risk.

 Before we begin stomping our feet and pointing fingers at the Russians, we have to ask ourselves what part we played. Because we are all connected, we each play a part. One type of participation would be believing the propaganda without question or research. We would have played a part if we did not vote because we were upset or overwhelmed. Russians can only manipulate us if we let them. It was a no-brainer for them. An inconvenient truth is we are either a part of the problem or a part of the solution. If you are starting to feel pangs of anger, feeling you are being accused…STOP. If you are feeling guilty because you fell victim to the propaganda…STOP. None of this will undo the past. What we can do is change what we do in the future.

But it's not just about elections, it's about every decision we make, every thought we choose to hold. Albert Einstein first pointed out: *"We cannot solve a problem with the same thinking that created it."* What do we do? We do the same things in a different way. Within us we have the courage to change.

There is another consideration. We now have a crisis even bigger than the opioid epidemic. It's a crisis of consciousness. It doesn't have a quick and easy answer, but the answer is guaranteed to work. The answer is faith and hope, found in the upper quadrants of consciousness.

Every day we hear people talking about the 1%, in other words the super-rich who pull the strings of politicians to promote their own agendas. Look at it this way: 99% is far greater than 1%. Even the financial wealth of the super-rich is not greater than our combined wealth and spiritual power. To change course in our country we have to shift our focus from fear to faith. We can stop looking at the overblown 1% and turn to God—Spiritual Principle—Universal Truth, and immerse ourselves in the power of God-all good.

Don't be intimidated. Realize we are a part of the 99%. Our job is to encourage and engage the rest of the 99%. Not all are ready or confident enough to act, but the good news is that many are. As we live and speak our truth, those who are ready to hear will come on board. The energy will build. We all have to know that our future is not a spectator sport. If you are thinking, *somebody ought to do something*, that somebody would be you! Feel free to share that thought with folks who tell you somebody needs to do something. What begins in consciousness can only change in consciousness.

Righteous Judgment: This is not personal, it is Principle. Please try to read it from that perspective. Lack of integrity weakens the whole system. Donald Trump filled his administration with people who are politically under-educated, inexperienced, and unprepared. Many are unfit to do the job they have been appointed to do. Nepotism raised its ugly head, unchallenged, as he appointed family to government positions, by finding a weak spot in the anti-nepotism law. (CNN article February 26, 2018: *This Ivanka Trump answer is exactly why nepotism laws exist.*)

THE EFFECTS: The first year and a half of the Trump administration has had record-breaking staff turnover of 34%, and as of March 8, 2018 an NPR article has the percentage of top position turnover at 43%. Protest marches have become a regular occurrence. Gun control measures are weakened while the administration drags their feet on making changes, and mass murders by weapons of war have become the new normal, with 35 mass shootings (3 or more victims). From January 1, 2018 to February 26, 2018 there have been 35 mass shootings, killing 65, including 14 high school students and three school employees on Valentine's Day, and injuring 137. An attempt to arm *well trained* teachers has so far resulted in three accidental discharges of firearms in schools, and two children wounded.

The mental and emotional fitness of the President is questioned on a regular basis. These are instigated by his own behaviors, including daily, erroneous, inflammatory internet tweets, blatant lies, questionable ethical behaviors, and threatening devastating nuclear war.

In recent weeks, the President has made announcements without first consulting with his staff. He decided to impose tariffs on steel and aluminum despite his advisors telling him that would hurt citizens. In April, 2018, per Trump's direction, via US Attorney General Jeff Sessions, ICE (Immigration and Customs Enforcement) started separating children from their families at the Mexican border. When the American people, including many Republican lawmakers stood up and spoke out and an uprising was imminent, he signed an Executive Order stating families would no longer be separated. What was not a part of the order was the reuniting of the families who have been torn apart. Is that intelligence, or insanity? You decide.

At the G7 Summit in June, Trump estranged the US from the other participating countries, and left early to attend a summit with North Korean Dictator Kim Jong Un. While he demanded North Korea to get rid of their nuclear weapons, and boasts about growing our nuclear arsenal, when he met with Kim Jong Un, there was talk but no solid decisions of nuclear disarmament. Yet Trump agreed to stop the training drills the US has done South Korea for decades, which keeps our own military strong and well-trained. Upon his return, he has done nothing but praise the murderous dictator. I ask you...what's wrong with this picture?

These are a few low-lights of the administration, as it moves forward from the great land of opportunity we once were, to dystopia.

Again, it's not about blame. It's about cause. If we keep doing the same thing we've been doing, we'll keep getting what we are getting. The Law of Increase will escalate our problems. Suffering will grow until we stand up and say ENOUGH! If we want different effects, we will need to create different causes. We have to stop looking at *them* and not fall into the traps of laziness, narcissism, apathy, and ignorance. While it is not flattering to hear, many of us have gone from dumbed-down to stupid thinking.

The light in this dark time comes from the surviving students of the 2017 Valentine's Day Massacre in Parkland, Florida. They are marching, protesting, and speaking out. They are sending out a strong, intelligent call for gun reform. Their message and courage are inspiring people of all ages around the world, setting an example we all can follow. It comes from the people of America—all ages, cultures, colors, religions—who would not sit back and let families seeking asylum in our country be torn apart. It comes from each of us who is willing to stand up for what is good and true.

WHAT'S NOT WORKING ~ WE'VE GOT TO THINK OUT OF THE BOX!

One reason we have difficulty solving our problems is that we're trying to fix them from a traditional, limited perspective. We treat symptoms rather than the dis-ease itself, the effects rather than find the cause. This solves nothing. Neither does it find a cure for the dis-ease called the human condition. If we want to change anything we must seek the cause, not find fault. Consider how this plays out in an auto-accident: The cars crash, the drivers get out and yell at each other, fingers point in blame. Nobody gets up in the morning wanting to have an auto accident. They are inconvenient, uncomfortable, and expensive. Yet, since the first head-on crash, on a straight, clear, 2 lane road, in good weather, when cars collide, a clash frequently follows the crash. We have the power to break that mold.

Years ago my job required me to go to what was called the *bad* part of town to pick up new students for the vocational classes they were taking. One day, I went into one of the worst neighborhoods to pick up a student. It was low-income-high-crime by definition. As we drove to the school, a van in front of me suddenly slammed on its brakes and started to back up. The student and I sat, horrified, as I tried to collect myself enough to blow the horn.

The van rammed into the front of my new car, and the hood bent and popped up. The young man driving the van came out and yelled at me, *"Didn't you see me backing up?"* I said, *"I wasn't moving."* Once he saw the damage he'd done and realized it was his fault, he said, *"Oh my God, look what I did to your car!"* I asked him, *"Did you do this on purpose?"* Now it was his turn to be horrified. He said, *"On no! I'm so sorry."* I smiled and replied, *"That's why it's called an accident, not an attack."* From that moment, the rest of the issue was resolved easily and with no bad feelings. It is doing these small, practical things that make a difference.

Jesus is a prime example of what we would call an *out-of-the-box thinker*. There are frequent Biblical reports of Jesus facing religious and political leaders who would challenge him from within their *box* of confining legalism—laws, rules and regulations. Jesus wasn't in a box though. To a world of literal interpretation of the law, he brought the moral and metaphysical interpretation. He added the heart to the letter of the law. That was more than two thousand years ago, and here we are, still arguing between letter and heart.

Another example of out-of-the-box thinking is a story about when the Buddha was approached by a warrior with a sword. The warrior said, *"Do you realize that I could run you through with this sword?"* The Buddha replied, *"Do you realize I could let you?"*

SOME THINGS THAT ARE NOT WORKING, OR NOT WORKING WELL:

EDUCATION: The problems with our educational system are not the fault of teachers. The great majority of teachers have a sincere love for their students and a desire to teach and inspire. But the hand of false gods has been stirring the pot, putting emphasis on false standards that discourage real learning. Many teachers work with budgets stripped to where they provide materials for their classes out of their own pockets. Teachers are not to interact with students as they see fit. They can neither discipline nor hug them. Yes, there are bad teachers out there who have done terrible things, but the behavior of a small number does not justify classifying all teachers as potential abusers or pedophiles.

While school systems jockey for funding, they compromise our children's learning. Education is not valid if its focus is on students spitting out answers to standardized tests rather than being stimulated to think and create. Over 16 countries score higher in various areas than the US in quality of education. Legislators and sometimes school boards cut funding for arts and music programs while funding sports. Atrocious behaviors of students with high achievement in sports, including rape, are punished with a slap on the wrist. Favoritism runs rampant. This is the influence of Mammon and Baal in action. One additional issue is the now normalized practice of giving participant trophies to everyone who played. Parents may not want to see their child disappointed, but children do not learn to overcome losses if they never have to face them.

A bit of out-of-the-box thinking that I see as brilliant would most likely meet great resistance. In Japan, the students also do the work of the school janitors. This is not seen as child abuse, it's seen as building character and learning to be a part of the community. There actually are a few schools in the US who teach these values. When Newt Gingrich proposed this during his 2011 presidential campaign, it did not get a very positive reception. We do have lots of challenges with school funding, and most of us bemoan the fact that the arts and music programs are the first to experience loss of funding. Just consider what the possibility would be if janitor fees were eliminated to fund arts and music?

INSURANCE: Here's a hot topic—insurance. Health insurance is an area of contention these days. People argue about benefits, beneficiaries of services and products, and their high cost. I remember when I was in the hospital over 40 years ago. When I looked at my bill, noted a $12 charge for an aspirin. Seriously! The concept, the Divine Idea of insurance is positive: *Let's all put aside money, and if someone gets sick, it will be there for us.* How could anything be wrong with that? There can't. Until the false gods show up, aka greed and fraud. Insurance and disability fraud are big and serious problems in our country. As is overcharging for medicines and services. Greed and fraud are fixable problems, but the solutions, Universal Principles don't work if we don't work them. Remember, while we are griping about our health insurance, doctors and hospitals are griping about malpractice insurance. We start to fix problems by living in integrity and calling for others to come up higher. There is so much more; it is complex and overwhelming, but that is no reason to not address it.

All forms of insurance are subject to fraud: auto, property, etc. Fraud increases insurance company losses and our premiums. But at the root of it all is the most challenging part. It is the consciousness this happens in. If we want to change it, we will need to be a part of the change. No matter how tempting it may be, we cannot afford to commit fraud. The Universe will claim any perceived gain we receive. It is also our collective responsibility to prevent fraud being perpetrated by others. Maybe you don't want to be a *tattle-tale* as we said in elementary school, but if we see something and do not say something we are a participant in the fraud. So…guess what? We will suffer the effects of our error.

MARRIAGE: A good marriage is the cornerstone of a happy, healthy family—a place where people can feel safe, secure, and loved unconditionally. Under the influence of false gods, marriages are very difficult to establish and maintain. The powerful bonds required for a strong, healthy marriage have taken a back seat to ego, emotions, romance, and the wedding. Our paradigm of what marriage requires: commitment and meaningful vows is unrecognizable.

We are conditioned to spend outrageous amounts of money on weddings, while there is little interest in what it takes to establish, build and maintain a marriage. The average wedding, as of 2017, costs about $36,000.00. Wedding showers, and bachelor parties were once comprised small groups of friends and family members. They were intimate and fun. Women shared wisdom and laughs, played a few games, and enjoyed little sandwiches and Jell-o molds the hostess made. They have now exploded to huge, costly extravaganzas that make intimacy impossible. It's all about money and ego. The mark of Mammon and Baal are all over them. Today, a shower, or *Jack and Jill* party can average over one hundred and fifty guests, and resemble the wedding itself. Original showers helped the couple get started with gifts like toasters and dishtowels, or sexy lingerie for the bride. Today, registries list gifts starting in the hundreds of dollars. Brides can become Bridezilla if their every whim is not met.

With about a fifty-fifty chance of success in marriage, there seems to be little reason to invest $50,000 with such high odds for failure. If that occurs it would add a costly and painful divorce. The divorce rate has declined but so has the marriage rate, so it balances out. The ease of divorce today gives little incentive to staying married.

The divorce rate skyrocketed from the nineteen-sixties through the nineteen-nineties. During that period, the sexual-revolution changed traditional relationships and conduct. Marriage was no longer the expected path of a relationship. Nor was parenthood. This created an environment that led to tragic results for the family.

During this time, the nuclear family suffered, and was for many, dismantled. We can point fingers of blame, yet there is little support working through difficulties in marriage, and abundant temptation not to. The prevailing thought is *everybody's doing it*. Divorce and infidelity, once feared and avoided are common. This is not a reason, it's an empty excuse. Songs like, *If Lovin' You is Wrong, I Don't Wanna Be Right*, planted seeds of discontent in the hearts of many married people.

Before moving on I should share that I have been married twice without success. My marriages were based on my own neediness, self-delusion, and false beliefs. In spite of every effort I made, they failed. I did not address the healing I needed between marriages, and experienced disaster in my life, my mind, heart, and ability to make good decisions. Finding Unity was a life saver for me, because I learned the Principles behind my mistakes, and my healing as well.

Failure does not invalidate marriage as a Divine Idea. It highlights the need to learn from our experiences so we don't repeat them.

A 1999 article in House and Garden, *Infidelity Comes out of the Closet*, by Joseph Hooper, points out that adulterous behavior of parents, affects the children. This underscores the scripture that states the *sins of the fathers will be cast upon their sons for four generations.* One could presume infidelity is generationally contagious. It is a selfish act, of immeasurable damage to all involved.

There are many causes of divorce. In 1969 California legalized no-fault divorce, removing further incentive to remain married. Now, no-fault divorce is legal in every state. The divorce rate continued to climb. What we haven't yet realized is that the mandates of humankind, made from the perspective of carnal mind, are flawed. It doesn't matter that *everybody's doin' it,* or that psychologists tell us how resilient children are. When a marriage ends in divorce, a family falls apart, and it hurts like hell. Like it or not, it puts an indelible mark on the children.

Marriage vows, when seen as a sacred commitment, provide a safe, secure foundation for a happy, healthy life and family. When one or both partners see their personal carnal or emotional cravings as more important than their vows, suffering follows. When that becomes the norm, the problem becomes, as it has now, overwhelming.

There are cases where divorce is the only answer. This would be the case of abuse, addiction, other valid threats to family members, and the refusal of the other partner to cooperate in maintaining the marriage. But before divorce, every couple—every parent—owes it to the family unit to do everything possible to create a healthy family. As Dr. Phil frequently points out, you have to earn a divorce. Then, the decision will be clear. One thing that would help secure a solid foundation would happen before the wedding. That would be getting to know the person you are about to marry. As a minister, I encourage couples to take advantage of the premarital counseling I offer. Not all do unfortunately, because couples occasionally realize they avoided terrible mistake.

I tell engaged couples marriage is the hardest work they'll ever do—and the most rewarding. You must be realistic. Marriage is not about romance and roses; it is about the ability to stay together through the difficult times. The romance and roses are the reward. Divorce divides not only the couple, but the children, finances, etc. Couples who stay together and work through their problems have a greater opportunity for financial stability, and happy, secure children.

WELFARE: There are two schools of thought on this. One is recipients are lazy and taking advantage of the system. The other is people need a chance to get back on their feet after unfortunate circumstances. Great efforts are being made to cut welfare programs, based on the first. The other fights to expand programs. With each *side* grounded in their belief, unable to consider the possibility the other side may have a point, there can be no resolution. Both sides are right. It is a good and helpful program a *small number* of *people* abuse. Instead of cutting programs, rooting out the abusers of the program would save money, while serving those less fortunate.

Welfare itself is much deeper and more complex than it appears. Welfare is an effect with many causes. To change the effect, we must change the cause. Causes can be: divorce, lack of education, unemployment, disability, drugs, generational poverty, and apathy regarding one's own worth and ability. We are each born with a desire to create, express, and live a productive life as a part of a greater whole. With children born in poverty, to a mother on welfare, it is difficult to maintain a belief that this is possible for them.

A common opinion of those who don't understand the welfare trap, is that the people are lazy. They might see someone with luxury items in their grocery cart and assume they're abusing the system. If we were to step back, and see a bigger picture, we might see that yes, there are luxury items, but sometimes a steak softens the reality they that live in low income housing, in a dangerous area, easier to bear. It's not that the system is without flaws. Fixing it will require a lot of work, but we have to start by changing cause, so we can have a positive effect.

Imagine what would happen if we helped people to see their true worth and helped them contribute to the greater whole? What if we infused young people with hope and open their souls to their potential? Because the job is big and difficult, does not mean it's impossible. What if we learned how to hold people accountable without shame and degradation? What if we had programs to educate people about the welfare program and how it works? The possibilities are endless and exciting!

POLITICS: Mammon and Baal are actively engaged in politics today. Ego-centered lust for power, financed by money from people with self-interest agendas are far from the vision our forefathers had when they drafted the Constitution. Needs of the citizens, the greater whole, is not in the current game plan. It would be more correct to say the game plan, is a *gain-plan,* where the wealthy enrich themselves at the expense of citizens and the planet. While this is not something new, abuse has escalated to dangerous levels, which point to impending global disaster.

The major players, the Democratic and Republican parties, are becoming more estranged daily. Instead of working together for all people and balancing freedom and responsibility, this has resulted in division among the people. Politics are becoming a complete disaster as the refusal to work together for the highest good of its citizens and the planet, puts us all at risk. Instead of being leaders we can look up to—an example of integrity—they bicker and refuse to work as a bipartisan team.

Oneness and interdependence is the Truth of our being. Separation spells doom. A prime example of this is a terrible event that happened in Charlotte, VA on the night of Friday, August 12th, 2017. White supremacists groups including the KKK, marched with torches, yelling hateful words directed at Jews and Blacks. Counter-protesters faced them. A car slammed into the peaceful counter-protesters, killing one person and injuring many. As of this writing, nothing notable has occurred to prevent future occurrences. One of the most outspoken supremacists is broadcasting his messages of hate from his jail cell. He has been given his 1st Amendment right, but when the rhetoric speaks of hate and division rather than the unity we are trying to achieve, we are far from one nation for all.

America has much to be proud of. Our country is founded on liberty and justice for all, with all people seen as created equal, entitled to life, liberty and the pursuit of happiness. We had a great work ethic, and a melting pot of cultures, colors and faith groups. We are not perfect, and made a difficult journey make these promises a reality. Even within our own country we had to fight for equal rights. We had to fight for the vote for women, and the end of segregation. We may never make it up to the indigenous people whose land we flat-out stole, but they're at least getting compensation via the large sums of money we leave in their casino coffers.

With all the good things our country has to offer, we have begun a perilous slide at the siren song of false gods. Like the pride of Narcissus, we fell in love with our own image. We saw ourselves as the best—Number One! Although our country has been blessed with vast resources, the insatiable greed of Mammon, the craving for riches is threatening our own environment and life of Mother Earth. Those who hold the purse strings, aka rich donors, are the ones who own the politicians who make decisions in our country. This is not the way it was supposed to work. Many politicians are more often bought with tax dollars rather than elected with honesty. They talk about building walls of separation rather than bridges of brotherhood.

Please don't assume this is anti-patriotic. I love my country. I have traveled to several countries around the world and would choose to live here. We can't change what we don't acknowledge. The division brought by the current administration, while not new, has escalated. Division is everywhere: Democrats vs Republicans, Liberals vs Conservatives, etc. What started during the campaigns, and has further separated us during the first year. Divisions are now increased beyond our borders. We no longer cooperate with countries in trade or efforts to save our environment.

The way to return to the great country we were so proud of is to break free of the bonds of false gods, to put the good of the whole above self-interest, and to cooperate to assure equanimity among humankind. We can *be* a leader in integrity, truth, and justice for all. We can embody the words of the Declaration of Independence and the Constitution, and exercise compassionate cooperation with our fellow inhabitants on Planet Earth.

The four quadrants of consciousness apply to governments and the individual. Seeking the good of the whole and doing the right thing show a high consciousness, putting self ahead of the whole, is coming from carnal consciousness. Personality and ego rule carnal mind etc. Principle and integrity are inspired through compassion and benevolence.

Another reason politics is not working is accountability. Do the politicians do as they promised? Do they work for the good of everyone or just special interests groups? Does their behavior reflect the best qualities of what it means to be American? And we must address the important issue of creating a level playing ground for all candidates, by taking the money out of politics. With all the campaign funds raised, who profits? The people, or the producers of commercials, lobbyists, etc.?

PRISON: Mostly, the prison system is not working. The United States has the highest incarceration rate, with 2.2 million behind bars. Of those, 6% are from abroad. Prisons are filled with broken people. Some want help and can't get it, others don't want help, or don't believe they can be helped. Of all who are released two thirds, return within three years, often for a serious and more violent offense. Over time, up to ninety percent are re-incarcerated. What's wrong? The broken-ness remains. (Source: New York Times article) We need to learn to identify and fix the brokenness.

One of the greatest problems we have regarding prison reform, is our eye-for-an-eye perspective on crime and the perpetrators. If we, or someone we love, is a victim of a criminal, that definition is understandable. We believe they need to be punished. Even the punishment they have received may not appear to be sufficient. But if the punishment is not fixing the problem, we are perpetuating it. Yet we want retribution. We either can't see another way or choose not to. This is error; emotion is fueling our thoughts rather than Principle. This locks us into our intellect, not wisdom. We see or hear *convict* or *prisoner,* and jump to the conclusion the person is evil.

If we broaden our scope, and see the prisoner or convict as a human being who has problems, mental illness, addiction, or is the victim of abuse, we can see locking them up is not the answer. In fact, that makes the problem worse. Neither is letting them run around free to commit more wrongdoing and victims. The condition of the person is an effect, the behavior of the person reinforces our opinion. To stop the crime and punishment cycle, we must change the cause and work toward healing. To change the cause is to change the effect.

James Gilligan, a clinical professor of psychiatry and adjunct Professor of Law at New York University published an article in the New York Times, stating: "The only rational purpose for a prison is to restrain those who are violent, while we help them change their behavior and return to the community." He states that generations of studies have revealed when children are punished with severity and violence, they become violent adults. (Source: New York Times, December 19, 2012)

A powerful deterrent to re-offending is education. From elementary school through graduate school, education has been one hundred percent effective for years or even decades in preventing recidivism. A complication in getting the education to the prisoners is that many have learning disabilities and cannot read.

With low re-incarceration, tens of thousands of dollars would be saved by the taxpayers. If a thing seems too good to be true, it probably is. Change is difficult, but can be done. The current plan to pull back on supporting education in prison is sabotaging both the prisoners and the taxpayers, as the revolving door turns and costs of incarceration increase.

Privately run for-profit prisons may further complicate our problems. When Mammon is imbedded in the system, million trade hands, lobbyists push their influence, and politicians make money in the deal. The prisoners often become a commodity to for-profit prison. The advantages and disadvantages of private prisons involve cost, efficiency, and effectiveness. When a private prison is operating with best practices and focused on rehabilitation, it can be a beneficial addition to a community. Unfortunately, many corporations have a reputation of focusing on profits over purpose, which can create numerous hardships. (Sources: journalistsresource.org article by David Trilling, and Vittana.org article Feb. 28, 2018)

Believe change is possible. We can shift the paradigm and see others through the eyes of God. When we look at convicts, we can't see them as they are, abused children in adult bodies. Easy? Heck no. Healing? Absolutely. Crime is an effect of cause sent forth. To change the effect, we must change what is behind it. This is our only choice. No, I am not wearing rose-colored glasses and an airy-fairy pair of wings. It is a real mess. A serious mess. That's all the more reason to utilize the wisdom at our fingertips.

A cautionary note: The more than 2300 children that were taken from their families at the Mexican border were most likely traumatized by the event. Trauma changes who the children are. We don't know what the outcome of this will be down the road, but I was reminded of a line from the movie *The Help*. Aibileen, one of the maids, is telling Skeeter about the loss of her son, and how disrespectfully he was treated after his accident. She said, *"A bitter seed was planted in me that day…"* And I wonder how many bitter seeds were planted as those children were torn, scared and screaming from their parents. Will the boys who were taken grow a bitter seed of hate for America or Americans? Consider the Law of Cause and Effect. What will be the effect of this cause?

TAXES: Taxes are a way each of us can pay our fair share of our mutual expenses. But when false gods make their presence known, greed and personal power look for loopholes in order not to pay their fair share. Like everything else, it is not as simple as it looks. We all look for deductions, but if we cheat, we are stealing. It's easy to justify our actions with rationalization, aka rational-lies. Doesn't everyone do it? I'm sure your mother said when you were a child, "If your friends jumped off the Brooklyn Bridge are you going to as well?" When we understand the true purpose of taxes, and doing our part, paying our share with pride and integrity, change will begin. Imagine if your salivary glands decided to withhold saliva? Eating would be impossible, and the body would sooner or later suffer the consequences.

WHAT'S YOUR EXCUSE?

For clarity, in this section, I am defining the word, *reason*, as a logical and true basis for a course of action or inaction, and *excuse* as a fabricated explanation to defend or justify action taken or not taken. A valid reason is truth and an *excuse* is a lie. There are valid reasons we can or can't do something. There are also invalid excuses, or lies we tell ourselves.

As children of God, we have the potential to grow into living expressions of our creator, manifesting and sharing our inherent divine nature. During our journey through this life experience we will have opportunities to grow through experience. Some of it will be challenging, like going to the gym to build a strong body. Problems, or challenges, require us to overcome the tendencies of our lower nature, and we often opt-out of the growth opportunity. Consequently, we stay stuck. We will, however, be presented another opportunity (problem or challenge), more difficult to overcome. This is the proverbial *cosmic* 2X4—if we ignore the lesson, then comes the *cosmic 4x6*—a *figurative* whack on the back of the head to get our attention.

Achieving spiritual maturity requires moving beyond our comfort zone and overcoming the excuses that allow us not to. We may declare that we will get back in shape, but if we make excuses, telling ourselves we really don't have time today and will start tomorrow, we're only lying to ourselves. The old favorite excuse was, *"The devil made me do it!"* That's true, since *devil* spelled backward is lived, and making excuses, is living backward. We can never achieve mastery with excuses. Habitual excuse-making, aka lying, can lead to difficulty in being trusted by others.

A MATTER OF AUTHORITY

All false gods require to get a foothold in our minds is denial of a greater power—God. While God is never separate from us, our focus can shift from God, all-good, to carnal thoughts and concerns. The first commandment tells us *I AM the Lord, your God*. If we break this statement down metaphysically, *I AM, (note, upper case letters)* is the Spiritual Identity. First it represents God, and second, as Children of God, it represents each of us. We must keep in mind, however that while we are a part of God, we are not the all-ness of God. For example, your liver may be a part of you, but it is not the all-ness of you.

Next comes *the Lord,* Defined as *someone or something having power or authority over another.* In historic terminology, the Lord, through his/her position of authority, issues and enforces the law of the land. These mandates assure universal good. Abiding by laws makes us all safer, more secure, and happy. Authority must accompany influence and power. It requires mastery and understanding. An author is one who originates or creates, based on knowledge and expertise. God, being Omniscient, or all-knowing, is the author of Divine Law, or Principle.

Since God is good by nature, the Commandments of God are good. They are for the good of all. Therefore Spirit, our Lord—Law—is our good. Living according by the Commandments will bring good, because God is good, as is God's will for us.

Original Sin, false belief that we are separate from God and each other, rebels against any form of authority. The rebellion has increased in the past 50 years. Authority is either denied or ignored. The rebellion is not just in our day-to-day lives, but also regarding spiritual authority. Defiant behavior has become normalized. This includes civil and spiritual law. People hurt others without thought of what the result will be. Unabated, humankind will drift farther and farther from our potential as Children of God. There will be an ache in souls who can find no way out of their suffering. Sounds like hell, no?

Gun violence alone is an ominous example of the sin of separation. If someone from the 1950's awakened one morning in today's world, unaware of all that has unfolded in the past sixty years, I don't doubt they would be horrified. Many abominable examples have unfolded since October 1st, 2017 when one man murdered 58 people, and injured 851 by showering bullets down on a concert crowd. From January 1, 2018 to January 28, 2018, there have been 1,095 deaths from gun violence, 48 of those were children under the age of 11. Just six weeks later, on Valentine's Day 2018, a 19-year-old man killed 15 high school students and 3 teachers. (gunviolencearchive.org)

On New Year's Eve 2017 I was saddened to see the security measures taken in Times Square to assure safety of the crowd. This included barriers and snipers posted on upper stories of hotels and other buildings. This happens when no strong, healthy authority will stand up for the people and what is right. Authority does not mean authoritarian, it means, having full knowledge, understanding, integrity, and grasp of what is in the best interests for everyone. This includes the world community, and its members, from the richest to the homeless.

In the Bible, Jesus tells Peter to put his sword away, because he who lives by the sword will die by the sword. (Matthew 26:52) Can we not see this message is for us? It is telling us that if we live by violence and death, we will create more violence and death. We witness this every day.

Consider the possibility that Spirit is not out to make our lives miserable, but to help us grow, and be strong, happy and fulfilled. Spiritual Principle is meant to support us, not bind. Would you rather learn how to operate your computer by someone with authority—expertise—or your cat? Who would you prefer to entrust with your health, happiness, and that of all you love—false gods, or Spirit, all-knowing, all-powerful, everywhere-present the good, Omnipotent?

Now we should have a basic understanding of living in Truth or facing consequences. We have the opportunity to apply what we have learned, and observe the results. We can watch them working all around us. This will help us see both what has to happen, and how we may bring negative consequences upon ourselves, through the causes we send forth. Remember, it is both individual and collective. Once we have this realization—learning, living and sharing—it is imperative for victory over false gods.

Here's an example: A student receives a test back from her teacher. It has a failing grade. The grade is an effect. If the student realizes this, she can ponder what cause was behind the negative effect. It could be the student didn't study enough, or she is not comprehending the class material. This is an opportunity to think about what caused the failing grade and get help. Once the student realizes what caused the failing grade, she can make changes to prevent this from happening again.

SURRENDERING TO VICTORY

If you are feeling overwhelmed by what you've read this far, try to let that go. Know you will *get it*, and claim victory over the false gods. Breaking free of false gods is simple, but I won't lie to you, it's not easy. Remember the last time the batteries in your television remote control died? When you would push the buttons and nothing would happen? Then you opened the battery compartment and wiggled them and tried again to no avail. Maybe you shook the remote, or banged it against the arm of your chair. None of those actions worked, because they did not address the cause of the problem, which is dead batteries. That's what spiritual transformation can feel like sometimes. To have the victory we want, we must surrender. We must let go of the tyranny of our carnal self, and the perceived conception we are in control.

J. K. Rowling, author of the Harry Potter series, had great challenges in her life. At one point she realized she'd hit rock bottom. She didn't give up though. She decided to carry on. Later, in reflection, she said *"So, rock bottom became the foundation upon which I built my life."* She decided to claim her own power in life and followed through.

The first step to claiming our power is to take a long, hard look at our lives. We ask ourselves what matters most. Our experiences should support what matters most to us. They connect us to our Spiritual self and each other, and leave memories which hold the feeling. Stop for a moment and note everything you'd take if you had to evacuate your home immediately and would not be returning. After family and pets, people say photo albums, because they preserve our memories of wonderful times.

In August of 2017, Houston, Texas and surrounding towns, experienced widespread, devastating floods. They could not take anything more than they could carry, which came down to a pillow case or trash bag filled with whatever it is they couldn't part with. I'd venture to say it might have included medicine, or other critical items. Yet the one thing they had in common, was gratitude for their lives and the people who rescued them. They were happy to be alive, safe, and dry.

In the disaster in Houston as in all times of shared crisis the soul of humankind emerges in the name of love and humanity. No thought was given to race, religion, immigration status, age, gender, economic standing, political affiliation, or any of the things that separate us. Supplies and money flowed in from people across the country. What matters most? Life. Compassion. Helping.

Many of the people helping had also lost much. They were helping because it is what we do. It is who we are. There were also misguided souls trying to profit from the tragedy of others. They broke into evacuated homes to steal valuables left behind. Nothing they took can enrich them because true riches come from right of consciousness. Yet, they risked their lives. Many were caught and will find themselves in jail.

The two Chinese characters that make the word for *crisis* represent danger and opportunity. We can pray those who came together will find their lives enriched, and maybe one day those who are still in bondage to false gods will realize it's not about money and personal power.

We can we let go of the trappings of false gods: manufactured rather than valid needs or requirements and promises of personal power, we find freedom beyond anything we can imagine. When we surrender items we have held for years without being used, to someone who will love and use them, we feel good, prosperous, and satisfied—victorious! When we find confidence in who we are, there is no need for power struggles.

IT'S NOT ME ~ OR IS IT?

A beloved television character named Steve Urkel was a clumsy young man, who'd trip over something, which would then crash to the ground. Looking up in surprise, he'd say, *"Did I do that?"* In our everyday lives, when something crashes to the ground we look for someone else whose fault it might be—including God. There are those of us who blame ourselves for everything that goes wrong. What's wrong with this? It's not helping us find what happened behind the scenes, in mind. Because *that's* what has to change. We cannot have different results without different actions (causes).

Many years ago, the rebel in me made the decision to attend the rock opera, Godspell, which the Catholic Church banned. It was a life-changing decision. As the story unfolded, I had a new, deeper realization of what Jesus was teaching. Truths in Jesus' teaching went off in my heart and soul like fireworks. That night, I came to understand why Jesus taught in parables: Spiritual Principles presented a story format. He would say: *"There once was a man..."* It was impersonal and non-accusatory. The people could let down their defensive guard. Listeners could identify with the characters in the story from a safe distance. They could see it was about Principle and not personal. The parables are about everyday life, making right choices, and the consequences of not doing so.

God created us to be His children—cocreators. What did God create? Good! What are we here to cocreate? Good, of course. To do this, we must develop our true nature. We're like rosebuds. The bud is just an undeveloped rose. As it matures, the petals open. When the rose is in full bloom, its color is exposed, and fragrance wafts calling bees to come enjoy their nectar and spread their pollen. As we mature, we blossom, sharing all that we have and all we are with anyone in need of it. To mature as a spiritual being is to learn, and then live according to the law, and break free of the spell of false gods. When we listen to the parables or any Bible story, we can listen for the message it has just for us.

The parable of the prodigal son, is a story about a man with two sons. One day the younger son went to his father and asked for his inheritance in advance. He then squandered it on extravagant living. When a famine came, the prodigal—wasteful son had to take work as a swineherd. This would be abhorrent to a person of the Hebrew faith, since pigs are considered unclean. One day the young man, hungry and destitute, had an epiphany. He realized even the servants of his father's house had something to eat, when all he has was corn husks. He decided to return to his father and beg forgiveness, offering to be as a servant, since he did not deserve to be a son.

When his father saw the boy coming, he ran out and embraced his son, calling servants to bring him a robe, and a ring, and to kill the fatted calf for a feast in honor of his son's return. The older brother, who had stayed and worked with his father while the younger brother was wasting his inheritance, was jealous and angry. He complained to his father and said he wouldn't attend the party. The father reminds his older son he still has his inheritance, and will receive everything after his death, but for now to celebrate the return of his brother.

Without exploration, this is a good story. If we delve in, this simple story can change our lives. *Where am I in this story?* We can ask. *Am I the prodigal son? Or the father? Or the resentful brother?* Chances are we'll find ourselves in one role on one day, and another the following day, depending on our circumstances and the lesson we are being called to learn. Sometimes it is us. The story has no evil. Just people living their lives, making both good and bad decisions, and paying the price, or receiving the reward accordingly.

The wisdom for us is that the prodigal son learned a lesson. He accepted the consequences of his actions. He wasn't a bad young man, but he was in the grips of Mammon and Baal—money and lust. Yes, sometimes it's us at the center of our circumstances. One of my mother's frequent comments was *"You brought this on yourself."* Often, that is the case. We have to be honest with ourselves. Observe our life from the perspective of cause and effect rather than good and evil. Once we acknowledge we had a part in it, we can change.

YOUR CREDO: A POWERFUL TOOL FOR TRANSFORMATION

The word *credo,* means *I believe.* If I asked you to explain your belief system concisely, could you? We may all think we know what we believe, but until we go through a discovery process, we probably aren't clear. We have to sort our actual beliefs from what others taught us. Consider these questions:

Who or what is God?

What do you believe about God?

Where did your beliefs come from?

How can we know what we believe is true?

Have your beliefs about God changed during of your life?

What do you believe about life and death?

You can explore these questions yourself using the Credo Exercise in the back of this book. One of the most important questions, is where our beliefs came from. Once we are very clear about our beliefs, we will stand on a firm foundation of faith. On this foundation, we can build a consciousness that can face life's challenges. It will change our lives and the world we live in.

Once we have established our own credo, we can apply the same process to that of our nation. The greater question then, is: What does the collective mind of the United States believe about God? Government? What does it believe about freedom and responsibility? Now *that* is a head-scratcher. Is it possible to find consensus in our divided country? It's not just possible, but to overcome false gods that separate us, it is necessary. Let me show you how. Here are two overlapping circles. Each circle represents individual thoughts, feelings and beliefs.

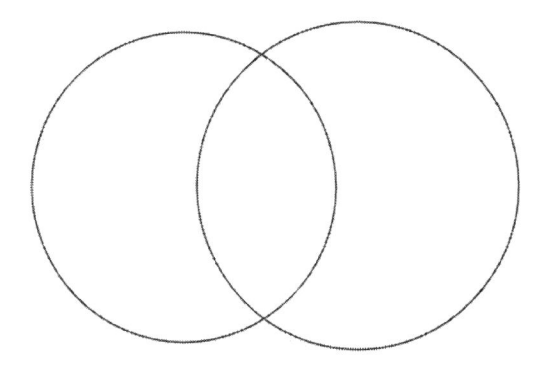

The space formed where the two circles overlap, would represent shared or collective thoughts, feelings and beliefs. This is where the Credo of the United States would be formed. While individuals may have many religions, or no religion, we all agree that people should be free to worship according to their beliefs. We come from many cultures, but we agree that all have the right to life, liberty, and the pursuit of happiness.

There are sticky issues including things like lifestyle, sexual preference, abortion, gun control, etc. that we haven't been able to find common ground we can all agree on. This is where our work lies It *is* possible. We just have to get about the business of rebuilding, cocreating the Re-United States of America.

PART SIX – CLEANSING AND RESTORING THE TEMPLE

In metaphysical interpretation, buildings represent states of mind, body, or awareness. The building is the manifestation of mind. A mansion might represent a rich, expansive state of mind or body, while a tiny shack might represent a poor or needy state. A temple, could represent our spiritual state of mind. A building is where we live. Our consciousness is the spiritual *house*. I use the words *might* and *could* because one interprets by the whole picture, not just one word. A serpent, using metaphysical interpretation, could either be lust, temptation, or wisdom. It depends on the context in the story. Manifestation begins in mind, and appears through the creative process. The condition of the structure is also important. In the Bible, we learn the enemies of the Hebrew people attacked the Temple in Jerusalem 52 times, recaptured 44 times, besieged 23 times, and destroyed twice.

When false gods, error thoughts and beliefs, invade our temple of mind, it becomes cluttered with toxic concepts:

"And he taught, and said to them, (Jesus is speaking) 'Is it not written, My house shall be a house of prayer for all the nations? But you have made it a den of robbers.'" (Mark 11:17) At that point he drove out the money changers, overturning their coin changing tables.

False gods have invaded minds of humankind through ego, personal power, greed and all that is not like God. Sometimes we feel encircled with depressing headlines or significant adverse conditions. Sometimes the conditions are so painful, we may feel desolate. To evict these things from the temple of mind, we must recognize and banish them from returning. To do this, we must fill the void created by their exit, with Truth.

A helpful technique is the process of affirmation and denial. To affirm, means to *make firm*. We affirm God's presence and power in our lives through speaking affirmations, such as the Unity foundational statement:

"There is only One presence and One power in the universe and in my life, God, the good, omnipotent."

When we use denial, we do not deny the reality of something painful in our lives, we deny that it has any power beyond God. If we find we are upset by an insult, we might say, *"What you think of me is none of my business. I am a beloved child of God."*

The trick is not just in thinking or saying it, it is in both thinking and feeling the affirmation and denial. When we establish this healthy habit, over time we restore our lives to wholeness. This process employs the Law of Mind Action because we take control of our thoughts and feelings.

"Unless the Lord builds the house, those who work, labor in vain. (Psalm 127:1) Achieving spiritual maturity is work, but the result is priceless.

The temple also symbolizes the state of our nation. While we are experiencing difficult times and great challenges, we have an opportunity to grow. Like the temple in Jerusalem, we are building our body/mind temple on freedom grounded in Principle. We've been through a lot, torn apart and segregated. We can and will overcome. Separation and segregation can't keep us apart because God is greater.

The temple, the essence of America will be restored by us, we the people. The enlightened, committed people, not a handful of privileged politicians. People from every walk of life, all races, all economic levels and lifestyles will build a new America with bridges to connect all people on the planet. There will be no walls of separation. Together we will restore our values, and emerge The

Re-United States of America, built on the secure foundation of Truth and Integrity.

When we emerge from our collective dark night of the national soul, if we do our work now, we can build something enduring. This can happen if we build on Truth as our foundation. For now, we can prepare by learning from our history, and freeing ourselves from it.

A TIME TO HEAL

One of the Unity teachings claims, *"Whenever we declare something for our life, everything unlike it comes up for healing."* A perfect example is the declaration that we will get in shape. We make a plan to pay attention to our diet and establish an exercise routine. Off we go in a blaze of glory! The next thing we know, we confront an obstacle. Temptation may appear when a friend invites us to dinner. The dinner turns out to be a calorie laden orgy of fats and carbs. The next day we wake up late for our exercise class. From there, procrastination rules, or we give up entirely.

There are examples of this in every situation in our life. We want to be debt free, and get our finances in order, and every compelling reason to overspend hits like a tidal wave. It could be an irresistible sale, a broken appliance, or other unexpected expenses. A plan to enhance our marriage may find our mate starts to display every irritating behavior, almost daring us not to react. Then there's the ever-present desire to improve our spiritual life with a regular prayer routine. But each day, some interruption or distraction throws our plan off schedule.

Does this sound familiar? I'm sure it does, for most of us anyway. The key here is the word *healing*. Do we want to be healed enough to do our part? Whatever comes up is something to heal. Our suffering is a symptom. It comes to us so we know what we need to transform. Each example stated has at its root in self, all about *me first*.

Contemplate the story of Jesus healing the man on a mat near the healing pool of Bethesda. He had been there for 38 years. Jesus asked him, *"Do you want to be healed?"* When the man told him he did, but couldn't find anyone to help him get to the water, Jesus said: *"Pick up your bed and walk."* (John 5:8)

Nobody can do our spiritual work for us. We each must do our part. In taking charge of the behaviors, we become strong enough to conquer them. We may feel overwhelmed by the time and effort required to overcome old ways. But a simple shift in our thinking process, and a single word, can make it much easier. Want to know how? Turn our problems into projects.

Problems may not seem to have an end, but projects do. Let's say we have a problem with anger. There are several things we can do to turn our problem into a project. Establishing daily prayer time is a good start. Journaling every day let us review mistakes, how we responded, and what we could have done. We have to remember when journaling to recognize our victories as well as growth opportunities.

My mother was right, when she told me I'd brought a problem on myself, and it is just as true today. We do cause our own problems. We do bring it on ourselves. But it's not about blame and fault. It is impersonal. It is about cause, and effect. We did it when we chose to be non-participants, or minimal participants. Ignorance is not bliss. We cannot hide from Truth. The mistakes we've made for years, whether in our personal lives, or as a country, have come up for healing. While some of us put out energies of indifference and negligence, others of swallowing lies and allowing the cravings and emotions of mortal mind to consume them. So now, our errors—might I say sins—cover us like hives. It is a systemic infection, begging the question: *Do we want to be healed?*

Unity's cofounder, Charles Fillmore, also said *"The mind of peace precedes all healing."* If we want healing, it is important to establish a mind of peace through prayer, affirmation and anchoring our thoughts and feelings to faith in God, where we find the peace that passes understanding.

WHY CONFESSION IS GOOD FOR THE SOUL

A New Look at an Old Tradition

In my days in the Catholic Church, to receive Holy Communion it was necessary to be in a state of grace. This means, to have no sin on your soul. This requires going to confession.

The process begins with an examination of conscience. The person reviews the time since their previous confession to collect sins to confess to the priest. When it was our turn, we would enter the confessional and listen for the priest to slide open a little window so we could speak to him. It was dark in the confessional, so we would have a sense of privacy or anonymity, I suppose.

Confession begins with: *"Bless me, Father, for I have sinned."* We would then recite our litany of sins, receive our penance, say a good act of contrition, and exit the booth to recite the prayers prescribed. This means, to acknowledge our sin, and commit to not doing it again. Which meant, until next time, often before we arrived home from church. But I always left the confessional feeling light and holy, assured that if a car ran over me before I reached home and I died, I'd go to heaven.

The church is right: confession is good for the soul. In fact, Carl Jung said he had fewer Catholic patients than any other, because they dumped their sins on the priest.

Behind the process of confession and repentance stand powerful Spiritual Principles. To confess is to acknowledge what we have done. To repent, is to recognize error and change our thinking.

When we change our thoughts, we change our world. Once we understand Spiritual Principle—we will no longer want to break spiritual law.

SONS OF LIGHT VS SONS OF DARKNESS

It would not be possible to clean our house well in the dark. We couldn't see what to keep and what to discard. We wouldn't be able to wash away spots, and would trip over items out of place. It's the same with cleansing the temple of the mind. Much of the clutter in the darkness is error thoughts.

Over 600 years before the birth of Jesus, members of the Qumran community hid their sacred documents in caves. After being discovered around 1946, they became known as the Dead Sea Scrolls. In the years that followed, scholars pieced together the fragments they had. They interpreted them to the best of their ability based on what they had to work with. A story emerged from one scroll. It told of the great battle between the Sons of Light and the Sons of Darkness. The story is considered be an apocalyptic prophecy, predicting the ultimate war between the forces of good and evil.

Mysteriously, just prior to the discovery of the scrolls, theologian Reinhold Niebuhr published a book titled, *The Children of Light and the Children of Darkness*. While the book was about democracy, it paralleled the story in the scrolls. The book, and the scroll are about the battle of light, aka enlightenment, and darkness, or ignorance. Describing the children of darkness, one identifying trait is there is no law beyond self.

The battle between ignorance and enlightenment has raged for eons—maybe even since the dawn of man's appearance on the planet. The root of our problem is in not understanding evil; rather than defining it as a thought, word or action, we impose it on a person, culture, religion, etc. as a character trait, or a part of who they are. Consider a new possibility. What if we looked at it in a different way; what if we looked at others intending to understand them? We could learn why they think and act the way they do. Consider what could happen if we learned how to enlighten instead of judge and contradict? This is how light can overcome darkness.

Consider what happens each day when the sun rises. Light emerges from below the horizon and soon it is everywhere. It does not have to fight darkness. Note, that the sun must rise above the horizon. Likewise, in order for light to come into our awareness, we must also rise above the horizon of our own current level of understanding. We need to be teachable, and flexible enough to change ourselves. To realize our connection, we must live it.

Much of the battle between the so-called forces of good and evil happens within our own minds and hearts. Consider the *seven deadly sins:* pride, sloth, envy, wrath, lust, greed, and avarice, and how they block the light. Sin is not who we are. It is what we think, say and do. Even during the sun's daily journey from dawn to dark, there will always be shadows. See them for what they are, only illusions caused by objects that hide the light.

LOST SHEEP–OUR SEARCH AND RESCUE MISSION

Lost sheep are all around us. They are lost in plain sight. Metaphysically, lost sheep symbolize the most harmless and innocent of animals. They represent our trusting, innocent thoughts, flowing with life, following the shepherd. Thoughts, like sheep, can get lost. They are easily distracted and sometimes drift away. How often have you been doing a routine chore, or even in a conversation, when you realize your mind was elsewhere? Sometimes in Jazzercise class I put my mind on auto-pilot as I think about what I need at the grocery store. This is what lost sheep are like.

The lost sheep can be our own thoughts, or collective thoughts. They can also be the thoughts of someone who has wandered away from their path. Not all thoughts or people are seen as lost sheep. We name them: homeless bums, druggies, crooks, or jailbirds. There are many more names, like murders, sluts, white trash, or crack heads. But they're not—not in God's eyes—and they shouldn't be in ours either.

To look at those whose lives may seem unworthy and see them as irresponsible, lazy, or leech, is to judge by appearances. It's like looking at the tip of the iceberg and thinking that's all there is. With others, we have to consider, as with an iceberg, the huge mass below the surface. Each person we tag with disrespectful names came into this world with the same dreams and desires we all share, and the desire for love, acceptance and appreciation. Then something went wrong—for whatever reason—their life went off course.

Behind the appearance that repels us, if we look deeper we will find pain. They did not make the decisions that put them in their circumstances intending to live on the streets, or in jail, abusive relationships. They did not think they would become addicted, shunned, and condemned to never-ending suffering. They did not decide consciously to lose their dreams and self-respect. I believe many decided to use drugs as a way of escaping a world that has become frightening and hopeless.

In America today, we are suffering from an opioid epidemic. Staggering statistics reveal that drug overdoses now kill more people than guns or car accidents, with 63,000 dying in 2016 alone. This is 21% higher than the previous year. (Source: NY Daily News, December 17, 2017, by Terence Cullen) For the second year in a row, the life-expectancy of Americans has dropped. The main cause for the decline is death from a drug overdose.

It's easy to look at drug addicts and see them as weak, lazy, even evil people who just want to get high and live off of others. We cannot judge by appearances. A closer look may reveal the cause behind the behavior. We have to look to cause. While authorities are trying to block the drugs from getting into the country or people's hands, they are treating symptoms. If the cause remains, drug abuse will always prevail. It is a losing battle. Imagine what would happen if the cause was eliminated? There would be no market for illegal drugs and they would go back to use as necessary for medical treatment. Yet there's more. It goes even further than this. Drugs are cash crops for underdeveloped countries whose lands and people have already been exploited by multinational corporations and agribusiness, leaving people with no other ways to support their families.

If our thoughts of the homeless, drug addicts, and troubled people changed to lost sheep rather than worthless and evil, everything could change. We'd see an opportunity to reach out to them and bring them back to the flock. It is not an easy task, since a disdain for these lost souls has been long-established in our thoughts. Even the lost sheep see themselves as worthless and unredeemable. But that is not the truth of their being—because they are God's children—even if it seems they don't want salvation, freedom from their suffering.

Overwhelming as it may seem, this is not an insurmountable problem. We must, however, have patience and endurance to shift our ingrained way of thinking. Rev. Eric Butterworth said we have to *see* things right before we can *set* things right. When we hold right, truthful thoughts, we begin the process of manifestation. We will draw like-minded people and opportunities to us, which will bring the quantum shift we desire. We can work with others to find treatments that work, not just get them clean and send them out to temptation. If we do not address the primary cause, we can expect relapse.

FROM FATAL ATTRACTION TO FAITH-FILLED ACTION

Once the temple is clean and full of light, we want it to stay that way. Whatever undesirable thoughts, words or habits are found in cleansing our temple, we can banish from our domain. Constant upkeep is necessary. This is accomplished through conscious living. We pay attention to our thoughts and feelings. We eliminate anything that does not support our spiritual growth and the good of all creation.

It is important to understand the compelling call of carnal mind, which operates both in the appetites of the flesh and the survival instinct. In the chocolate cake example, the commercial on television—the cake looks moist and sweet. The chocolate frosting glistens with a sheen so beautiful and tempting we can almost taste it. In fact, we may salivate. Before too long we'll find something chocolate to eat. Even if we have to bake a cake. Seriously, I've done things like that! The first thought attracted like thoughts—supporting thoughts—and nucleated creative energy resulting in manifestation.

That may be an amusing story, but it's amusing because it's so true. During the commercial, images come before our eyes. They link, one to another, each one binding our attention. Through the Law of Mind Action, each thought makes our craving for chocolate cake stronger. This works in every area of our lives. If something stimulates anger, chances are the experience will attract like thoughts, and images and anger increases. I saw a cartoon once that said, *"I know the best way to stop temptation. Give in."* That is too true!

The actual best way to overcome temptation is to remove its power by replacing the temptation thought with a good thought. *"Do not be overcome by evil, but overcome evil with good."* (Rom. 12:21) We can look away from the temptation to something else that is pleasing. If the temptation is chocolate cake, think about the weight you are losing. Imagine being your perfect weight—buying clothes, playing sports games, seeing the scale reading your ideal weight. We can be like athletes and do pull-ups on a bar, so we raise our spiritual bar. It will cause us to pull hard and stretch, but it will make us fit.

RAISING THE BAR

To raise the bar, we raise our consciousness—moving from carnal mind to the mind of Spirit. Let's take another look at the 4 quadrants of consciousness chart:

Superconscious	Mind
Spiritual Higher Mind Intuitive	Spiritual Higher Mind Sensing
Carnal Lower Mind Thinking - Thoughts	Carnal Lower Mind Feeling - Emotions
Subconscious	Mind

The area above the quadrants represents the Super-conscious—All-Knowing, and the area below the quadrants represents the Subconscious—Unknowing. The quadrants are areas we know of and have the ability to move through. This example applies to individuals and groups, cultures, etc. all the way to the collective consciousness of all the beings on Planet Earth. To raise the bar for all, we must begin by raising the bar for ourselves.

When we are in the lower, or carnal quadrants, we are being ruled by human mind. In our day to day lives, without practice, it can be very difficult to rise above the lower mind. Like the pull of gravity, the pull of the lower nature is strong. We must strive to rise above it if we are to escape its influence. Regular spiritual practice provides the strength and discernment to do this. A great start is daily prayer and meditation. This is not as daunting as it may seem. Over time, it will become your favorite part of the day. The critical factor is to establish it as a daily practice.

NOTE: Throughout this book you will notice I use the terms *higher,* or *upper,* and *lower* when speaking of consciousness. This is for simplicity and understanding. As *heaven* and *hell* are states of consciousness not physical or geographical locations, consciousness is not linear. At the same time, *up* and *down* are valid metaphors to define states of consciousness. For example, when we are sad, we literally feel *down.* Our shoulders slump and we feel the weight of our sadness, on the other hand we feel lifted up, or in *high spirits* when we are in a positive mood. These are physical responses to spiritual energies.

The terms *lower,* and *carnal* do not mean that part of our consciousness, including the physical body is bad. It is good. It is the vehicle through which we are expressing and cocreating with Spirit. Consider the automobile. We should not be driving if we are impaired. As much as I love my cat, I wouldn't let her drive either. Nor do I favor the new cars that drive themselves. I want to be in the driver's seat of my life. I want my body and mind to work with me in agreement. Imagine what it would be like to push your car everywhere you went, rather than driving it.

Instead of forcing our will on our lower self, we only need to train it by bringing it into the light. This would rid us of things like addictions, being controlled by our emotions, and self-indulgence.

Did you ever leave dirty pot on the stovetop overnight? Even though the flame is off, the residue in the pot will stick to the surface. The same thing is true in eliminating old, sticky behaviors and beliefs. There are three ways to handle this. We can scrub the pot. It will take considerable effort to remove the residue. The second way is to soak the pan in water with a little dish detergent. Soon, the food will get soft and easy to wash away. The third way is to soak the pan after cooking, so nothing will get stuck while you are enjoying your meal.

The first method most of us can relate to. Its name is procrastination. We delay addressing something because it is inconvenient or uncomfortable, then we wake up one day to find a problem in our life has gotten out of control. Have you ever seen the people scrambling to get to the post office before midnight on April 15th?

The second method is easier but it takes patience and extra time to fix. This might be like rushing to the post office before midnight to file for an extension to complete our taxes. While this may seem like a good solution, when we consider the amount of effort exerted in stress and anxiety that drained our ambition every day we carried it, was it worth it?

The third method works best—handling responsibilities—because staying on top of things and accountable has an energizing effect. Try it!

It's the same thing with prying our attention away from the relentless grasp of the carnal nature. The difficulty of the task decreases with the time and effort invested. We have to learn to say a firm *NO* to that part of us that wants to procrastinate. If you don't think you're a genius, just start the process of taking quiet time. Observe how many creative ways your little self can come up with to distract you. We may say *little* self, but it the little self is powerful and can be insidious.

I have been practicing a daily prayer time for over thirty years. There are occasional days I miss, few though. I look forward to it every day. On vacation, I may take less time, but that doesn't mean

I forget about God/Spirit in my daily life. I still take time to pray, maybe a little less. Yet during the day I find countless moments of joy to say *Thank you, God,* for the wonders of the day.

We can't let distractions tell us we don't have time to pray. We all have the same twenty-four hours every day. It's what we choose to do with them that matters. It's unnecessary to deprive ourselves of television or technology—just reassign their importance, and the time we give to them every day. False gods drive us using distraction. They want us to focus on our own little lives and concerns, getting lost in technology, immerse ourselves in our physical appetites. This is the opposite of what we need. In fact, Charles Fillmore said, *"The more I have to do, the more time I need to pray."*

FROM PEOPLE PLEASING TO PLEASING GOD

Every human being shares some basic needs. We all want acceptance and love. Note, the word used is *love,* not *like.* To like, is conditional. We can like a person today, and not tomorrow. Yet the word *love*, implies the spiritual faculty of love, which is absolute, eternal and unchanging. We want others to accept us and never reject us. This is evidence of our inherent interconnection. We are a part of a greater whole—One with God, one with each other, and all creation. Spirit wove us together as one and we each depend on the other. Whether or not we are conscious of it, we all want to take part in the life of our oneness. Wholeness is living from that Truth. Since wholeness and holiness mean the same thing, it would then be true that acknowledging and living our oneness will make us whole—holy.

Earlier, we explored *original sin* through the story of Adam and Eve. Their banishment from Paradise shows the great cost of losing awareness of our bond with God. God did not *like* what they had done, but still *loved* them, and gave them the opportunity to redeem themselves through the sweat of their brow. This means

Spirit required them to earn true knowledge and wisdom, through experience and realization, instead of stealing it, which is what they tried to do by eating the fruit.

Here we are thousands of years later, having made little progress. Why? Despite the pain and suffering of living in carnal mind, making the same mistakes, and wondering why things keep getting worse, we refuse to surrender our *free will* to the will of God. Even the reality of God is in question for some. It's not all our fault. Over time, well-intentioned leaders have not presented an appealing image of God. Because of our religious instruction, we fear God. They teach that we must follow the rules or suffer, and that God is an angry, vengeful God, who would condemn us to hell in a heartbeat. It is interesting to note that Bible scholars say the correct translation of fear, should be *respect*. The word respect would seem fitting for the creator of all good.

The material world, the realm of false gods, is much more appealing to most people. Free will provides a license to do whatever we want. We have rights. We believe we are in control, and can manipulate others without consequence, enticed by our appetite for money, possessions, and personal power, and so we give up our true spiritual power. When we exercise our free will as self-will, disappointment will follow. If we curry favor with people we believe will provide the things we want, including love and acceptance, we will not receive genuine love. What we thought was freedom became a prison.

Sometimes the right thing to do is put the requirements of others ahead of our own. But when we put others before Truth and integrity, we have worshipped false gods. We have locked the door to Paradise on an individual and collective level. No relationship is worth that. Nor is any job worth it, nor any amount of money.

People pleasing today has become a widespread epidemic. Sometimes pleasing others, is a tool to get what we want through manipulation. Narcissism, which is the polar opposite of Oneness, demands its own way and places itself above anyone or anything else. The narcissist is mean-spirited, while being hypersensitive to any criticism. This behavior will never bring the lasting love, acceptance and appreciation they deserve.

When we are able to see things as they really are, we can free ourselves from people pleasing, and turn to pleasing God, our true source of all good. As we reunite with our true self, we begin to live the life we desire. This applies on all levels of consciousness and to every situation in life.

In the current (2019) administration of the United States, despite his classless, crude comments, dangerous behaviors, and 8,157 documented, blatant lies and misleading claims, Donald Trump maintains his base. Many republicans continue to support him. We shake our heads and wonder why. What is in it for them? Job security can be seen as a reason, despite the unprecedented turnover. Others see it as a vehicle to getting their agenda passed. For too many it's propaganda-based revenge against real or perceived wrongs of the government—a government they did not take part in, even if that was their choice.

What do you think America would look like if we put pleasing God before self, tribe or party? What if we lived as *One nation under God, indivisible?* Not a Christian God, or a Jewish God, or Buddhist, etc. but God—creator of all-good. It can be. Where there's life, there's hope. As each one of us lives in integrity, serving God and each other, strong and re-united in the name of all that is good, we *will* recreate what we love most about the American ideal. Everyone has a part in creating a new world. The apostle Peter said faith, or hope, without works is dead. We don't have to do it all, but we each must do our part.

NOW IT'S GETTING PERSONAL!

No matter how spiritual or intelligent we may be, one thing we never want to be is wrong. Our pride can't handle the thought we are not as perfect as we'd like to believe. Heaven forbid anything should be our fault. Well, not according to our ego. Here's a wake-up call for everyone, myself included: If we were already perfect we would not be here. We are here because we have things to do and learn.

The collective soul of humankind is suffering atrophy from lack of exercise. Despite millions we spend for timesaving devices, how much time have we saved? We fill every moment in our life with demands of ego and pursuit of *more*. We think we need more of everything. When we get the next thing, and the next, we need a place to store it! What we need is time and space. Unscheduled time and space to get still, to clear our minds and drink from the well of living water. It's impossible to have a spiritual life without solitude. To see for yourself, answer a few questions: how many hours of your day provide you with solitude? How many minutes are you free of distraction or activity? In the *exercises* section, you will find how to create your own prayer time and process.

Self-Examination is an important part of our spiritual path. As false gods play the game of distraction, our life slips by, and with it precious moments we could spend living the life we desire. One problem with self-examination, is that it is very difficult to dig for our flaws. I don't think it is so much we avoid thinking about our personal flaws. I think we fear them. We fear that if others knew our flaws we would be rejected.

It is crucial to remember we're all Children of God. We may not behave like it, but we are. If we are not acting like it, all we need to do is change our mind and act like it.

Where to start? We come to understand it's not a personal judgment. It is a process of discernment. When a teacher presents his or her students with a test, it is to determine comprehension of the lessons, not to judge or punish. It's that simple. Good news: if you don't 'pass' the exam, you will get another opportunity—and another—and another, until you master the lesson.

It's not personal, its Principle. How we work the Principle is, however, personal. We can practice what we learned or not. In the exercises section, you will find a self-evaluation to complete. Once you have completed it, you will know which areas you are excelling in, and which you want to work on next.

CLAIM YOUR POWER OVER FALSE GODS

Since we have determined we are being called to be *the one*, it is time to explore how to go about it. We can begin by taking action to free ourselves from the grasp of lower mind. It is not unlike taming a wild horse. This does not mean to treat the lower self with disrespect but to lead, like a horse whisperer.

False gods thrive in the realm of lower mind. Their intention is to influence based on human cravings, presenting them as requirements to the lower, self-obsessed mind. We absorbed in the allure of the physical world, influenced by senses and emotions. It's everywhere we look, and in everything we hear. We have confused expensive luxury items with needs, not a frivolous waste of money. Advertisers tell us we must have whiter, brighter teeth, when the average person's teeth are the off-white color they should be. We purchase expensive cologne or after shave with the promise it will attract members of the opposite sex. This appeals to the carnal nature, that is of the world.

How do we escape and overcome the false gods? We begin by accepting that greatest detractor is ourselves, and we need to make some changes. Most of us don't like that thought because we may fear it means we're wrong or evil. Let go of that. Consider this: *"Do not be conformed to this world but be transformed by the renewal of your mind, that you may prove what is the will of God, what is good and acceptable and perfect."* (Romans 12:2) This process is called repentance, another *Ouchy* word that we misunderstand. It means to re-think our current beliefs and way of life. After we evaluate, we may make another choice. God is Principle, therefore good will manifest. It will take as long as it takes for us to make the change. We can expedite the change when we do our part—renewing our own minds. We can choose transformation by the renewal of our mind.

Transformation builds a bridge between the mind of self and mind of Spirit. Remember, our mission is not to eradicate our human self, but to put it under direction of Spirit. It's not a matter of this *or* that, but this *and* that. The wonderful thing about transformation is that it brings only good. The part of us that balks and complains is the part that is resisting change—resisting our own good! Transformation through self-discipline makes us happier.

"We only grow strong in the crucible of adversity." Cavett Robert

We begin the process by determining what matters in our lives. We want to discern what matters most, and in which quadrant of consciousness it is located. Carnal thoughts and feelings may compel, but we make the choice. We can strive for integrity, love, peace, and joy that come from Spirit-centered living. This is where we find our meaning and our mission in life.

The philosopher Socrates said, *"The unexamined life is not worth living."* These are words of Truth. We all ask ourselves the question, *what is the meaning of life?* We wonder if our life has a purpose, or is it a random event. The older we get, the more pressing the question becomes. Most likely because after we pass the halfway-mark of the average lifespan we're more concerned regarding what we came here to do.

Without examining our life, we won't know if we are fulfilling our life's purpose. What we will notice is a disturbance—divine discontent moving within us. If we don't explore what we are being called to do and if we don't look around at potentiality that excites us, we could even die. Think how often people reach retirement age, and if they don't have a plan for their future, within two years they have left the planet. As for me, I don't want to die with the music still in me.

It's time to face our demons, which are error states of mind. Exposing error to light transforms it. If you want to determine what matters most, observe how you spend your time, money and energy. What do you see at the end of your day, week, or—dare I say month? Glance at your bank statement. Where did the money go? What kinds of items are on your to-do list? How many of these support your goals? Do you have goals?

We can look into the future as well. Am I struggling to buy a bigger car, house, or vacation home? Can I afford these, considering the price I will pay of time and quality of my life? There are so many questions to ask ourselves. Should I shop by labels or value? Do I keep my children overburdened with dance or sports and no time to be a child? Is my house a home? What impact does my lifestyle have on the planet? These things can help determine what we are giving our life, and our power to.

Cornell University psychology professor Dr. Thomas Gilovich conducted a 20 year study that analyzed how product purchases versus experience purchases make us feel. The research showed that purchasing trips, tickets for activities and events, and/or other experiences leads to greater happiness than buying a tangible possession. The bliss associated with adventures lasts longer, too. This is about living our life, not having *stuff*. We believe having stuff is a measure of our worth, when it is the quality of our life that is more value than the quantity of things we have.

False gods promise what they can never fulfill. The immediate thrill of buying *a thing* lasts about as long as it takes to sneeze, leaving in its place a hunger for more, for the next thrill. Yet the false god's bait is put before us, bringing on a never-ending stream of waste-producing *next-best-hottest-whatever*. We believe this will be *the one that makes me happy or satisfied.* There's just one thing that will satisfy our soul: developing our potential as a Child of God. We are here to express our divine qualities, cocreating with God, manifesting, sharing, bringing joy.

In the holiday classic television program, *Rudolph the Red Nosed Reindeer,* Rudolph makes friends with an elf named Herbie. The elf is very unhappy because he doesn't fit in with the toy-maker elves. He doesn't want to make toys; he wants to be a dentist. Rudolph, with his red nose, is also a misfit. They decide to seek the Island of Misfit Toys where they believe they might fit in.

If you've ever felt like you didn't fit in, consider the possibility it's a good thing. Each one of us is an individual expression of God, created to fulfill a particular purpose—to express our divinity in our own unique way. If we spend all of our time trying to fit in, we are ignoring our uniqueness. False gods keep us in a state of measuring ourselves against *them,* whatever that might mean. There is no need to measure ourselves against anyone else, based on the criteria of false gods. That includes income, social standing, fame, attractiveness, or how many letters of distinction precede or follow our name.

Another way that false gods distract and drain our ability to complete our mission is people pleasing, which we addressed earlier. Our job is not to please other people; its pleasing God. This can be very confusing. We want to serve or help others. This is a good thing, until we find we are helping them as a form of manipulation, or to get what we want. This is where we can sort out which things are people-pleasing, and which are being of service. My rule-of-thumb: *"You will know them by their fruits."* (Matthew 7:20)

We can ask ourselves, *"Is what I am doing helping to fulfill my mission?"* Here's an example. I am a writer. My personal mission statement is to *know, love, and serve God, as I inspire others to do likewise.* One way I do that is through my writing and preaching. If I busy myself with distractions like spending hours giving my attention to interruptions, from someone who just wants to chat, or attending to minor household or business tasks, I'm not fulfilling my mission. On occasion this can be helpful, but we can't make a habit of anything that is a distraction to completing our mission.

REVENGE OF THE FALSE GODS

As pointed out earlier, false gods make the unimportant seem important, and the important unimportant. Recalling the quadrants of consciousness, important things would be in the upper boxes and unimportant things the lower. As the gravitational pull holds us to the earth, the wiles of false gods hold us to lower consciousness.

Under the influence of false gods we see:

Important: Physical Beauty
Unimportant: Character and a beautiful soul.

Important: A large bank account.
Unimportant: Wise use of all resources.

Important: A fancy house, cars.
Unimportant: A home filled with love and connections between family members, reliable and eco-friendly car, both big enough to meet our needs without being excessive.

Important: Individuals unlimited access to all types of guns.
Unimportant: the United States has one of the highest instances of violence and death from firearms in the world!

Important: how much richer the rich get.
Unimportant: how depleted the planet and poor are getting.

Important: how much junk food the President eats.
Unimportant: how many people go hungry in our country.

A careful look at these duos will show that the pull of the false gods draws us to self: I, me, my, mine, rather than we, us, ours. Because we are all One, we will thrive as we look to the good of the whole, rather than the individual. This is a good thing! We will be happier because that's the way Spirit works.

False gods won't just let go of the grasp they have on our lower nature. We must reach and grasp on to our highest self, as we pull ourselves out of temptation. A great device for overcoming our own resistance to old habits and weaknesses is denial and affirmation. Example: We do not deny the lure of exceeding the speed limit, we deny that the temptation has power over us. We affirm *I am a safe and conscientious driver*.

There was a time I had a great weakness for sweet pastries. When I went to the bakery it was difficult to overcome the mouth-watering fragrance and mounds of fluffy icing with caramel drizzled over it. I had to deny its power with: *You have no power over me,* as I walked past the counter. Okay, I had to look at the pastries and call them salt patties at first. Does it matter? It worked!

Whatever temptation or weakness we may face, we *are* greater. Even if we find ourselves inundated with visions of sugarplums, that which is within us is greater than the object of our craving. Keep in mind the word *discourage,* means a lack of courage. We can give ourselves back our courage through *encouraging* affirmations, people, places and things. It is said, God hates a void so, whenever we release something from our lives, it is wise to replace it. This leaves no space for the removed habit to settle back in. Decide in advance, if we give up sugary treats or soda, what will we replace it with? If we don't, we will feel depleted, or that something is missing, which will breathe life into our old temptations.

FOUNDATIONS AND FRAMEWORKS

To restore a temple, whether made of stone or mind (consciousness) we must start with the foundation and structure to see if its sound. The foundation of our spiritual temple is Faith. Is there a crack of doubt in our foundation? Can we mend it, or do we need to tear it all up? We each must discover that for ourselves. Developing a clear, concise credo, or belief system, is the first step in building a strong foundation. There is a credo exercise at the end of this book to help you.

The framework is the structure we build on. It holds everything together. There are many beams to the construction, which include integrity in thought, feeling, honesty and truth. Building blocks of the temple include marriage, family, relationship, religion, and all connections that bind us to one another. The most important building block is the cornerstone. In ancient building practices, the cornerstone was the principal stone placed at the corner of the building. It was the largest, and most solid in the structure.

Jesus described Himself as the cornerstone that His church would be built upon, a unified body of believers, both Jew and Gentile. This means that the cornerstone represents first the Christ, or spark of divinity within each person, that Jesus embodied, and the Universal Principles of Truth He taught. It was for all believers, Jew and Gentile, which I interpret as applying to all God's children, even all creation. The cornerstone in our lives would be our consciousness, and the strongest cornerstone, Christ consciousness, our spiritual center.

Keep in mind as we explore cornerstones and foundations that this paradigm has no limits. It applies to personal lives, humankind, the economy, ecology, and our government. The cornerstone, or strongest element of our government, is the Constitution. Our forefathers built America and developed the law of the land and shared values to protect it.

Based on the activities and decisions made by the current administration, it is chipping away at the cornerstone with chisels of the false gods, powered by self-interest, greed, separation, and rebellion against the values we hold collectively. When we compromise the values of a people united, everyone suffers. As the cornerstone of the temple of consciousness must be the universal good, so must be the cornerstone of our lives, and the government.

THE POWER OF FAMILY–SACRED BUILDING BLOCK OF THE TEMPLE

Next to the Cornerstone, I see the family as a critical part of building a temple that can withstand all challenges and challengers. Family is a Divine Idea in the mind of God. In its purest form, it is an interdependent, supportive, protective, loving, safe and secure unit. It is a stepping stone to creating a world that works for everyone.

MARRIAGE–FOUNDATION OF THE FAMILY

As false gods have infiltrated our families, wooing them with self-interest and distraction, they've become weaker. More than half of all families fall apart. Blended families struggle to reclaim the Divine Idea of family, creating blended step-families. These fall apart at an even higher rate. It was 67% as of a 2012 study, and 73% for third marriages. There are many reasons, such as the distraction of technology, ease of divorce, adultery, marriage, and manufactured beliefs about what constitutes happiness, which we have confused with pleasure. The primary reason for failure is it is built without a foundation.

A healthy marriage forms the foundation of a strong family. If it's not strong and Spirit-centered, it will crumble. With more than half of all marriages ending in divorce, one might assume we do not marry well. It is imperative to understand, because a marriage didn't work, doesn't invalidate the Divine Idea of marriage. The Divine Idea, which is perfect, can't fail. Our expression of it can. If we consider Fillmore's explanation of manifestation, we recall he said an idea is like a nucleus, or particle, giving off a vibration that *nucleates,* or attracts like energy which culminates in manifestation. The quality and duration of the marriage and family that emerges from it will depend on the idea behind it.

If a marriage forms in the lower quadrants, which would include romance, emotion, chemistry, dysfunctional families, codependency, money and ego, it will fail. There is no foundation. How does this happen? A woman may feel that her biological clock is ticking. Maybe a man feels he should get married to show stability and climb the ladder of success. Or a child may be conceived, and the parents want to provide it legitimacy and a home. These reasons are not sufficient as a foundation to build a family on.

For marriage to serve as the cornerstone of a family, it must be established in the upper quadrants of consciousness: intuitive and sensing. The focus is the bond, not the self. In a healthy marriage, the couple shares beliefs and values. It doesn't matter which church they go to, or if they even go to church, as long as their values are shared. This marriage does not exclude carnal and romantic pleasure, but they should complement the union, not initiate it.

The way people marry today reminds me of a little plaque my mother had on her kitchen wall. It said *"We grow too soon old, and too late smart."* Having a good and enduring marriage is too important to leave to our ego-self. As a minister, when I counsel engaged couples I make it clear a good marriage is not about roses, wine, and romance. It is about the ability to stick together and support each other during life's challenges. I advise them marriage is the most difficult job they will ever have, and the most rewarding.

FAMILY–BUILDING BLOCK OF OUR FUTURE

We cannot underestimate the power of a strong, functional family. A functional family fulfills the purpose or intention of the Divine Idea behind it. The nucleus or divine energy behind it is love. The basic components are: respect, acceptance, safety and security, commitment, a sense of belonging, clear boundaries, and most of all, faith as its foundation. This doesn't mean there won't be moments of disagreement, frustration, difficulty or acting out. It means each member of the family is assured they have love and respect despite it.

As the divorce rate spiked, the nuclear family splintered. All members of the family suffered. Children lost their sense of safety, security and belonging. I believe this has led to all kinds of suffering, and dysfunction, including antisocial behavior and the opioid crisis. Please understand, this is not about blame, it's about getting to cause, where we can make changes to stop the downward slide we are experiencing. The information below underscores the power and importance of family:

An article titled *How Iceland Got Kids to Say No to Drugs,* published by the Atlantic on January 19, 2017, reported how they attacked the very serious problems of substance abuse they were having with their adolescents. Harvey Milkman, an American Psychiatric Professor assisted in the project. They started with surveys asking students 14, 15, and 16 years of age, from every school, questions regarding teen substance use, home and family conditions and relationships, and activities outside of school. Based on their findings, a program was developed called *Youth in Iceland.*

The surveys revealed a link between the drug abuse and changes in brain chemistry. This was caused by the substances which either stimulated or sedated it. The intent of the program was to provide activities that changed the child's brain chemistry naturally. They did this with activities such as dance, music, sports and other groups or clubs. Involvement was voluntary stressing that participants should not be forced. Nor should they take too much space in the child's life. Balance is key. Parental presence and involvement was an essential part of the program. They discovered that quantity of time parents spend with their children was more important than small periods of quality time. The experiment covered more than twenty years.

Because of the extent of time required, parental involvement and financial output that would be necessary by the government, it was determined the US would not be likely to try. That speaks volumes to where we are relation to lower mind and the false gods. In Iceland, short-term grants provide funding. Meanwhile, here in the US we put Band-Aids on bullet holes, addressing not the cause, but the effects.

Consider the possibility the division in our country is a magnified image of what is happening in our families. Imagine what could happen if we pulled our minds out of the lower, self-focused state of mind, into the realm of unlimited potential and the universal blessings, above self. What could the lessons learned in Iceland do to reduce the staggering death rate from addiction, crime, and lives ruined or wasted away in prison?

Have you ever noticed how often violent crimes and mass murders describe the perpetrator as a loner or a victim of bullying? It's common for them to have suffered mental, physical or sexual abuse. Maybe this is a desperate cry of rage or loss caused by absence of the support a family can provide.

Those who don't have supportive families at home often seek them elsewhere. People marry, under the illusion they can create the family they never had. Without healing the wounds and scars of their dysfunctional or broken family, it is most likely they will recreate what they were trying to escape. Gang members call their fellow members their *family,* as they try to get the acceptance and approval they didn't get at home. Remember, this is not about blame, it's about Principle: cause and effect. Alienation is another negative cause. Everyone wants love and acceptance, even people who commit crimes. They are people, first and foremost. How do we cross that bridge?

What about billions spent in rehabilitation that doesn't succeed because we're not addressing cause? A core issue in a family is connection. Technology has separated us. While it has its benefits, it is abused and out of control. A current television series called Undercover High, shows candid video of students, in classes ignoring the instructor as they Snapchat or have video calls. Is this the tail wagging the dog? The teachers were ignoring the students. Why? Is no one stopping this waste of valuable time, energy and money? Where is the authority of the teachers? Why don't school boards ban phones from classrooms? This is the insanity we are living.

Drifting farther and farther apart, it's time to put down the technology and reconnect. It's not just the kids fault. Parents are often absent, or worse, sucked into their own world on the other side of the phone or computer screen. Discipline is missing, and guilt over leaving the children often leads to spoiling which leads to entitlement, bullying, etc.

Somewhere between the helicopter parent and the absentee parent is a realm of potential called high touch. In the beginning it will be difficult to designate the time and attention to enable the family to reconnect. Our experience is the effect of our own ignorance and lack of involvement. The small effort involved in establishing new behaviors will reap benefits of love, respect, higher grades, and more successful family units.

Stronger, healthier families create stronger, healthier people, and bring our country back to the respect it once had. We may not yet be able to replicate Iceland's program, but we can strengthen our families. It will be uncomfortable and inconvenient at first, but the result will enrich our own lives, and the lives of those we most love.

BEYOND FAMILY–IT TAKES MORE THAN A VILLAGE

WHO WILL TAKE CARE OF THE CHILDREN?

There is an old saying: *The hand that rocks the cradle rules the world.* Consider that possibility as we ask: Whose hand is rocking the cradle today?

From 1958 to 2018, we have experienced a radical shift in the entire paradigm of family. The traditional two parent family included one parent, a full time homemaker providing love and nurture, the other taking responsibility for the family's financial needs and protection. This was replaced by either a single-parent home or a family where both parents leave the home fires to provide for their needs. This left children with a less-than-desirable family experience. There is neither the time nor energy left to provide the love, nurture, guidance and boundaries a child needs to thrive and develop as a healthy adult.

If asked, *how did this happen,* a typical reply in the single parent household would be *I have to provide for the family.* In the two parent household it would be, *you can't raise a family on just one paycheck. Everything has gotten too expensive.* There is an unfounded belief two paychecks are required for a family today. A more likely reason is that false gods are afoot. Baal seduces the ego to seek self-interests and carnal adventures taking them out of the family unit, while Mammon spews never-ending demands for *more*—more money, more stuff, the latest stuff, etc. Meanwhile, the children try to find new ways to get their needs met—not the basic food, clothing, shelter needs—but love, support, security and guidance. Many children, influenced by false gods through television ads and peers feel they must have, which guilt-ridden parents provide.

We find answers as we peel away layers of change that happened over the years. It's always a good idea to keep in mind the original cause, also known as *original sin*, which is separation from God, each other, and what matters most in life.

Is the family just another Humpty Dumpty we can't reassemble? Or can we restore this integral building block of the temple of wholeness? What can we do next? Let's start with love, the nucleus of the true family. We can make our house a home, a safe, loving, and welcoming place. A place of unconditional love and support. Our families can thrive in a place of guidance and healthy boundaries.

A favorite book of mine, *Simple Days*, by Marlene A. Schiwy lets us peek into her journal, where she spent one year exploring what matters most. I'd like to share a few passages:

"Lately I've been thinking about the role of homemaking in our fast-paced modern lives. One thing for certain: in our rightful and necessary quest for economic equity and a public voice and presence, 'something's lost, and something's gained,' in the words of Joni Mitchell's much-loved song. What's gained is clear; some measure of progress toward equal opportunity for women and a he social recognition that derives from involvement in public life. What's lost is more elusive, insidious, even. There's no one home to tend the hearth; indeed, there is literally no one home-making. Relieved to be rising in the ranks of the gainfully employed at last, we discover that Athena's gain (goddess of wisdom and protector of cities) is Hestia's loss (goddess of hearth and home)."

"At the end of the day, what we go home to is not the welcoming aroma of a freshly prepared meal shared with dear familiars, but a kitchen full of appliances and gadgets, the better to expedite dinner-on-the-run before we head out to meet our personal trainer at the gym or rush to yet another committee meeting. Who wants to spend the evening inside a home-that-isn't, after all.

It would be naïve to think we can just snap our fingers and the nuclear family would return to 1955. First, while it was—from personal experience supported by statistical data—better than our current experience, it was not perfect. As we evolve, our paradigms of what a family looks like evolves as well. The Divine Idea remains the same, but we transform the expression. Children learn what they live and live what they learn. We can create an environment where the children—who will one day be running the world and caring for us—will cocreate a world better than we can imagine, IF we can overcome the false gods through the renewal of our minds.

There are resources all around us to use as we mend our brokenness. We begin with working on our own lives, as we reach out to others. We do this to both give, and receive support. We become what we surround ourselves with. Experiment as you go through the next week. Notice if you are talking to a friend in a bad mood, complaining and blaming, you might add a few of your own complaints and problems. Can you see where that is going? Observe what happens if you try to turn the conversation around, seeing potential good outcomes. This may seem magical, but it is metaphysical. Behind everything seen, or felt, or experienced, is the unseen Principle. It is important to build connections with those who inspire and encourage, not those who influence and bring us down.

We have resources through connection with family and friends, school, church, clubs, activities. Establishing or restoring positive relationships create an amazing support system. Invite people to your home to visit and strengthen connections. It takes a village to raise a child; likewise, it takes a village to build a world community.

After the 9/11 terrorist attack, I was inspired to establish relationships with people around the world. I found sites to make pen pals, and wound up with connections in Singapore, Russia, Egypt and other places. It was important to me to repair the fabric of humankind. These are things everyone can do.

Technology separates us. It's much greater and more devious than we may realize. Before television, people would entertain themselves by playing games, making music, having barn dances, having neighbors over to play cards, and sports. As time went by, television became a part of our daily lives. Families gathered around the television after supper to watch together. Then came the TV dinner and tray table, which eliminated dinner table talk.

Next, multiple televisions separated the family altogether. Cell phones and computers widened the distance as we became more captivated by technology; instead of the level and quality of communication increasing, it decreased. The impersonal communication via text diminished skills in communication and vocabulary. Selfies have become the ultimate self-focus, as we join the ego-urges to keep up with the Kardashians.

To restore family and community, we must move from being high tech to high touch. It won't be necessary to banish all forms of technology, but it will require self-discipline in its use, reducing the number of hours and depth of involvement. With technology, it's not what we've got that matters, but what we do with it.

We can restore high-touch and reduce high-tech by limiting our involvement with it—claiming control through self-discipline—and setting boundaries for children. At first, there will seem to be a void, a black hole we once filled with technology. This is the time to fill the void with something positive to prevent a relapse, letting technology seep back into the space and reclaim the piece of live we won.

A song from 1977, *The Greatest Love of All* composed by William Masser and lyrics by Linda Creed, gives us the solution we need today. The lyrics are like a manual for putting family back together. I cannot publish the lyrics here because of copyright law, but I would like to share what the song teaches us:

> While children may seem small and maybe childlike now, they are the future.
> They need to have confidence in themselves, and healthy pride.

> We all need heroes, someone to be a role model for us, to guide and inspire.
> If we can't find that, and are lonely, we can find comfort within ourselves.
> We need integrity and faith in ourselves, and not be a follower.
> Win or lose, it is important to live as we believe.
> Finally, the greatest love, love for ourselves, is within us.

If we hear the messages within the song, we see these are all things family can provide. We're not there yet, but we can get there. It will require patience and persistence to restore the nuclear family, the re-United States of America, and the World Community. We can be a part of it, reaching in to discover the power within us, and reaching out to reconnect with our brothers, sisters, and all creation on Planet Earth.

Even if we are able to restore the family, many don't have a family to provide for their needs. This can be due to many circumstances. These are the times we create a family of choice. We can connect to like-minded people who will support us in being our best self. They will hold us accountable while accepting us as we are. We can establish traditions with our family of choice. Celebrations, rites and rituals that support our shared beliefs.

There are abundant opportunities. We can begin right this minute to strengthen the families we have and build new family units based on Universal Principles of Truth. A great start can be your church family, provided it feeds your soul. If your church doesn't feed your soul, you may want to find one that does.

BUT WHAT ABOUT *"THEM"*

As a part of facing our own needs to heal and restore our union, we need to acknowledge and address *them*. These are the people on the other side of the wall of consciousness that separates us. If we are to become One, even oneness in diversity, we must remove the bricks in the wall. The bricks are ugly and dirty. They carry the names Prejudice, Hate, Jealousy, Partisanship, Homophobia, Islamophobia, Differences, Social Standing, Popularity, Poverty, Sexism, and more. The wall is as big as we will allow.

Most of us have our own *them,* and the reasons we have put up mental or emotional walls to separate us. This is as dangerous as a clogged artery in the physical body. The things *they* say and do that annoy us represent lessons we need to learn. If we cut off the flow of our unity, we block our ability to see and learn. It's as much about us as it is about them. Each person is a Child of God, perfect in Spirit and potential, yet still working out imperfections. It's difficult to accept that Jesus taught us we must love our enemies. We think only how undeserving of our love they are. We fear the wrong we only imagine they might perpetrate in our lives.

Instead of looking at others and judging by appearances, we can see the things that bother us, as effects. Behind every appearance or behavior, lies a cause. What we are seeing and perceiving is the symptom of the cause. The cause may go back years, or lifetimes, but they—just like the rest of us—want healing, and to help others heal. Judgment is not healing. Nor is hate. Without exception, everyone I have met in this lifetime has issues to heal. That's why we're here, and why we're in this together.

We need to address unacceptable behaviors, but without judgment. Issues separate us, not the people themselves. Jesus was right when he told us to pray for our enemies. Anyone can love people they like. What about when we can't bear the sight of them? It's not a matter of *what* but *how.* H. Emilie Cady, author of *Lessons in Truth*, said any time we get a *serves him right* attitude, we can know we have not forgiven completely. When we pray for our enemy, we do not pray they get what they want, or what we perceive they deserve. We pray for their enlightenment, and that they will find their way.

PART SEVEN - EMERGENCE OF THE WARRIORS

In the book *Spiritual Warrior*, Author John-Roger defines Spiritual Warriors as *"people, men and women who confidently make choices about where to focus their internal attention, even when the external realities of their everyday lives are chaotic, troublesome, or just plain annoying."*

ARE YOU THE ONE?

One day when Moses was watching over his father-in-law's flock, God appeared to him in a burning bush. God told Moses that he had seen and heard the distressed cry of his people, who were afflicted by taskmasters in Egypt. God told Moses that he would send him to Pharaoh to demand the people be released from their captivity. Moses said: Who am I that I should go to Pharaoh to *release the people?* God told Moses not to worry, because He would be with him. Then Moses said the people would not believe God had spoken to him. So God showed him signs to prove to the people what he said, so they would believe. Next, Moses said he was not an eloquent speaker, being slow of speech and tongue. Then God said he would be Moses' mouth. Moses replied, "Can't you send anyone else?" God was not pleased, but said he would allow Moses' brother Aaron to go with him.

What if you were walking down the street today, and saw a bush burning but not consumed by fire, and God told you to go release your people from their bondage; to free them from hate, war, poverty, disease and every terrible thing, how would you respond? Would you think you could be the one?

Well, I believe you are the one. And so am I. Your neighbor is the one, and the homeless person you walked by on the street. The drug addict is the one, and the prisoner. How can this be, you wonder? We are each the one because we are all one. We are all Children of God, working out our salvation. Oops! Did you freeze up at that word? Let's look at it from the metaphysical perspective:

Salvation, according to Charles Fillmore, is: *The restitution of man to his spiritual birthright; regaining conscious possession of his God-given attributes.* Our physical bodies share our parents' DNA. As children of God, we share the DNA of God. DNA=Divine Nature Attributes, in this case. Fillmore said the belief that Jesus in any outer way atoned for our sins is not salvation. Salvation, is based solely on an inner overcoming, a change in consciousness. It is a cleansing of the mind, through Christ (Spirit, the spark of divinity within us) from any contrary thought.

We are not alone in the process of salvation. Each person we encounter is both our teacher and our student. Our kinship with God presents us opportunities to live the Universal Principles of Truth taught by Jesus and other enlightened beings. There is a saying: When the student is ready the teacher will appear. Our consciousness will draw the people we need to teach or be taught by. This happens by right of consciousness. Spiritual energy will attract like a magnet with those with a similar spiritual energy, or vibration. In Truth, your vibe attracts your tribe.

We agree the world could use great change. Most of us could use a little refinement as well. I believe we all are being called upon to bring the change we desire. We can do that by being what I call Change MACR's. A Change MACR is one who lives a life of Mutual Accountability and Collective Responsibility.

The story of David and Goliath can inspire us as we take on false gods. When instructed to battle Goliath, David ran out to find him. He killed the giant with a stone and a sling. The odds seemed impossible, but when we know God is with us, we can slay any giant in our path. You have power over false gods. You have the power to think, discern, and make new choices based on Principle rather than personality. We can do as Jesus taught, *Lift up your eyes*, to see Truth, and take Principle-based action.

CHARACTERISTICS OF SPIRITUAL WARRIORS

Below, are the characteristics of a Spiritual Warrior, while we may not have mastered them yet, aspiring to do so qualifies us as a *warrior in the making*.

A Spiritual Warrior is:

Fearless: In his book, *Spiritual Warrior*, John Roger, says fear is a form of atheism. If we believe in God, Principle, there is nothing to fear. We focus on God. When Jesus walked on water, he reached out to Peter to join him. As long as Peter stayed focused on Jesus he could do it also, but when he looked instead at the impossibility, he sank. Spiritual Warriors are fearless through their focus.

Lives the Law: Understanding law is Principle, desiring to create positive effects, the warrior does not vacillate. With practice, this becomes easier.

Has Integrity: A Spiritual Warrior is consistent in thought, word and action under all circumstances.

Is a Peacemaker: From the foundation of our unity, the Spiritual Warrior tries to see the Truth at the center of any real or perceived conflict, speaking words of Truth, with love.

Is Truthful: Living the Law, a Spiritual Warrior can be trusted to tell the truth, while honoring confidences. The Spiritual Warrior speaks their truth with love, but not compromise, willing to risk rejection for the will of God.

Is Reliable: If a promise is made, a Spiritual Warrior can be counted on to fulfill it.

Is Selfless and Generous: Understanding God is the source of unlimited good, the Spiritual Warrior supports the good of all, and his or her own good.

Is Self-Aware: Having developed their spiritual DNA (aka mission, vision, values and core beliefs) the Spiritual Warrior embraces and demonstrates their highest expression, with the realization they are still striving toward the goal of Mastery.

Is Patient: Trusting the work of God through Principle, the Spiritual Warrior waits with faith and patience for desired results, while continuing to do the work that is his or hers to do.

Lives their Beliefs: With integrity and focus, the Spiritual Warrior practices what they claim to believe, in every aspect of life.

Stays Grounded: Through regular, dedicated and consecrated daily practice, the Spiritual Warrior maintains focus and revives the Spirit within.

IS LIKE A BEACON OF LIGHT: Standing tall, true to their values, and shining forth the light from within, Spiritual Warriors are like a beacon of light in the darkness of ignorance. Those who search for Truth are drawn to them, for enlightenment and guidance.

THE DUTIES OF THE SPIRITUAL WARRIOR

The duties of the Spiritual Warrior vary depending on spiritual gifts and inner call. There are common duties Spiritual Warriors share, which include:

Put God first, strive to live through higher mind, rather than carnal.

Turn angst and anger into action, be an agent of positive change.

Build bridges not walls. To work continuously and tirelessly to mend the connections and relationships among people of every race, religion, gender, and lifestyle.

To be a role model, and beacon of light for those who are searching.

Develop self-discipline for holding focus, fighting distraction, and manifesting good

Is God calling you to be a Spiritual Warrior? Look at it this way: is God calling your heart to work for the health of the whole body? Or your kidneys? Or skin? Of course the answer is yes. I believe this is what Jesus was talking about when He said, *"These things I do and even greater things shall you do, if you believe, and Follow me!"* John 14:12 Each of us is here for a reason. We share moral responsibility in an increasingly amoral world.

GOD: WHO SHALL I SEND? US: HERE I AM, LORD. SEND ME!

If you found the title and subtitle of this section intimidating or fearful, relax! You don't have to visit the local purveyor of armor or weapons. Nor do you have to sign-up for a tour of duty. That was done when your Spirit made the journey to planet earth.

And as Wordsworth put it so beautifully:

> *Our birth is but a sleep and a forgetting;*
> *The Soul that rises with us, our life's star,*
> *Hath had elsewhere its setting*
> *And cometh from afar;*
> *Not in entire forgetfulness,*
> *and not in utter nakedness,*
> *But trailing clouds of glory do we come,*
> *From God who is our home…*

We've all had moments of absolute knowing, in life. We knew- without knowing how we knew. We knew God. Not the anthropomorphic God introduced to us by parents, clergy or Sunday school teachers. We felt God in the beauty all around us, in the embrace of parents, in the joy of laughter and song. We had an inner sense of something greater than all of it, and a desire—a yearning, or homesickness for Heaven.

If we think back—as far as we can, we feel the clouds of glory from our early lives, when all things were possible. When there was no doubt our dreams would come true. We felt invincible and gifted. I believe we all felt that way until something happened that changed our mind. Many of us got stuck there and remain there today. No matter how it happened, the clouds of glory fizzled out. Yet deep within, is the unquenchable spark of divinity. It waits for the breath of the Holy Spirit to burst into flame and set us back on our path. We may not know our reason for being right now. But if we pray and listen we will find out. Until then, we live every day dedicated to living the Principles we do know.

Simply because you are reading this book indicates you are one who has heard the call of Spirit. While the Bible says, *"Many are called, few are chosen."* Matthew 22:14 I believe there was a misinterpretation. I believe it should say: Many are called, few choose. In reading these words, we have the opportunity to choose. Will we? This is a Divine Appointment.

YOUR MISSION, SHOULD YOU CHOOSE TO ACCEPT IT...

Considering the multiple crises we face today, changing anything can feel overwhelming. It's easier to point out what's wrong than change it. Beyond appearances though, is the truth that all is created by Spirit, so all is good. Our circumstances are the result of our own errors. They are the result of our choices, and using our free will for self instead of all creation. The circumstances can change when we surrender our will to God's. We can see them right, which will set them right.

Fret not, there is good news. First and foremost, God is in charge, and with God all things are possible. Second, we don't have to do it by ourselves. We are like organs or cells in the body of a greater whole. In *1 Corinthians 12*, there is a beautiful definition of spiritual gifts. While it is too long to include here, I do encourage you to read it. In essence, we learn we are all One in Christ—one body many members. Each member serves the whole body. We see this in the working of our own bodies. Each part, no matter how small or insignificant, supports the whole body according to its design. In the physical realm, organs serve the natural, or carnal body in specific ways, whether it be through the senses, nourishment, communication, healing, etc. In the metaphysical realm, each of us has spiritual gifts we bring to the whole. Our spiritual gifts are abilities or talents we are endowed with for that purpose. It's what we have been created to do.

The best thing about spiritual gifts, is that they came with a desire to use them—in fact, using them fills us with joy. They include: Administration, Encouragement, Giving, Hospitality, Teaching, Wisdom, and many others. In the exercises section at the back of the book, you will find an activity to determine your gifts, and other resources you can use to explore your gifts and use them.

As a spiritual warrior, the first thing we should know in our crusade to overcome false gods, is that they cannot die. They must be transformed. Since false gods live in the shadows of ignorance and ignore-ance, they are transformed by exposure to light. That makes light our greatest weapon. It is the light of God—knowledge—wisdom. While Jesus told us not to hide our light under a basket, this is not an easy thing for many of us to do. When we share our light, we expose ourselves to the possibility of rejection or opposition by those who do not want to change. To overcome this, we can learn to always speak our truth with love.

Many people don't like change. It's uncomfortable and inconvenient. There are parts of us that don't want to change. In fact, the change we would be best to start with is our own need for transformation. We don't have to wait until we've reached perfection, but we must acknowledge we have our own work. As spiritual warriors we live our beliefs whether or not popular. We remain moral in a sea of amorality.

SIMPLE–BUT NOT EASY

Every time I get a new computer, upload a new program, buy a new phone, or sometimes when I make a new recipe, I have to gain knowledge and understanding. If I don't, it will be impossible for me to use the new thing. It's frustrating as I claw my way up the learning curve, trying to follow the *simple instructions.* When I hear, *so simple a child could do it,* I want to go find a child to do it for me. Mastering new things and applying them in our lives is a one-person job. The one person would be ourselves. When I reach the apex, and slide forward, pleased with myself, I realize it was easy. It took work, but was worth it.

It seems today we want everything to be fast, easy, and to have immediate results. That only works for things like point and shoot cameras. We may take pictures, but not the amazing photos a good, adjustable camera can produce. Yes, achieving spiritual mastery is simple, but it is not easy. If we want empowerment, we have to do the work.

That said, it's as hard as we make it. Dreading the task makes it harder, resistance and procrastination make it more difficult. Our expectation it will be easy makes it harder. Trying to force growth is not just frustrating, it's impossible. Lack of patience is a real drawback. I planted carrots once, so I know this is true.

Carrot seeds are tinier than grains of rice. They are thin and hard and once planted take quite a while to sprout. It felt like nothing was happening. Then one day, after faithfully tending them for many days, feathery little shoots appeared. The shoots grew bigger, fluffier, and gorgeous. They looked so big and fine I was sure they were ready to harvest and pulled one up out of the ground. There, at the end of the beautiful green top, was a tiny, white thing, no bigger than a newborn's pinky finger. It took several weeks for the carrots to grow big enough to eat, and my lack of patience resulted in a nice little bowl of baby carrots. Waiting without patience, is simple but in no way easy!

If, there was a knock on the door, chances are you could stand up and answer it. But consider how long it took to learn to walk. Consider how many times babies fall down as they attempt their first wobbly steps. The persistence of a little one learning to walk amazes me. Especially when I think of how many times I have given up a pursuit because it is not as smooth and easy as I thought it should be.

What can we learn from the baby? The child sees people walking, so it knows it's possible. There is a desire to be like them, and they believe they can do it. When they fall down, they get right back up and try again. Keywords are: the idea (walking), thought (I want to do this), expectation (I can do this), persistence (don't look at a fall as a failure), patience and practice (Maybe I can do it this time). What do you think would happen if we followed Jesus' teaching to become as a little child? It's simple, even if it's difficult!

The baby saw people walking and knew this was possible. There are many times we know according to our beliefs that Spiritual Principle works, but there are no demonstrations—no results to validate the belief. These are crucial times to stand firm, speak our truth, and pray believing we have already received. Spiritual warriors live their beliefs despite appearances to the contrary. This is faith.

The Bible tells the story of when King David's infant son became ill. The king prayed night and day his child would be healed. He fasted and didn't sleep. He did this for seven days, and then the baby died. When David heard this, he got up, bathed, shaved, and went to worship at the temple. Then he went home and requested food. Stunned, the people asked how he could do this. He told them as long as the baby was alive the Lord might feel sorry for him and let the child live. But now the child was dead. He said, Now the baby is dead, why should I fast? Someday, I will go to him, but he cannot come back to me. A while later, he and Bathsheba had another child, who David named Solomon. (2 Samuel 12)

Even when we pray, live right and follow every rule, bad things can happen. This does not mean we give up. It doesn't mean God is not in our lives and stopped loving us. It means that there are things we don't understand. Jesus said, *"There are things I have to tell you, but you cannot bear to hear them now."* (John 16:12) Until then, we can find comfort in our faith. We cannot be pitiful and powerful. The good news is, it gets easier with practice, and it is as hard as we make it.

There is no question of faith. We all have it. What matters, is where we put our faith—what we have faith in. One reason we are in a precarious political and cultural crisis today, is our faith is misplaced, or misunderstood. What does it mean to stand on our faith? Does your church have a creed you had to recite? Does it match what you think you believe? If it doesn't, you may be in the wrong church. You can find out by developing your personal creed, or credo.

PRAYER – ANONYMOUS – ATTRIBUTED TO ST. FRANCIS

Lord, make me an instrument of your peace:
where there is hatred, let me sow love;
where there is injury, pardon;
where there is doubt, faith;
where there is despair, hope;
where there is darkness, light;
where there is sadness, joy.

O divine Master, grant that I may not so much seek
to be consoled as to console,
to be understood as to understand,
to be loved as to love.
For it is in giving that we receive,
it is in pardoning that we are pardoned,
and it is in dying that we are born to eternal life.
Amen.

USE YOUR GOD-GIVEN TOOLS!

We are not here on earth to battle with false gods. We are cocreators with God, of all that is good. We are equipped and empowered. Each person has twelve spiritual faculties to help them. They are: Faith, Strength, Wisdom, Love, Power, Imagination, Understanding, Will, Order, Zeal, Renunciation, and Life. As stated earlier, this is a basic presentation of spiritual concepts—an introduction.

The definitions provided assume the positive aspects of the faculties. In the upper quadrants of consciousness, they empower us to cocreate our lives and reshape life on planet Earth. In the lower quadrants, which focus on self, the negative aspects. In the upper quadrants, Faith is being faith-full, trusting God, and knowing. In the lower quadrants faith is experienced as faith-less, or belief in the material realm and false gods.

The following is a brief definition of the twelve faculties. You can study them in depth in Charles Fillmore's book, The Twelve Powers of Man. The faculties are within everyone. They work through the lower mind until they become quickened by spirit and function in harmony with Divine Mind. I have provided an affirmation for each faculty to assist you in its development and use in your life.

FAITH: Faith is more than belief. It is an inner knowing. It is cultivated through denial of all doubt and fear, and affirmation of God's presence and power. Affirmation: God is in charge. God's will is for me is good and only good, and all is well.

STRENGTH: Strength is physical, mental, and spiritual. Through strength we can overcome temptation, develop character, and the ability to stand strong and see our challenges and accomplishments through to the end. It is the faculty of strength, coupled with Faith that provides the power to keep our focus on right thoughts and ideas. Affirmation: The strength of God flows through me, as me, and no challenge is too great.

WISDOM: Worldly wisdom is the ability to use knowledge. Spiritual wisdom is divine insight, comprehension of Spiritual Principle and its workings. We can develop this faculty by letting go of limited thought. Affirmation: The wisdom of God works through me to make right decisions.

LOVE: The pure essence of Being (God-Spirit) that binds together the whole family of humankind. It is impersonal. The quality of love sees good in everything and all people. Love is the great attracting power of Spirit. It will draw good things to us when we stay grounded in love. Affirmation: God's unconditional love flows to me, through me, and touches everyone whose life crosses my path.

POWER: Power is man's innate control over his thoughts and feelings. The power faculty within us, allows the universal power of God to move through us. One way we use our faculty of power, is through the spoken word. Words can hurt, words can heal. Words aligned with Spirit lead to manifestation. Affirmation: I have the power of God within me, I practice it through self-discipline, and bring forth good through my thoughts, words and actions.

IMAGINATION: Imagination is the imaging faculty. Ideas received through Divine Mind are fabricated through the imagination, which will, through the creative process manifest. Affirmation: *Through the faculty of imagination, my dreams and desires take shape, and manifest in unlimited ways.*

UNDERSTANDING: Understanding is the faculty through which the intellect and knowledge are clarified. It operates in the realm of ideas and builds a strong foundation upon which to build the consciousness. Affirmation: The faculty of understanding works in me empowering me to the right use of Spiritual Principle.

WILL: The executive faculty of mind. It is the directive power that determines what the person will do. It is the faculty that assures completion of a project. The will is intended to work in alignment with God. Affirmation: I now align my will with the will of God and bring forth good in my life and the world I live in.

ORDER: Order is the faculty that ensures everything will go right. It assures unfoldment through a systematic procession of steps or events leading to manifestation. Sensitive to the working of divine order, the individual will have a gut reaction to make things right. Affirmation: Divine order is now manifest, unfolding my life according to His perfect plan, and all is well.

ZEAL: Zeal is the urge behind all things. It is enthusiasm. Zeal is the vitality to complete our goal despite obstacles. Affirmation: The zeal of Spirit fills me with enthusiasm, I achieve my goals with joy and *passion*. At the age of 94, Charles Fillmore said: "*I fairly sizzle with zeal and enthusiasm, as I spring forth with a mighty faith, to do that which is to be done by me.*"

RENUNCIATION: Renunciation, or Elimination, is the ability to release and let go of old, error thoughts, habits, feelings and beliefs. This creates space and openness to receive new ways of thinking, feeling and being, in harmony with Spiritual Principle. Affirmation: *I release and let go of all that is not for my highest good, assured God will fill the void with good.*

LIFE: Life is divine, spiritual, and its source is God, Spirit. We have a body, but we are not our body, we are spirit. Our body is the out-picturing of our consciousness. Our body and mind are vitalized—filled with life—by consciously contacting spirit. This is done through prayer, meditation, and good works. Affirmation: The life of God flows through every cell of my body, every thought in my mind, every word I speak, and every action I take. I am the life of God in expression.

The Twelve Powers—or spiritual faculties work alone and together as need in our work to achieve mastery. For example, the power of renunciation helps us to release old habits. When we do we feel light, clear, and filled with zeal to get about our purpose.

THE GIFT OF GUILT

Imagine giving someone a wonderful gift. The gift assured a lifetime of peace of mind, health and happiness. Instead of using the gift, they stashed it in the closet. They didn't like it. They didn't like the way it made them feel when they tried it on. What a disappointment. Do you think you would refuse such a gift? Many of us do every day. The gift, is guilt. The Bible tells us, "I will put my law within them. I will plant it in their hearts." (Jeremiah 31:33) The word *heart*, when used in the Bible, means the combined thinking and feeling faculties. We read in scripture, *"You will know the Truth, and the Truth will set you free."* (John 8:32)

Within each of us, there is a moral compass. It points to Truth. When we veer off course, we experience a very uncomfortable sensation. The feeling is a response to impending or actual sin. Since the word *sin* means missing the mark, this would be a very appropriate word. Through the gift of free will, we have the choice to either continue on our journey off-course, or to steer back to True North.

If we are operating from the lower quadrants of consciousness, when faced with temptation we will feel a warning twinge of guilt. We may then try to shut down the sensation. We might try to anesthetize it with drugs or alcohol, or soothe it into submission through rationalization—rational-lies, or quell it with a promise it's *just this once*. If we don't heed the warning of guilt, and give in to temptation, the disappointing outcome will be compounded with regret.

If we are operating from the upper quadrants of consciousness, have a greater sensitivity to perceive guilt as a warning, and handle it with wisdom. We can remove temptation with denial, saying: You have no power over me, and affirming: God is my strength and source of all good. We can also remove ourselves from the source of temptation if perhaps it is the bakery when we are on a diet.

When we see guilt as a gift and not a form of punishment for a real, perceived, or potential sin, we open and use the gift as intended. Guilt is like the rumble strips on the side of the highway that alert us we are driving off of the road. They are there to save lives. Likewise, guilt helps to keep us on our straight and narrow path.

THE POWER OF FORGIVENESS

Forgiveness is a very misunderstood concept. We think if we forgive, it's like saying the offense or suffering we experienced is okay. But it's not okay. When someone hurts us, we are in pain. The pain could be physical, emotional, or mental. Un-forgiveness hurts the offended person and the (real or perceived) offender. This is true even if the offending party isn't aware of what they've done. This is because of the energy factor. Energy is vibrational. Whenever there is a discordant vibration anyone involved can feel it. This energy is not healthy, and must be neutralized as soon as possible.

Here's an experiment: Bring to mind a recent disagreement, argument, anger you have felt with a friend, family member, or co-worker. Who was the offender? Who was the offended? Can you feel the negative energy pulsing through your body? Maybe you feel sick to your stomach, your heart is racing, or you're trembling. Many emotions surge through us, everything from rage to remorse. You may want to blast the other person, or you may feel rage coming from them. It may feel impossible to fix this. What if that's true?

Many of our conflicts are due to misunderstandings and miscommunication. Before we react, we should assure that is not the case. We can ask: *"What did you mean by that?"* Or *"Did you mean...?"* This can end the misunderstanding. We can then turn it around.

If we are the knowing or unknowing offender, and are being called out on something, we can often stop it in its tracks by saying: *"I'm sorry, that's not what I meant"*. If we said or did something we meant to do, we can still say: *"I'm really sorry that we don't agree on this. I did not mean to offend you. I would like to agree to disagree."* It's frequently the only thing the other person needs to hear.

Then there are the times when we've been flat-out wrong. We are human. We make mistakes. The first instinct of human consciousness is to assign blame and get defensive. This is the exact opposite of what we should do. Five simple words work like magic to drain anger from someone who is angry with us: *"I'm sorry. I was wrong."*

There are cases where no apology, explanation, reason or excuse will work. Our job is to offer it. Their job is to accept it or not. A perfect way to handle this is found in Scripture: *"As you enter the house, salute it. And if the house is worthy, let your peace come upon it; but if it is not worthy, let your peace return to you. And if anyone will not receive you or listen to your words, shake off the dust from your feet as you leave that house or town."* (Matthew 10:13-14)

When we have an *interpersonal* problem, and are certain we have done everything in our power to make things right, without success, we must let go. To shake the dust off of one's feet symbolizes moving into the future and leaving the residual negativity behind you. If we don't let it go, it will ride on our back, and mind, and heart, which will keep us bound to our suffering. If you're having difficulty letting go of offense or being able to forgive, consider the advice of Jesus, *What is that to you? Follow me!*

Another thing we can do to remove *residual dust* from our feet is with a forgiveness affirmation. We can do this on our own. Just close your eyes and bring to mind the person you are experiencing disharmony with. Say: *"I forgive you, and you forgive me now."* Repeat slowly, feeling a sense of love, peace, and release. It is very important to not only think, but feel the release and forgiveness. To retain the thoughts or feelings will just stimulate reappearance of resentment. When you have found a peaceful place, release it and find something more pleasant to occupy your thoughts and feelings. A walk outdoors can do wonders.

Every night before he went to sleep, Charles Fillmore would forgive anyone who had offended him, and asked for forgiveness from anyone he had offended. Here is a forgiveness exercise you can use:

"I now forgive and release from any animosity or criticism everyone I need to forgive, and everyone who needs to forgive and release me from his animosity or criticism now does so, and we are all happy." (Happiness Now, by Mary Catherine MacDougall)

HARD QUESTIONS AND LIVING WITHOUT THE ANSWERS

There are many hard questions that don't seem to have answers. Our problems are often far more complex than we make them. Sometimes we think we have the answers, but don't dare to put them out for exploration because we fear rejection. Or, the answers are situational. It's a paradox of black and white, confused by gray. Jesus was trying to show that when the Pharisees would question him, trying to catch him breaking religious law:

> *"And behold, there was a man with a withered hand. And they asked him, 'Is it lawful to heal on the Sabbath?' so they might accuse him. He said to them, 'What man of you, if he has one sheep and it falls into a pit on the Sabbath, will not lay hold of it and lift it out? Of how much more value is a man than a sheep! So it is lawful to do good on the Sabbath.'"* (Mt 2)

Paradoxically, making an exception for a holy purpose, is not breaking the law because you used it to perform an act of goodness and mercy. This does not invalidate the law. Here is where the difference comes in between excuses and reasons. False god consciousness would encourage breaking the law for our own pleasure, while Spiritual consciousness honors each moment, centered in God.

We must each come to terms with our own beliefs and behaviors. The law will bring justice because it is law. It's Principle not personal. Whatever question regarding right or wrong we have, we can find the answer within us. Ask questions and don't be afraid of discovering your thoughts were incorrect. As you ponder, consider the cause and effect, and what will you be reaping from what you are sowing. What fruit are you growing?

It is the practice of Mohegan tribe elders to project the effects of actions they were considering by looking forward thirteen generations, to see what impact their actions would have on the tribe. We need not be a psychic to predict the future, only to consider the law. Learning and living the Principles will assure we will make right decisions and take right action.

Although it may appear there are no answers, we can't let our discomfort regarding hard questions prevent us from exploring them. To do so would be like letting a wound become infected and fester, eventually poisoning our whole system. We each must come to our own conclusions and live them, open to the guidance of the Spirit of Truth. Sometimes the Spirit of Truth will open us to new ways of thinking, but to get there, we must question our own beliefs, weighing them in the balance of cause and effect.

Hard questions are not just about ourselves, they concern the common good. We can't drink poison without the whole body being affected; we can't exercise without the whole body being strengthened. Consider the cause & effect. Below, you will find a few examples of hard questions that don't seem to have answers. We all have several unique to ourselves. Because each life affects another however, healthy discussion—not debate or argument—allows us to consider another opinion, and share ours. The purpose is not to convince another, but to talk it out, even if we agree to disagree in the end. Consider these hard questions:

ABORTION: What do you believe about abortion? Is it murder? At what point does it become murder? What if it's a life-or-death emergency, or convenience? Would allowing the baby to be born be a healing choice? When does life begin? What caused the pregnancy? Is there a lesson to be learned for all humankind? Does abortion respect life? Whose life? What, if anything, could prevent the need for abortion?

THE DEATH PENALTY: Where does the commandment Thou Shalt Not Kill come in? Or: Revenge is mine, sayeth the Lord? Is there an act heinous enough to take a person's life? Should a vile murderer escape punishment for his or her sin? What about An eye for an eye? What will be the effects of causing this person's death? If reincarnation is a reality, would this soul come back angrier or enlightened? Who has the right to decide? What caused this person's sin? Are they evil or damaged?

SEXUALITY: What is the purpose of sex? Is it to have fun, or make babies? What's wrong with recreational sex? Is there a positive and negative way to enjoy our sexuality? Are STDs punishment from God, or biology? How does the Law of Cause and Effect figure in our sex lives? Do we need intimacy for sex, or sex for intimacy?

That was just a starter. Discover your own answers to the hard questions of life. On an individual level, the hard questions bring turmoil to our mind and heart. On the collective level, they breed debate and separation. Sometimes we need to find peace without the answers or agreement. If we're in a position where we must choose we can try to *feel* the right answer. First discern the question, i.e. *"Should I complain to my boss about the vulgarity in the lunch room, or should I mind my own business?"* Paying attention to our higher sensing nature, state each option. One will give us a sense of peace. The other will give a sense of anxiety, or urgency. With this question, concern about rejection would not be a sense of anxiety because that is a natural response. Even through our fear, doing what we believe is the right thing, will give us a sense of peace.

Here are a few other areas where hard questions lurk: legalization of marijuana for recreational use, war, sexual harassment, gun control, doping in sports (and use of steroids), immigration and tax reform. That should give us food for thought to last a year!

PART EIGHT—RETURN TO PARADISE

GOOD NEWS!
"Then I saw a new heaven and a new earth; for the first heaven and the first earth had passed away, and the sea was no more. And I saw the holy city, New Jerusalem, coming down out of heaven from God, prepared as a bride adorned for her husband; and I heard a loud voice from the throne saying, "Behold, the dwelling of God is with men. He will dwell with them, and they shall be his people, and God himself will be with them; he will wipe away every tear from their eyes, and death shall be no more, neither shall there be mourning nor crying nor pain any more, for the former things have passed away." And he who sat upon the throne said, "Behold, I make all things new." Also he said, "Write this, for these words are trustworthy and true."
(Book of Revelation 21:1-6 RSV)

ANOTHER DAY IN PARADISE

Enlightenment and Paradise are not places you visit,
But you can live there…They exist in consciousness.

What will we see in Paradise—will there be pearly gates and streets paved in gold? Will angels float by on fluffy clouds? I don't believe that's God's plan. Just as we have always tried to make the image and likeness of God into our own, I believe we base our images of Heaven on mortal concepts, rather than spiritual. For many years, Unity and other new thought philosophies have taught Heaven is a state of consciousness, as is Hell. In fact, in 1999 Pope John Paul II agreed. That should not diminish their nature. I've had hellish encounters that caused me great suffering. I have also had many heavenly experiences. Given my 'druthers, I'll take Heaven.

The good news is we decide where we will abide. Since heaven and hell are states of consciousness, we have the power to choose and put our spiritual powers or faculties, to work. Free will, allows us to make decisions that can bring us directly to hell, which is as eternal as we make it. When God banished Adam and Eve from paradise, He told them they would have to earn their way back through the toil of their hands and the sweat of their brows, and the woman would bring forth her children in pain. They had to learn through experience what they tried to take without permission.

Here we are, thousands of years later, still trying to figure it out. What's taking so long, we wonder? I'd venture to say our mortal minds are still wrestling for control while the false gods cheer them on and promise material and carnal rewards—that rust and moth can consume. Just because we haven't overcome yet, does not mean we will never overcome. It's difficult, and it is uncomfortable, and if we want to live in paradise, we can't be lazy or narcissistic.

We've made more progress than it would appear. For many of us life is good. We have not only necessities, but many luxuries as well. Our goal is to have that for everyone, that death will be no more, and every tear will be wiped away. Once we make up our minds, and begin the work, knowing we will experience success and failure, it will get easier. We will one day have more successes than failures. This process will repeat, until we look around one day to find we've arrived at the gates of Heaven: the life we desire! But we're not there yet, so let's continue.

We can look at a blueprint for a house, but that doesn't make it a house. If we put the blueprint away and tried to build the house without looking at it, or try to cut corners and leave pieces out, we would not have a safe, secure house. The same thing is true about the spiritual home we create daily with the blueprint of Spiritual Principle.

Every today we are creating our tomorrow. Our thoughts, words, and actions will materialize according to their nature. What do we want to manifest? What is it based on? If we don't answer these questions and get grounded in the vision, we can only create more chaos. Start with your vision, then connect with others. We need not rush to find others. We have eternity, but if we make poor choices, we will have poor results. Visualization assists in developing a focus on what we want to create. A Treasure Mapping Exercise can be found at the back of the book.

THE REMNANT–HOPE FOR THE FUTURE

When we're in a dark place, it is difficult to see the light. The future can feel discouraging, but that's the work of false gods, attempting to extinguish the light of hope. It's easy to become discouraged. It happens to all of us, and we can feel overcome. We're not alone. We may think we are, but if we get our thoughts and feelings out of the lower realm of mind, we can access the part of mind connected with God-mind, and with all possibilities.

In the prophecies of Isaiah, the word *remnant* is found 84 times. The literal meaning, is *left-over* or *what remains*. It is the piece of cloth at the end of a bolt that is too small to sell. The metaphysical meaning is being small or irrelevant. But Isaiah sees the remnant as a holy seed. From the remnant, the nation of Israel is restored. Leaving a remnant was always the promise of God. The positive message this gives us, is no matter how dark it seems, or how insignificant we feel, is that we too can make a difference.

CAN WE GET THERE FROM HERE?

Our country is shattered. If we could describe what that looks like, a post-fall Humpty Dumpty would be an accurate depiction. It would appear that we can never break through the wall of consciousness that separates us. That belief is coming from lower consciousness, influenced by the false gods of separation, Mammon and Baal. Listen to the rhetoric. It's all about money, ego, power and self ahead of the common good. We have to face the unpleasant fact that through our own actions and inaction, this could come to pass. As Physicist Albert Einstein said, we can't solve a problem at the level it was created.

The splintering of our country did not happen overnight, although it was exacerbated and enlarged by the 2016 elections and their outcome. History will show that the inability of the current administration to reunite the people in spite of their differences, can only have a negative result. When we add to this a constant stream of blatant lies, there is a distrust of the government and each other. Lack of cohesiveness and cooperation only makes things worse. What to do?

The first thing we can do is stay grounded in Spirit. We have to affirm—to make firm in our minds and hearts—God—the Spirit of Truth and Goodness is ever present. We remind ourselves this is all a learning experience. Observe, think and act from Principle. Strive to stay in the upper quadrants of consciousness. While being informed, we must not get pulled down and tangled up in the drama. When we buy into appearances, focusing on human thoughts and emotions, we will nucleate what we obsess on. Instead, we look at effects and seek cause, where change can happen. There's a lot of talk about the 1% running the show, but we have to remember an engaged, motivated 99% is significantly larger than the 1%. It will be necessary to wake up this sleeping giant, and to encourage others to do likewise.

Our greatest work will be in dissolving the invisible wall that separates us from those who do not share our beliefs. We may seem far apart, but they are still a part of us. How can we do this? One way we can't do it is through force. Even the greatest Truth can't be imposed. It must be exposed. We will dissolve the wall of separation as we discover and express the things we hold in common. Every one of us has the same basic needs and desires.

The needs of the body are food, water, clothing and shelter. The needs of the soul are love, belonging, approval and purpose. We begin dissolution of the wall that would separate us, by establishing, and building on what we have in common. We can demonstrate this with the Venn diagram seen earlier:

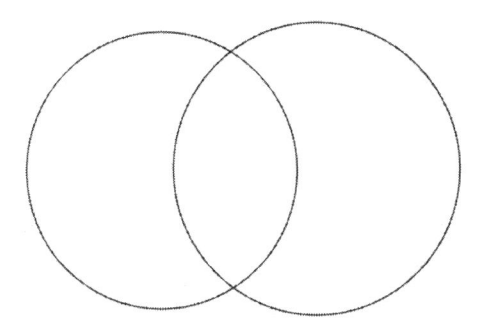

The two circles above represent two individuals. Each has their own thoughts, feelings and beliefs. The overlap of the two circles creates a third space, which represents what we have in common. For example, one person may abstain from alcohol and the other does not. But both agree that exercise is healthy for the body. On one side, one would put *alcohol-no,* and on the other side, *alcohol-yes*. In the middle it would say *exercise*. Applied to guns, on one side *guns-no,* on the other side *guns-yes,* yet in the middle it could say, *safe schools*. It's a start. As we establish common ground, it grows. There are things we will never agree on, and that's okay. These areas are where we agree to disagree. We are one. But our oneness includes diversity.

This same diagram can illustrate how political parties or citizens can come together, establishing common ground as a starting point for reuniting our citizens. It can even be effective in healing our relationships. As we establish relationships with those of differing opinions, without focusing on what makes us different, doors of receptivity open. This is the out of the box mindset where new solutions can be found for old problems. We CAN get there from here, but we can't break down the door. Learning to discuss without dispute opens doors of understanding. We will disagree from time to time. The more critical, the more important it is to stand our ground and speak our truth with love.

The Venn diagram is also an important reminder of our interdependence.

SMALL FOOTPRINTS

In paradise, everyone will have very small feet. Well, I mean a very small ecological footprint. Planned obsolescence is replaced with the circulation of resources. Our lust for excess and perceived need for the latest and greatest must be replaced with reduce, reuse, and recycle. We will respect Mother Earth and banish the abuse she has suffered so long. The sustainable environment we create will assure us of generations and lifetimes of cocreating with the Divine.

ABUNDANCE, TO HAVE AND NOT HOLD

"Do not lay up for yourselves treasures on earth, where moth and rust consume and where thieves break in and steal, but lay up for yourselves treasures in heaven, where neither moth nor rust consumes and where thieves do not break in and steal." Matthew 6:19-20

Prosperity and abundance are Divine Ideas in the mind of God. We will always be prosperous when we develop the consciousness and confidence of Spirit as our instant, constant, abundant, unlimited source of all good. Prosperity is not only about money. When we think about abundance and consider Spiritual Principle, it is not about accumulation; it is about circulation. The blood that flows through our body circulates. It provides oxygen and nutrients to the body while removing carbon dioxide and waste products. If the circulation stopped or became blocked the organism would die. Resources are meant to circulate, not accumulate.

Scripture tells us: *"As you give, so shall you receive."* If we are giving but still holding thoughts of lack and limitation in mind, this scripture assures *as* we give, we will receive, which would be a lack or depletion. In Paradise, everyone is cared for because we take care of each other. False gods tell us we need to accumulate, and *the one who dies with the most toys wins*. Yet our own greed and thoughts of lack deplete us.

A big mistake people make is in their investments. We have forgotten the purpose of investing, which is giving our money to something we want to grow. Instead, we give our money to something in the hopes our money will grow. Many investors and stock holders are not even aware of what the products *their* company does to make them money. Many of us have mutual funds, but do we know what types of businesses we are giving our money to? We have to ask ourselves if it would be something we want to grow.

Here's a *Pop Quiz* for you. Read the following true story and apply the Law of Cause and Effect to it. Record your thoughts in a journal.

In January 2018, Brenda Fitzgerald, head of the Centers for Disease Control and Prevention, resigned from her position after allegations of conflict of interest. The woman, who is a physician, had purchased stock in a tobacco company shortly after taking that position. She also had a history of tobacco investments prior to accepting the position with the CDC. Smoking is the No. 1 preventable cause of disease and death in the United States. It would appear that she would make money from making people sick, then make money when they got sick, and would most likely get paid even if they died.

There are many socially responsible investment companies you can select for your investments. A simple internet search will lead you to many options. Call your investment firm to review what you are supporting. How would it feel to know your money was going to a tobacco company?

While we're on the topic, if we love the church we attend, and want its teaching to grow and spread to help others, it is a great place to invest. Don't look for a dividend check in the mail because your dividends will be spiritual rather than financial. Imagine though, how wonderful it would be if churches were supported as generously as sports teams?

As a minister in the field for over a quarter of a century, I can share that many churches have tippers rather than tithers. Everyone wants a church that has a great building with a talented, experienced, well-educated minister and staff. They want to be warm in the winter and cool in the summer. The church has bills, just like our households. If you consider it to be *your* church, then they are *your* bills too.

MYRTLE FILLMORE'S CREDO

To enjoy without possession.
To see without coveting,
To have without holding,
To be without seeming,
In short, to be myself, without desiring.
Knowing that all this is for me, for my pleasure
and the satisfaction of my immortal soul.
To say that "I am the monarch of all I survey.
My right to be here is none to dispute.
To be generous-hearted.
What I see, others may see.
What I enjoy, others may share also
on equal terms with me

TALK TO ME: COMMUNICATION IN PARADISE

Communicate, don't debate.

We limit our awareness of communication to words, while the most important part of a conversation is the idea behind the words, the unformed substance seeking expression. No longer limited by abbreviated thoughts and words in texts or tweets, in Paradise we now converse in a flow of thoughts and feelings, not unlike telepathy. To communicate in Paradise: Looking into the eyes of the one we are speaking to will stop the glut of meaningless words. Listening for tones and inflections that paint pictures words alone can't. Listen with authentic interest. We can give heartfelt consideration before responding. Speak words of truth and discern the words we hear without judging.

In Paradise, conversations are meaningful and productive. We may use technology in our communication, but we do not let it use us. It is our tool, not our toy or taskmaster. Healthy communication is powered by the energy of love that binds us together instead of tearing us apart.

GOVERNMENT/LEADERSHIP
BUILDING BRIDGES NOT WALLS

The current government of the United States has two established parties. When they are working for the good of the country, it works. If it is fraught with separation and divisiveness, it does not work. If it works for the good of the country, but not the good of the planet and its inhabitants, it does not work. If it ignores the reality of our interdependence with everyone on the planet, it does not work. The true need on Planet Earth is to build bridges, not walls.

Enlightened by the Spirit of Truth, in Paradise our interdependence is common knowledge. We will no more hurt another than we would hurt ourselves. Consider the words of the following declaration, written by Will Durant in 1930. Consider printing it and posting it where all can see.

DECLARATION OF INTERDEPENDENCE

HUMAN PROGRESS having reached a high level through respect for the liberty and dignity of men, it has become desirable to re-affirm these evident truths:

The differences of race, color and creed are natural, and that diverse groups, institutions and ideas are stimulating factors in the development of man:

To promote harmony in diversity is a responsible task of religion and statesmanship:

Since no individual can express the whole truth, it is essential to treat with understanding and good will those whose views differ from our own:

That by the testimony of history intolerance is the door to violence, and dictatorship: and

That the realization of human interdependence and solidarity is the best guard of civilization.

THEREFORE, we solemnly resolve, and invite everyone to join in united action,

To uphold and promote human fellowship through mutual consideration and respect:

To champion human dignity and decency, and to safeguard these without distinction of race, color or creed:

To strive with others in concert to discourage all animosities arising from these differences, and to unite all groups in the fair play of civilized life.

Rooted in freedom, children of the same Divine Father, sharing everywhere a common human blood, we declare again that all men are brothers and that mutual tolerance is the price of liberty.

Written in 1930, By Will Durant - https://web.archive.org/web/20120310225853/http://www.wildurant.com/interdependence.htm, PD-US, https://en.wikipedia.org/w/index.php?curid=38909249

A GUIDE TO CONSCIOUS VOTING

A Unity perspective…by Rev. Alicia-Leslie

Why Vote?

In a Presidential election, campaigns heat up. Claims and accusations are made. Emotions often rage. You may feel like going into hiding until it is all over. But as a responsible citizen of the United States of America you cannot. Why? Because it is our right and responsibility to vote. It is our opportunity to participate in the operation of our government. Don't just pray, move your feet. VOTE

Some people under the influence of apathy say that their vote does not matter. It does. While the Electoral College may cast the actual votes that declare the President, their decisions are based on the popular vote of their state. While in theory an elector can go against this commitment, this is very rare. Additionally, you will be voting to fill other important positions. The people you vote for can make a positive or negative change in your life and our country. They are the decision makers *we* have chosen.

Galatians 6:7, 10 "Do not be deceived; God is not mocked, for whatever a man sows, that he will also reap. … So then, as we have opportunity, let us do good to all men, and especially to those who are of the household of faith.

Barbara Marx Hubbard: "Conscious evolution inspires in us a mysterious and humble awareness that we have been created by this awesome process of evolution and are now being transformed by it."

The Consequence of Not Voting

"We are free up to the point of choice, then the choice controls the chooser."
Mary Crowley

Our first choice is whether or not to vote. If you do not vote, you put your future in the hands of those who do vote. Would you let a blind person take you out for a drive? Would you let a circus clown perform brain surgery on you? Do we really believe, as Abraham Lincoln said, that we are a nation of, by and for the people? If we say that we believe it, we must do our part. We cannot abdicate our responsibility to vote.

Why is it that two thirds of eligible voters do not vote? For one thing, it is not easy. Oh, it can be easy if you go unconsciously, ignorantly, or passionately misinformed to cast your vote. Typically that would be putting personality before Principle. Laziness causes many people not to vote, and apathy.

We in the United States of America enjoy countless benefits of freedom. But there is another side to the coin. It is responsibility. You are a part of a greater whole. You are an organ, or a cell in the body, or collective consciousness that we call *American*. Your vote helps determine what that looks like, whether it is healthy and whole or filled with dis-ease and broken.

The laws and programs that will impact our lives are made and changed by the people we empower to do so. Even if it does not turn out the way you wish it had, you did your part, and now can do your part to hold the feet of those who won the vote to the fire of accountability

How to Make a Conscious Decision

"Choose this day who you will serve...as for me and my house, I shall serve the Lord" (Joshua 24:15)

Pray first. Our mind is our connecting link with God – Spirit – Higher Consciousness. When we turn first to our higher power, we are more likely to make a conscious, rather than unconscious choice. Pray with positive prayer, not begging or coming from fear.

Educate yourself – Pay attention to news articles, outcomes of debates, and yes, even claims on the internet, PROVIDED you fact-check everything. Ask yourself: is this fact or opinion? The following sites are good sources, but the more important the issue is, the more thoroughly you should check it out. Sources: FactCheck.org, Politifact.com, FactChecker.com

Consider the source – Even news reporters have conscious or unconscious prejudices and opinions. Do not draw all of your information from a single source. Do not become over-involved to the point that your mind is saturated. The idea is to learn and sort, not to drown in a sea of information.

Which candidates reflect your own values? Is it personality that draws you or Principle - His or her charm, or the intelligence and value in his message? Are you voting a party line because your parents did? Are you voting for a particular candidate because you don't want to make another person angry?

Know the Candidate – Is s/he:

Qualified: Equipped, educated and experienced?

Independent National View with Interdependent World View – Seeking peace, harmony, prosperity, for all people everywhere, *including but not just* the US?

Grounded in Ethics, Character, Values and Conscience?

Making achievable promises and goals?

Courageous enough to go against influencers such as lobbyists?

Honest – What they did in the past, will indicate the future.

Understanding, Knowledgeable, or Wise?

Diplomatic?

Watch your habitual thoughts. The thoughts we hold in mind, manifest in and as our lives through the Law of Mind Action. Are you holding thoughts of fear or anger against the opposition, or positive thoughts about the candidate or party you prefer? This will influence your vote.

How To Know You Made The Right Choice

"I will put my law within them, I will write it on their hearts, and they will be my God, and I will be their people"
(Jeremiah 33)

"The test of Truth is that it satisfies the logic of the mind and the longing of the heart."
Charles Fillmore, co-founder of Unity

We all have built-in indicators that let us know when we are aligned with Truth and when we are not. We feel it in our gut when we are about to make a bad decision, whether we listen to the warning or not. In decision making: One choice gives you a sense of urgency or anxiety the other gives a feeling of peace. Go with the feeling of peace.

Pray before taking action. Expect God to do something, but do your part. Pray to make the right choice, adding "This or something better."

If you feel fear of guilt as you prepare to choose, you are being manipulated.

The Bottom Line

By right of consciousness, the American people will elect a person that will draw lessons needed for their collective growth. The election is a cause sent forth. The result of the election brings effects of that cause. The lessons can be painful or positive. Everyone will be affected in one way or another.

If money determines what you do or do not do then money is your boss. If God determines what you do or do not do then God is your boss. Richard J Foster, Money, Sex and Power

ARE WE THERE YET? – HOW WILL WE KNOW

> *"And the Lord' anger was kindled against Israel, and he made them wander in the wilderness forty years, until all the generation who had done evil in the sight of the Lord was consumed." (Numbers: 32.13)*

The actual journey the Israelites made to the Promised Land should have taken eleven days, yet according to the Bible, it took forty years. How can that be? Reflecting on my own life however, I can relate! Like when I think of the diets I was planning to start tomorrow, or how many times I've said: *"Why is this happening to me again?"*

Excitement filled me on the night before my twenty-first birthday. There was a great party planned. When I awoke the next day however, there was a sense of disappointment in my mind. It seemed like any other day. I didn't feel any different. Legally I had arrived, however I was the same twenty-year-old that went to bed the night before. I will say though, lessons were coming up to remind me how far I had to grow.

The first guest who arrived presented me with a thirty-three pound turkey which I later discovered he had stolen. The party went downhill from there. I stepped on a bee and a number of people got falling-down drunk. I was too busy taking care of my guests to imbibe much, as I recall. The next day my legally-but-not-actually grown-up self, faced a big clean-up job. That was over fifty years ago…fifty years of nonstop lessons or what we called AFGOs: *Another Freaking Growth Opportunity!*

The scripture above has the Israelites wandering the wilderness for forty years. Hebrew writers used numbers to symbolize ideas. The number forty is signifies trials and testing as well as completion. The people had to keep wandering and learning lessons until they earned the right to enter the Promised Land. Likewise, we must also continue to learn our lessons until we have mastered them.

There are no such things as report cards for spiritual growth so I have no proof I've made progress, except for the ways my life has changed. I do find comfort in the knowledge that each day I commit to, and do my best. In seminary, almost thirty years ago, I did find a good tool, called the Nine Incapabilities:

In Buddhism, there is a teaching regarding what they call the *Nine Incapabilities*. I believe we will know we have arrived when they apply to each of us. We might find some we've already accomplished, or we have a long way to go. Remember, the journey of a thousand miles begins with just one step!

NINE INCAPABILITIES

Words ascribed to Gautama Buddha

The arahant in whom the intoxicants are destroyed, who has lived the life, who has done his task, who has laid low his burden, who has attained salvation who has utterly destroyed the fetter of rebirth, who is emancipated by the true gnosis (knowing), he is incapable of perpetrating nine things: He is incapable of deliberately depriving a living creature of life.

He is incapable of taking what is not given so that it constitutes theft.

He is incapable of sexual impurity.

He is incapable of deliberately telling lies.

He is incapable of laying up treasure for indulgence in worldly pleasure as he used to do in the life of the house.

He is incapable of taking a wrong course through partiality.

He is incapable of taking a wrong course through hate.

He is incapable of taking a wrong course through stupidity.

He is incapable of taking a wrong course through fear.

A great source of inspiration in my life was Cavett Robert, who taught: *"School's never out for the professional."* Words of Truth for all of us, especially the Truth Student.

At the age of 94, Charles Fillmore said: *"I fairly sizzle with zeal and enthusiasm, and spring forth with a mighty faith to do the things that ought to be done by me."*

Psalm 13

How long, O LORD? Will you forget me forever?
How long will you hide your face from me?
How long must I take counsel in my soul
and have sorrow in my heart all the day?
How long shall my enemy be exalted over me?

Consider and answer me, O LORD my God;
light up my eyes, lest I sleep the sleep of death,
lest my enemy say, "I have prevailed over him,"
lest my foes rejoice because I am shaken.

But I have trusted in your steadfast love;
my heart shall rejoice in your salvation.
I will sing to the LORD,
because he has dealt bountifully with me.

Paradoxically, it will take as long as it takes, and how long it takes depends on us. The Principles in this book work if and when we work them. In the following section you will find exercises to help you!

EXERCISES

In the following section, you will find several exercises designed to assist you in digesting and assimilating the teaching presented. They can be completed on your own or in a class setting. The ultimate experience would be both attending a class or group study and then working with the teaching on your own, and sharing results with other participants.

LYRICS EXERCISE

Look up the lyrics to the top ten songs of 1967, and the lyrics from 2017. Note the differences in content. When you are done, ask yourself how each songs reflects the state of conscious from then, and now. Can you see the causes and the effects?

Top Ten Songs of 1967	Top Songs of 2017
To Sir With Love – Lulu	Shape of You Ed Sheeran
The Letter – The 4 Boxtops	Despacito – Luis Fonsi
Ode to Billie Jo – B Gentry	That's What I Like – B Mars
Windy – The Association	Humble – Kendrick Lamar
I'm A Believer – Monkees	Something Just Like This - Coldplay
Light My Fire – The Doors	Bad and Boujee – Migos
Somethin' Stupid – Sinatra	Closer - Chainsmokers
Happy Together – Turtles	Body Like A Back Road – Sam Hunt
Groovin on a Sunday Afternoon – The Rascals	Believer – Imagine Dragons
Can't Take My Eyes Off of You – Four Seasons	Congratulations – Post Malone

Note your conclusions here:

CREATING YOUR PRAYER TIME

Without solitude it is virtually impossible to live a spiritual life. *...We do not take the spiritual life seriously if we do not set aside some time to be with God and listen to him.* Henri Nouwen

Our goal is to learn how to be in the world without being of it. False god consciousness keeps us locked in mortal mind. We come to believe we have more important things to do, we have no time for God. *Maybe later,* we tell ourselves. When we give in to these lies, we are being led by ego, or as stated earlier, *Edging God Out.* This is the exact opposite of what is necessary for fulfilling our spiritual potential.

To create a personal prayer time is uncomfortable and inconvenient in the beginning. The object is to initiate and commit to daily prayer time. What you are doing is making a new habit. Keep in mind that every time we declare positive change in our lives, all that is unlike it comes up for healing. This way you will expect challenges and be prepared to handle them.

Begin your exercise by addressing the six basic questions: Who, What, Why, When, Where, and How:

Who: God and you. During your prayer time, you may invite angels, guides or loved ones in the Spiritual realm to be with you and support you in spirit. The important thing is God is always first and most important.

What: Devoting time to your spiritual life, learning Universal Principles of Truth and receiving guidance how to apply them in your life and share with others as directed.

Why: To enrich our relationship with God, receive guidance, and the ability stay focused on our higher consciousness, with authority over carnal mind. To claim and use our spiritual power.

When: That is up to you. What part of the day can you carve out time for prayer? Typically it's at the beginning or end of the day. The start of the day is easiest because there has been no opportunity for time for distraction. As for how long, that is up to you. I find that at least an hour works for me. Start with twenty minutes and build up. Just be sure to set aside sufficient time where you will not feel rushed.

Where: Find a place that feels right and comfortable to you. Walk around your house to find the place that seems to say *yes!* The space you choose should have sufficient light for reading, yet soft enough light for meditating and pondering.

How: Just do it. Start.

Assemble "Ingredients:" Bible, Devotional, Inspirational Reading, Journal, Pen, Paper

Music player–if you would like meditation or other soft music. I do not do this because I find it distracting.

Sacred Items (things that make you feel close to God, or inspired. This can include but is not limited to: figurines, religious items, prayer cards, white stones, etc.)

If a clock makes you feel comfortable, if you fear you will go over or under time, include that but try not to look at it too often, and A little blanket or shawl if you feel cold. Tissues just in case.

Arrange ingredients on a table or surface near you, creating your Sacred Space. Put the blanket or shawl within reach should you need it.

Try it and adjust to suit your needs. Go to the bathroom so you won't be distracted during prayer time. Turn off anything that will distract, such as phone, computer, or television. Settle in and give yourself to Spirit.

A Look at My Prayer Time

I'd like to share with you a little about my prayer time. I do my prayer time in bed, first thing every morning. My sacred items are on the top of my dresser, and I have inspirational pictures hanging in my room. I always have a picture of Jesus. I have my coffee at hand, which gives me the sense of having coffee with the Divine.

Some days, I begin by watching a religious program. While I do not fully embrace everything it teaches, I draw from the experience things that support my spiritual life. If what I hear is contrary to my beliefs, I simply turn off the TV.

I then speak my personal prayer greeting to God: I joyfully, joyfully dedicate and consecrate my life to Your will, Your work and Your way. Have Thy way in me, Lord. Have Thy way in me. Have Thy way in my thoughts, feelings, actions, decisions and words. Have Thy way in me, Lord, have thy way in me.

Next, I turn to my devotional. I have a little prayer book I've been using for over 25 years and love it as much as the first day I opened it. It's called A Guide to Prayer for All God's People. It includes a format including Opening Prayer, Scripture, Reflection, written and silent, Selected Readings, and Benediction. This book can be purchased online, see sources in resources section.

During reflection time, I read Unity's Daily Word, and a little from a Unity classic book, such as *Lessons in Truth*, journal, and write my gratitude list. The gratitude list is a very important practice for me. I have been doing it for many years, inspired by a book: *The Magic*, by Rhonda Byrne. Each day I list five things I am grateful for and why. The most important part is the why. It really is consciousness-changing, because it engages both the mind and the heart.

Also during reflection time I try to spend no less than ten minutes in silent prayer, just listening. It is amazing how difficult it can be to turn off the monkey mind that wants to chatter all through the prayer time. Don't let the chatter distract you. Just take a deep, cleansing breath and let the thought go. Consider the words of St. Francis De Sales, who said *Even if I spend the entire hour bringing my heart back to the altar, the hour was well spent.*

When praying, don't get hung up on words. Spirit doesn't require a high-holy monologue of fancy-schmancy words. It's okay if you like them and want to toss them from time to time. At the same time consider talking to the Divine as you would your own parent. If you're talking to Jesus, or Buddha, you don't need big words, just a big, sincere love.

Typically, my prayer time lasts about an hour and a half. That is my choice. It is not just the amount of time we spend but the quality of the time spent. We ultimately will receive out of the time what we give to it. Prayer is a way of taking care of ourselves, our spiritual development, and mastery. Through prayer, you can find inner peace amid adversity.

Our Prayer for All People

There are many names of God,
many faces of God,
many paths to God,
but there is only one God,
and this God expresses through all people.

Knowing this,
we bless people of every race, religion, cultural background, ethnicity, gender, sexual preference, rank, power, economic status, and mental or physical ability.

We celebrate the divinity of all people
and give thanks that this is so.

Path Ministries

A SABBATH-INSPIRED EXERCISE

The spirit of Sabbath is rest and spiritual renewal. The Jewish observance is sacred and beautiful, and it is theirs. Yet we can embrace the spirit of Sabbath by designing an observance based on the Principles we practice. It is simple—not easy at first, since change is necessary—and well worth any time or effort invested. This is a time to step away from the world and all its clamor, setting aside uninterrupted time to reflect and appreciate what our lives are all about.

I have prepared ideas for individuals and families. Because it is something new and different, there may be push-back from family members. It is important to try to work something out, as the process is beneficial for every member of the family. If the pushback is more stressful than the observance is helpful, you may need to devise a plan where you retire to your room, or office to practice by yourself.

Here is a suggestion for a personalized Sabbath practice:

Decide on the day and time. With today's varied work schedules, it's difficult to block out an entire 24 hour period. Review your schedule and set your Sabbath day and time. I, personally don't think God cares what day we choose, only that we choose and observe the Sabbath.

As for the time, a good suggestion is to start at the end of the day. Prepare in advance. Collect any reading or writing materials, books to read or study, etc. Do any chores the day before, and anything that might come up so you will be free to give the day to Spirit. Consider it a divine appointment. I fast from after supper the night I start, until supper the next day. I have my supper made and ready to heat and eat when I am done with my fast.

It is Jewish tradition to get dressed up in their best clothes for Sabbath, and to go to the temple for services before supper. If you are not going out, you can still dress in something special to mark the observance, or I like to put on special pajamas that make me feel warm, safe and loved for my time with God.

Begin with candles, prayer, and a great meal. If this is a family observance, encourage each member to participate in some way. Paper plates will result in fewer dishes in the sink. If you wish to fast, have coffee, juice, tea, or water available to drink. You can choose to fast

or not. Fasting is not for children, so if you have children, you will want to be sure there are things like cereal and sandwiches made the day before or another plan made.

Yet another part of Sabbath is fasting from distractions. This includes TV, phone, video games and computer. Music is optional although silence is an amazing spiritual practice. So, turn off all the *stuff,* and rest! With children, all hell will probably break loose when you take away the technology. If possible to stick to your plan, it will help them realize that there are other things to do.

This does not mean you do nothing. You can read, journal, pray, draw, etc. If you feel fidgety, move through it. Maybe color a Mandala, or take a shower. If you are doing this as a family, it would be a good time to spend an hour or so playing board games, or playing with Play-Doh. While you are playing, you might talk about beliefs, church, etc., or teach them to recite or write prayers or letters to God.

Go to bed! The next day, continue. Try to remain quiet and contemplative. This does not exclude going for a walk in the park. If you have children, let them run around outside and burn off their extra energy. It excludes technology, movies, etc.

At sunset, light the candles, say a prayer, have your end-of-Sabbath meal, and turn all of your gadgets back on! You will find yourself amazingly renewed.

SAMPLE SABBATH MEAL GUIDE

Candle Lighting & Opening Prayer: (If in a family setting, the mother lights the candle) *Sweet, Holy Spirit, I/we give myself/ourselves to you, during this sacred time. Be with me/us as I/we relax into your loving arms. May the light of these candles remind us always of the light of Christ we carry within, as your own children. We invite the presence of Jesus, or brother and wayshower, to join us in our prayer and rest.*

Spiritual Theme: (select one earlier) Suggestion:

> The Parable of the Prodigal Son Luke 15:11-32

Jesus said, *"There was a man who had two sons. And the younger of them said to his father, 'Father, give me the share of property that is coming to me.' And he divided his property between them. Not many days later, the younger son gathered all he had and took a journey into a far country, and there he squandered his property in reckless living. And when he had spent everything, a severe famine arose in that country, and he began to be in need. So he went and hired himself out to one of the citizens of that country, who sent him into his fields to feed pigs. And he was longing to be fed with the pods that the pigs ate, and no one gave him anything.*

"But when he came to himself, he said, 'How many of my father's hired servants have more than enough bread, but I perish here with hunger! I will arise and go to my father, and I will say to him, "Father, I have sinned against heaven and before you. I am no longer worthy to be called your son. Treat me as one of your hired servants."' And he arose and came to his father. But while he was still a long way off, his father saw him and felt compassion, and ran and embraced him and kissed him. And the son said to him, 'Father, I have sinned against heaven and before you. I am no longer worthy to be called your son.' But the father said to his servants 'Bring quickly the best robe, and put it on him, and put a ring on his hand, and shoes on his feet. And bring the fattened calf and kill it, and let us eat and celebrate. For this my son was dead, and is alive again; he was lost, and is found.' And they began to celebrate.

"Now his older son was in the field, and as he came and drew near to the house, he heard music and dancing. And he called one of the servants and asked what these things meant. And he said to him, 'Your brother has come, and your father has killed the fattened calf, because he has received him back safe and sound.' But he was angry and refused to go in. His father came out and entreated him, but he answered his father, 'Look, these many years I have served you, and I never disobeyed your command, yet you never gave me a young goat that I might celebrate with my friends. But when this son of yours came, who has devoured your property with prostitutes, you killed the fattened calf for him!' And he said to him, 'Son, you are always with me, and all that is mine is yours. It was fitting to celebrate and be glad, for this your brother was dead, and is alive; he was lost, and is found.'"

Blessing of the Food: (in a family setting, the father or oldest child would recite this) Thank you, God for this abundant blessing of food. We/I give thanks to you, and to all who have worked to bring it to our table.
AMEN

Silent Reflection or Discussion: If individual observance, reflect on reading and questions. If a family setting, discuss reading and questions.

Questions:

Do you think the father should have given the son his inheritance early?

How would you feel if you were the other brother? Why?

What do you think made the lost son change his mind and go home?

Do you think he really learned a lesson?

Would you have gone in to the celebration if your brother did this?

What did this teach you?

Prayer After Supper: I/we am/are overflowing with the food that fills my/our body/ies, the love that fills my/our heart/s, and gratitude that fills my/our soul/s. What I/we have received will sustain me/us as I/we enter our time of prayer and contemplation. Thank you, Spirit of Love and Truth.

If this is an individual Sabbath, follow with recording your thoughts from the theme in your journal. If it is a family observance, you can play a board game, do a craft, or each find their own way to rest, relax and renew.

CREDO EXERCISE

You will need a journal and a pen or pencil to complete this exercise.

What is a credo? A credo is a statement of what an individual, or group believes. It is a fundamental set of beliefs and is sometimes called a Statement of Faith. This exercise gets a general idea of what you believe, and why. It is a starting point, from which you can do further exploration.

What are the benefits of developing your personal Credo?

   * We can define and articulate our belief system.

   * We will be better understood by others, and able to share our beliefs effectively.

   * We will be free from bondage to a belief system taught to us by others, that we don't believe in our hearts and souls.

   * We can sort out what is true for us and what is not.

   * We will be grounded and confident in our belief.

Everything we do in life is influenced by our belief system. Whether a devout follower of a religion, or an atheist, our actions are based on belief. The beliefs we were taught, are not necessarily the beliefs we hold in our mind and heart. Until we come to know our beliefs, we will be subject to what we were taught by others.

To get in touch with our belief system and to make any adjustments, it's necessary to get it out where we can take a look at it. That is what this exercise is about.

Your true credo never changes, it blossoms. It is the Truth that is "Written on your heart" as the prophet Jeremiah told us. (Jeremiah 31) Unfortunately, this Truth has often been occluded with error thoughts and beliefs, taught to us with both the best and worst intentions. Our goal is to realize how our beliefs have been formed, so we can decide for ourselves what we believe.

Our belief system is a blend of five formative factors: Experience, Revelation, Culture, Tradition, and Reason. Below, there is a brief explanation of each of the factors. This information will make it possible to explore where and how we came to our current beliefs. It will also provide the opportunity to establish an authentic credo, based on inherent Truth.

Before we begin, answer the following questions. There are no right or wrong answers. Be as honest as possible because the answers to these questions will provide you with information to help as you establish your credo.

Do you believe in God?

Why? Or why not?

How did the Bible get written?

Do you believe it?

Do you believe in heaven and hell?

What do you believe about Jesus?

These can be very challenging questions, especially if we either don't have an answer, or it's something we were told, and not what we really believe. Once we have developed our credo, we will be able to share it with confidence. After answering the questions, continue with the exercise, with formative factors.

CREDO - THE FORMATIVE FACTORS:

Where Our Beliefs Come From.

EXPERIENCE–From the day we were born, we received input from parents, teachers, clergy, and friends. We went to church, where we received a religious education. Or we did not go to church, which presented a different perspective regarding church. Most children have taken part in religious ceremonies and rites of passage. We accepted everything we were taught, since it came from a real or perceived authority. Both children and adults have widely varying beliefs about what *church* is, and what part it should play in our lives.

At some point, we perceived a gap between what parents, clergy, and teachers told us to believe, and the Truth that is written in our hearts. We might not define it like that, and consider it's all a bunch of lies. Many rebel during their teens. What looks like rejection of God, is the rejection of what was taught that does not resonate with their inner Truth.

It's through the formative factor of experience we come to 'own' our faith, as it emerges from inside out. Sharing our experiences can be very inspirational to others and in a very real sense becomes a formative factor in their life as well. Sometimes starting a conversation like this is difficult because we had been told ours was the only *right* or *true* religion. We will be most effective sharing our religious beliefs with others when we look for what we hold in common, rather than what we see as different. Once we have developed our personal Credo, we will find that there is no need to *sell* it to another, nor to defend it.

MEDITATION ON EXPERIENCE: Take a few minutes to relax. Breathe deeply and think about the origins of your beliefs, and answer the following questions:

Question	What I was told/by who	What I believe in my heart
Who or what is God?		
What are heaven and hell?		
Who or what made the world?		
Who are you and why are you here?		
Who is Jesus?		
What is the one true church?		
Why are there so many different religions? Where is God in all this?		
Does God answer prayer? How? Why, or why not?		

REVELATION–A revelation is an unveiling, a disclosure of Truth, making known that which is hidden. It is the *"aha!"* moment when we hear something and know beyond the shadow of a doubt it is true. We may not even know how we know, but we know. It is a moment that the Truth that is within us contacts our conscious mind.

Revelation is an experience of the activity of God. For example, Myrtle Fillmore, cofounder of Unity, was ill with tuberculosis she'd inherited. She was told she only had months to live. One night at a lecture by EB Weeks, Myrtle heard him say we are children of God, and therefore cannot inherit illness. She had a personal revelation and knew it was true Myrtle began a practice of prayer and meditation she would adhere to for hours every day. She blessed every cell in her body, including the ones that were diseased. Over a period of two years, she was healed. This was the beginning of the Unity movement.

The first time I stepped into a Unity church, my soul cried, *home!* I had a direct revelation of God's intention for my life one day while I was in prayer. Feeling discontent, the prayer had been given to me by a friend. I had been feeling discontent for several months. I had a job I liked, but something was missing. One line in the prayer said: *As I joyfully release my full potential to be used.* I raised my hands to the heavens. *What is it? What do you want me to do?* Then I audibly heard the words *Minister. Unity Minister* in my right ear.

I thought that was pretty strange, and wondered what my Catholic family would think. Then I realized that everything I had done in my life to date had been preparing me for ministry. I gave myself to God through Unity ministry over 25 years ago, with never a regret. I'd like to say Spirit speaks to me so clearly all the time, but I can't. I receive guidance for sure, just not so dramatically. Many people receive callings of all kinds—to teach, to practice medicine, to help the poor, etc. While not every call is to be a minister, we are all called to minister—to serve—each other.

Revelation becomes formative for your belief system when you have experienced a particularly significant individual revelation event, or when you focus on the revelation experience that has formed the movement of which you are a part.

MEDITATION ON REVELATION: Take a few deep, cleansing breaths, and again sit back and relax. Let your mind wander through time. Invite experiences to come forth that revealed God's presence in your life. It might be a thought or idea that comes at a moment you need it, or as a stirring in your soul when you heard something. It could be guidance. Was there a time when you had that moment of realization? The real-ization, or *aha* moment? Record any memories that come to you. Don't be surprised if more examples keep bubbling up from your memory. Note them as well.

THE PRAYER OF PURPOSE

My Heavenly Father is my source of all supply.
God answers my every need.
Each day I am guided and directed to all that is right and perfect for me,
As I joyfully release my full potential to be used.
Thank you, God For all the peace, joy, health, happiness, prosperity, and love I could ever want.

AMEN

CULTURE–The customs, skills, arts, language, concepts and institutions of a given people in a given period a *way of life*. Even though America is called the great melting pot, many of our beliefs were formed by the culture of our ancestors. The words we use to communicate, the analogies we draw, and the moral behaviors we practice are influenced by our heritage. Delving in to genealogy can be a rewarding quest in learning how culture of your ancestors may have impacted your credo.

Our beliefs are also shaped by the prevailing culture of the times. We have been deeply influenced by the collective consciousness of the American way of living and believing. In the past 60 years our beliefs and values have shifted dramatically. Unfortunately, they've become muddled for most people, which is resulting in the chaos and division that is putting our lives, and our planet at risk of extinction. This is where seeking Truth and Principle can save us.

Our culture becomes instrumental in determining our concept of self, our relationship to God, and our relationship to humankind. It is a deciding factor in honoring and respecting all people, all life, and the planet we share.

MEDITATION ON CULTURE - Relax again now. Let your breath be deep and slow as you consider your roots. Where did your ancestors come from? Did they bring customs and a way of life here from somewhere else? What do you know about your ancestry? Were families big, or small? What was your socio-economic status, and how did that affect your beliefs? As your mind presents memories, thoughts and feelings, write them down.

TRADITION - Tradition as a formative factor refers to those aspects of a religious faith that are repeated by an individual or a community because they have value. They are also called rites or rituals. Tradition can become an empty ritual. When traditions contain within them a deep spiritual meaning, they build a foundation of faith to pass down to future generations.

Traditions need to be released when they are not congruent with our true beliefs. An amusing story that illustrates this, tells of a woman who always cut the end off of the ham when she put it in the baking dish. Her husband asked her one day why she did it. She said that it is what her mother always did. After thinking about it for a while, the woman called her mother to ask why she did it. The mother said, *because the pan was too small.* So, you see, the daughter was performing what could be called an empty ritual that really had no meaning.

Traditions are worthless without knowing the Principles they represent or symbolize. Once we have a full understanding, they serve as spiritual food to help us be strong and grow. Religious or Spiritual traditions come in many forms, but the purpose is the same, to maintain our relationship with God and commitment to all that is good.

An example of a religious tradition is the Jewish celebration of Hanukkah. Here is a very streamlined and simplified version: When the Maccabees reclaimed the temple in Jerusalem from the Syrians, it had been desecrated. They cleansed it and needed to light the lamp. When they found the oil for the lamp, there was not enough for the eight days required to complete the cleansing. Yet the oil that was there, burned for the eight days. It was proof that God was with them and approved. Jewish people observe Hanukkah every year as a reminder of the faithful presence of their creator.

MEDITATION ON TRADITION – Bring yourself again to the quiet place within your mind and heart. Search through the days of your life, seeking your family or church traditions, rites and rituals. What celebrations did your church have every year? Did your family have similar celebrations in your home? How were new babies welcomed? How was death handled? Did you say grace before meals—or maybe just on special occasions? Do you carry on your own traditions? Are there traditions you would like to revive, or maybe even create on your own? Think on these things, and when you are ready, write them down, as well as your feelings about them.

SCRIPTURE – Scripture is not exclusive to the Judeo-Christian faith groups. Any book or body of writings, when regarded by a particular religious group as sacred would be called Scripture. Whatever your religion, there is most likely holy books or scriptures associated with it. Jesus' use of the Torah in his teachings show it was a strong formative factor in his credo.

If nothing else, most of us are familiar with the stories in the Bible about characters like Adam and Eve, Moses, and Noah. We may be able to recite parables. In many homes, the Bible is out on display, as if its mere presence declared the home to be holy. It may be used on special occasions or in daily prayer time. With each passing year, it seems the Bible is losing the interest of people. Why? Maybe we will get the best answer if we each ask ourselves that question. For me, while I loved the thought of this great holy book, whenever I would read it, it would scare the daylights out of me. There was violence, strict rules, and a punishing god. Reading it and engaging it are two different things. This is true of all holy books.

Scripture becomes significant for us in the development of our individual belief system when we use it as a central or primary reference point for contemplation or meditation, and when we use it as a source of spiritual guidance and understanding. As you proceed with this exercise, remember—there are no right or wrong answers. This is one component you can use to determine what your beliefs are, and if they are authentically yours.

MEDITATION FOR SCRIPTURE – Set aside anything in your hands, relax, and allow your breaths to become smooth and observe the thoughts and feelings that come up. Can you recite a passage you've always loved, or one that upsets you? Can you recite the Ten Commandments? What scriptures speak to you and guide you? Take time now to reflect, then write your thoughts in your journal.

REASON
The faculty of rational argument, deduction, judgment, etc.
Reason has had times of acceptance and rejection throughout Christian history. Of those who oppose reason, revelation is the most outstanding. True reason and revelation are not in conflict with each other, but support each other. Charles Fillmore, cofounder of Unity said, Truth satisfies the logic of the mind (reason) and the longing of the heart revelation). He called this the test of Truth.

Although reason is a good thing—the practicality of Practical Christianity—it is not possible to reason our way to God. If we do, we will create a God in our own image and likeness. We need both reason and revelation. They affirm each other. Reason can look at a tomato, slice it in half, and see many seeds, but it can't see the tomatoes in the seeds. The understanding of God's abundant provision through the tomato is revelation.

When I first found Unity, my soul cried *Home!* As I walked through the door of the first Unity church I attended, it was a revelation I felt, not reason. The rest of my experience confirmed it. I had found, for me, a religion that aligned with what I believed inside. Whatever church you attend, you should experience both the revelation—knowing this is your spiritual home—and reason, it agrees with what you already believe, even if you weren't consciously aware of it.

MEDITATION ON REASON – Relax one more time into the silence. See if you can elicit moments when you thought, *that makes sense,* as you listened to a sermon or teacher. Recall moments in elementary school when you realized one plus one equals two, and if Sally had two apples and gave you one, how many apples does she have? There was no doubt. She had one, you had one. When you are satisfied that you have reviewed the topic of reason sufficiently, note your thoughts.

It is now time to use these formative factors to examine your findings and write your first credo. Fill in the answers to the following questions, and *Voila* you will see your personal credo! As you move along your spiritual path, with further learning you may revise it, according to your ever-expanding awareness!

MY CREDO–I BELIEVE

About God (who or what is God?)

Who or what am I?

What is my relationship to God?

About good and evil

About the meaning of life

About life and death

About religion

About miracles

About science and religion

About sin and punishment

The future–heaven, hell, etc.

The Bible & Holy Books

SELF-EVALUATION

This evaluation defines which areas of our lives we excel at, and which areas we can grow in. While we may weigh these areas, it does not weigh the quality of a person we are. This is no place for guilt or feeling we don't measure up. It is simply a way for finding growth opportunities.

WHEEL OF VIRTUE ~ WHEEL OF OPPORTUNITY

VIRTUES AND OPPORTUNITIES

1. HUMILITY -- PRIDE
2. CONFIDENCE -- ENVY
3. PEACEFUL -- WRATH/ANGER
4. PURITY – LUST
5. GENEROSITY -- AVARICE/GREED
6. SELF-DISCIPLINE -- GLUTTONY
7. VIGOR/ENERGY -- SLOTH

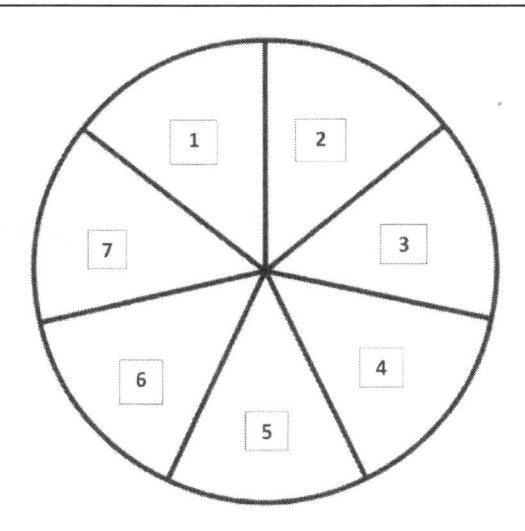

Each wedge of the pie chart above contains a number. Each number has been assigned a Virtue/Opportunity pair.

The center of the wheel has a value of 0, and the outside line has a value of 100.

Color each wedge, preferably using a different color for each. From the center, zero point, toward the edge, to show how fully you already express the virtue assigned to that wedge. For example, if you expressed generosity 50% of the time, you would color 50% of the wedge.

Complete all wedges before analyzing.

ANALYSIS: Each wedge colored provides guidance toward the next steps of your spiritual growth. The un-colored spaces are your areas of opportunity. The answer is in the other half of the pairing. If you scored very high on vigor/energy, sloth is not a big issue for you. It's a good idea to be alert to times when you might start to slide. These times can be warnings of depression or distraction. If you scored very low on being peaceful, you will want to look for ways to address your anger issues, and the circumstances you have drawn for your growth.

SPIRITUAL GIFTS EXERCISE

Part A: Check the items which best describe you:

_____ I like to work by myself, with my own tasks and projects. G

_____ People consider me to be a good resource, for information or help. A

_____ I do not have typical financial challenges and have sufficient resources. A

_____ I like to help people who come to me for advice or encouragement. D

_____ I am self-motivated and get things done. G

_____ I enjoy being a leader, assisting and directing others for a common task. A

_____ I am a people person. I love to show kindness. E

_____ I love to teach others and do it well. C

_____ People say I am inspiring and eloquent. F

_____ I give at least 10 percent of my income to churches and charities. A

_____ Advice I give is taken seriously and usually followed. D

_____ I like to research when I am preparing to teach something. C

_____ Finding people to take part in activities, and to lead, appeals to me. B

_____ I prefer small group or individual, more intimate relationships with others. E

_____ I am very creative and have many talents to share. G

_____ I have a strong sense of right and wrong and live according to God's Principles. F

_____ I like to have nice things, but do not value them above people and Principle. A

_____ People come to me to be lifted up when they fell down. D

_____ It's important to me to know the rules and live them. C

_____ I love to set goals and achieve them on my own and with organizations. G

_____ I care about others and want to help them live good and healthy lives. D

_____ I can make good decisions quickly, I feel when a decision is right. F

_____ I love to help those with less, or who have fallen on hard times. E

_____ I am grounded, and able to handle criticism and feedback. C

_____ I like to volunteer for worthwhile causes, sharing my talent and gifts. G

_____ I have confidence in myself and my abilities. B

_____ I do favors for others with love, and no concern for repayment. E

_____ I like to lead my team or group to victory. B

_____ When a question of spirituality or morals comes up, my answer is usually right. F

_____ I like goals with deadlines. The time limit excites me and I usually complete on time. B

_____ When someone is hurting, they find comfort in my presence and words. D

Tally your answers here, using the letter at the end of each question:

A _____ B _____ C _____ D _____ E _____ F _____
G _____

Recording a 3, 4, or 5 after a letter indicates a Spiritual Gift.

Like the other exercises in this book, this exercise is a jumping-off point for further exploration. There are other spiritual gifts, and tools to determine them online. Some of the gifts are active and the others in potential.

SPIRITUAL GIFTS DEFINITIONS

GIVING: Contributing comes naturally to you, whether you are giving money, time, or other material resources. There is no sense of lack, loss, or expectation of payment. You give because it is a joy to give, and you cannot even imagine not giving. You have confidence you will always be provided for as you have provided for others.

ADMINISTRATION: You are organized and goal-oriented. Through your leadership, projects get done. Setting goals, schedules, tasks, policies and guidelines energizes you, and you are able to share them without concern for criticism.

TEACHING: You love to learn and are passionate about sharing what you have learned with others. It is your desire to teach others things that will make their lives better and more successful.

ENCOURAGEMENT: Your gift of encouragement draws to you people who need what you have to share. To encourage is not to do the work for another, but to delight in helping them find their own solutions, and strength to do what is to be done by them.

MERCY: Compassion guides you in comforting those who are suffering. You have the ability to help hurting people. You are sensitive, giving, loving, and your energy is healing to them. Your words and prayers are like medicine.

PROPHECY: You have a natural ability to receive inspiration from God, understand spiritual law, and share it with others. You can discern motives and have strong convictions. It is very important to maintain your spiritual life, to enhance your gift.

SERVING: You are able to see areas where you can make a difference through service to others or causes. When you see a need, you are called to meet it. Serving others energizes you, although you prefer short-term projects, where you can work alone.

The Spiritual Gifts we have been given, are provided as a means to do the work of Spirit on planet Earth. We are cocreators, provided gifts and a desire to use them. When we are using our gifts as intended, we rarely feel drained or unhappy. Instead we feel vital and energized—filled with zeal—and when our day is done, we sleep peacefully, in the knowledge we are fulfilling our purpose in life.

We have another gift, the gift of free will. This means we can use our gifts in any way we want. For example we could use our gifts to control or manipulate, if influenced by false gods. When we do this however, we will find we feel drained, experiencing stress, and having a general sense of inner discontent.

CLOSING SPIRITUAL GIFTS EXERCISE: Review the gifts again, and explore how these gifts could be used in error, and what the likely results would be. Make notes of your thoughts.

EXERCISE–WHAT MATTERS MOST
The best things in life aren't things.

Our everyday lives have a way of distracting us from the things that matter most. Between the enticements of the false gods, to worldly fears and concerns, somehow what is most important gets moved to the back burner, and often forgotten. This simple exercise will help you to determine what is important in our lives.

INSTRUCTIONS:

In the box titled LIST A, make a list of everything you would like to do, a kind of like a bucket list.

In the box titled LIST B, make a list of how many you have done or worked toward recently.

List A	List B

INSTRUCTIONS PART TWO:

Review your past six months of bank statements. Make notes of expenditures other than those for food, clothing and shelter.

Of the items you have noted, how many are associated with what you determined to be most important in the previous lists?

You should now be able to determine which things in your life you are giving your time and money to, which would place them in the category of *Most Important*. Ask yourself what you would change and how.

TREASURE MAPPING EXERCISE

The purpose of a treasure map is to provide a visual tool for focus. It helps to keep the mind from drifting away from a goal or desire. Creating a treasure map helps us to sharpen our vision as we bring forth images and words that support whatever our treasure may be. It is fun to create, and you can do this on your own or with friends. Making a treasure map on your own allows you construct the map quietly and prayerfully. Making a treasure map with friends creates an energy of support and connection. They will hold the vision with you.

What you need
Old magazines with lots of pictures
Glue or paste
Sharpies, colored or black
Scissors
A piece of core-board, poster board or paper–whatever size you want.
A picture or small, flat object of Spirit, God, Jesus, Buddha or other religious symbol.

Instructions:
Look through magazines to find pictures and words that describe your goal. Cut them out.
Build your map by placing your religious symbol on the map.
At the bottom of the map, write, "Thank you, Spirit, for this or something better."
(use God, Spirit, Buddha or whatever spiritual name you prefer)
Next, glue or paste other images to the board.
Write an affirmation on the board with a Sharpie (ex: I travel far and wide and see many things)

Tips:
Keep your treasure map simple. Focus on ONE topic. To do more, only blurs your focus.
Put the map somewhere you can see it regularly. Don't let it go to the back burner of mind.

Spend some time meditating on your map daily. Even a few minutes will do.

Don't just look at the pictures and words, FEEL them. Act as if it is yours already.

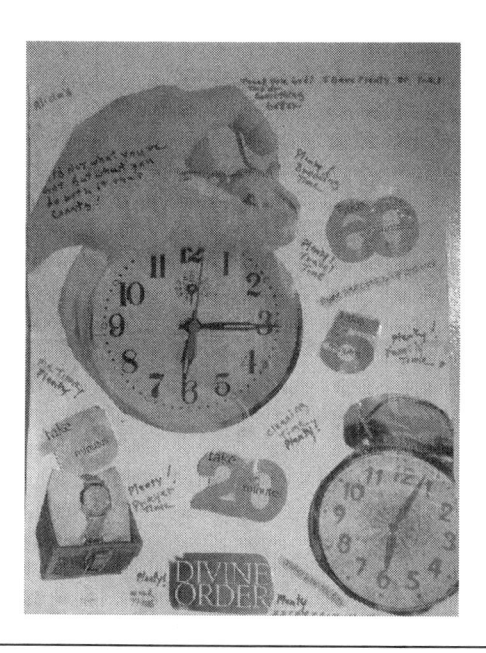

> This is a treasure map I made several years ago. I hung it right next to my desk, since I spent a lot of time there.
>
> It reminded me of the importance of taking time...not waiting for it to appear...to do the things that matter.
>
> I realized as I look at it, that I did find my treasure, I did achieve my goal. While I am as busy as ever, I DO have the time to do what I want.
>
> This is a great exercise to get what you want!

FOCUS-BUILDING EXERCISE

This is a very simple exercise. Draw the Four Quadrants of Consciousness illustration, shown below, on a piece of paper. Hang the illustration on your refrigerator or behind a door, etc., if you want to keep it private. During the course of the day, especially if you feel particularly happy, angry, confused, frustrated, etc., make a mark in the quadrant your thoughts or feelings are occupying. If you find you are in the lower quadrants, think of ways you can shift to the upper. This is a great way to build awareness.

Higher Consciousness Intuitive	**Higher Consciousness** Sensing
Lower Consciousness Thinking/Thoughts	**Lower Consciousness** Emotions/Feelings

CONSCIOUSNESS IDENTIFICATION EXERCISE

Below you will find an illustration of the four quadrants of consciousness, followed by a word-list. Write each word in the quadrant it belongs to. This is not as easy as it may appear. When you have completed the list, observe the outcome. You should have a clearer understanding of the quadrants.

Higher Consciousness Intuitive	**Higher Consciousness** Sensing
Lower Consciousness Thinking/Thoughts	**Lower Consciousness** Emotions/Feelings

CONSCIOUSNESS IDENTIFICATION EXERCISE WORD LIST

Addiction – Arrogance – Bondage – Confidence

Creative – Death – Disease (Dis-ease)

Enlightenment – Eternal – Faith – Failure

Fear – Freedom – Formative – Guilt

Gossip – Happiness – Health

Heaven – Hell – Ignorance

Illumination – Illusion – Inclusive

Integrity – Intimacy – Judgment – Lawful

Lies – Life – Love

Marriage – Me – My – Mine

Money – Oneness – Personality

Principle – Prosperity – Romance

Sensuality – Repentance – Purgatory

Purgatory – Religion – Separation

Sex – Sin – Temporal – Truth

Unlawful – Wealth – Wisdom

GLOSSARY

This is a simplified glossary of words used in this text. They are presented here because they sometimes differ from traditional usage of the words. The glossary will assist in your understanding of the material. The definitions are presented in the simplest, easy to understand wording. If you wish to explore more deeply, you can refer to The Revealing Word, by Charles Fillmore.

ANTICHRIST: That which is opposed to Christ and the works of Christ. It denies that the Christ dwells in, and is, the true self of every individual. Antichrist tries to delude people into the belief that this world is the only reality, and that death is the way to life. Jesus came to deliver man from death through a teaching that leads to eternal life. Antichrist thoughts must be persistently denied.

CARNAL: Pertaining to or characterized by the flesh or the body, its passions and appetites: sensuality. Not spiritual, merely human; temporal, worldly.

CHRIST: The divinity of God within man. It is every man's potential for perfection, that Jesus fulfilled and taught us to fulfill in ourselves. In Unity we teach that Jesus is the man, and Christ the spark of divinity which he came to express fully and teach us to do as well.

CONSCIOUSNESS: Awareness, pure knowledge, states of mind. There are three phases of consciousness: Conscious mind, what we know of in our day-to-day lives; Subconscious mind, ideas, thoughts, memories, and concepts we are not normally aware of, Superconscious, the realm of Divine Mind, where we may sense, intuit, or receive ideas from the Mind of God.

COLLECTIVE CONSCIOUSNESS (Race Consciousness): Just as individual cells of our bodies form the body itself, so do individual minds form the collective consciousness. I call this the *collective perspective*. Through its vibrational energy, it draws like energy—for better or worse. This is what is meant by the term: *your vibe attracts your tribe*. Consistently held thoughts attract like-minded others, and a group psyche manifests. The process works, on a collective level, through the Law of Mind Action, to create the KKK, and the Peace Corps as well. Our ultimate goal is to align the collective consciousness with Christ consciousness, manifesting life on earth as it is in heaven, the realm of all-good.

EGO: Human identity, personality—the lower nature. This is the part of us that needs to be transformed in order for our true self to express. Ideally, ego, or the human nature, experiences life: learning lessons and achieving understanding. This evolves the ego into the true individuality, Christ Consciousness. This is also called enlightenment. When the ego bonds to sense mind, through the call of false gods, it expresses as the Antichrist man, which causes all kinds of trouble on planet Earth. While there is no reality to this *being*, the individual suffers and causes others to suffer through greed and carnality. The way to freedom and transformation is found in repentance: the renewal of the mind. We must transform the ego, or face a future of self-defeating thoughts, feelings and behaviors.

"Man, duality of—Man is a duality in seeming only. He is a unit when he knows himself. His ignorance of himself and his relation to God is the cause of the seeming duality. When wisdom comes to him and he makes wisdom his own, there is no longer war between the ideal man in God and the becoming man in the Lord God." Charles Fillmore *The Revealing Word*

ENLIGHTENMENT: An awakening, moving from knowledge *of*, or *about*, to knowing, on a deep, personal level. This cannot be learned, it is realized within.

EVIL: Evil manifests through fallen human consciousness. The word *evil*, is *live* spelled backward. Evil is backward living. It is all that is not of God. Evil apparently results from ignorance (darkness), and when Truth is presented (light/enlightenment), evil disappears, as a shadow vanishes in light. If we look to cause when experiencing an occurrence of evil in our lives, we have the opportunity to look at it, discern the cause, and change it.

FALSE GODS: False gods are states of mind formed by the error thought of humankind. There are two primary false gods, or false belief of good; one is Mammon, or materialism and the other Baal, or carnality, i.e. the sense consciousness. The basic natures of the false gods are money and ego.

FLESH (the): This refers to the yet-untransformed human part of us, in particular the senses and ego. It is the part most susceptible to the temptation of the false gods. They say the spirit is willing, but the flesh is weak, yet, if the flesh is so weak, why is it so hard to overcome? The way to overcome the flesh is to spend time daily in prayer, meditation, a study of metaphysics or inspirational material, and avoidance of input that includes violence, promiscuity or messages contrary to Spiritual Principle.

GOD: All-good, Principle, Truth. The attributes of God are love, peace, understanding power, and all good things. God is immanent, or within, and yet transcendent. God does not have gender. God is Spirit.

HEAVEN and HELL: Are states of consciousness, one uplifted and aligned with the Divine, the other, in a state of suffering and misery. Heaven and Hell are as eternal as we make them.

IDEA: The original, primary thought of Spirit—archetype—perfect pattern for all manifestation. Everything starts as an idea in mind which we bring into manifestation through the creative process.

HOLY: To be holy is to be whole in body, mind and spirit. While it is possible to touch on moments of holiness, however, transformation of the lower consciousness is required to retain and express a state of holiness.

LAW: Is the systematic unfoldment of manifestation. It is Principle—the paradigm or framework of creation. Whether scientific or metaphysical, it is a structure upon which everything is built. The primary Principle is called the Law of Cause and Effect although it has many other expressions. Every expression of spiritual law is based on a cause we send forth, and the effect of that cause. This can be positive or negative.

METAPHYSICS: Metaphysics is the study of that which transcends the physical. It is a clear understanding of ideas and their legitimate expression (Charles Fillmore, *The Revealing Word*). It is the study of Universal Principles of Truth, or Spiritual Laws (see Law). Metaphysics is a philosophy based on the premise that the world makes sense.

MIND: Our mind is our connecting link with God. We communicate with God through prayer and meditation. It is the receptacle, vessel, and channel of the Divine Ideas received from Spirit. We manifest through mind, according to our current state of awareness.

MIND - DIVINE: The Mind of God. It is the creator of all Divine Ideas. Principle. Omniscient, all-knowing.

MIND - CARNAL: The word *carnal* is not commonly used today, but expresses exactly what we are dealing with. This is the earthly, or sensuous mind. It is also called the Mind of the Flesh. The carnal mind's belief is based on error thoughts that the physical experience is the most important thing, and it must survive by being in total control, and having its every want fulfilled. It is the author of error thinking.

PRINCIPLE: God as Principle is first cause of all manifestation. Principle, as God, is everywhere present. It is absolute, eternal and unchanging. While this may seem contradictory, it is not. The law or Principle does not change, but its expression can change. It is paradoxical. What may appear as change is often blossoming or expressing at a higher level. When Jesus addressed the Sabbath, and his disciples picking grain or healing, Jesus pointed out the higher law or Principle—*"The Sabbath was made for man, not for the*

Sabbath." Jesus was not negating the law, only teaching that sometimes the law works on a different level. Also: Law—Lord.

PROPHET: One who speaks forth the word of the Lord. In the Old Testament, this would be someone who advised people based on communication received from God. Metaphysically, it refers to one who comprehends Divine Law, and shares it with others. This works on an individual level as well, as we come to assimilate the teaching into our thoughts, words and actions. We can then discern Divine Will. Rather than turning to a prophet, we become our own prophet.

PROPHET–FALSE: From a charlatan trying to manipulate, to mis-guide others, to our own self-centered desires, we may receive error guidance. This can be selfish and dangerous. Before acting on guidance, always consider the source, and likely effect of any action taken. "You will know them by their fruits." Jesus Christ.

REAL/REALITY: While the words *real* and *reality* are synonyms for Truth, in the lower, or human consciousness, they are more perceptions of what is believed to be true. In metaphysics, we use the terms, "little 'r'," and "big 'R'," when clarifying what we are talking about. *Little r,* would indicate perceived reality, where *big R,* would indicate Truth.

REPENT/REPENTANCE: A realization of error and regret, coupled with the intention to *sin no more*. To repent is to re-think; it is to change one's mind, committing to a new way of being. Prior to the knowledge of Divine Law, it would appear to be imposed by God or religious leaders. Once awareness and understanding are grasped, comes the realization that this is not imposed from without, but exposed from within. The law now benefits us.

RESENTMENT: To re-experience (re=again, sentir=feel) the feeling of a real or perceived offense, which results in holding another responsible for the act. To continuously hold on to negative emotion, coupled with the causative thought, will draw like vibration and impair healing of an otherwise good relationship.

SACRIFICE: The origin of this word indicates its meaning as giving something up, usually to a deity, to make it, or yourself holy. In the process of spiritual transformation, we give up old beliefs and ways of thinking we have come to know are error. We give up ways of living that are not harmonious with our highest good, or the highest good for all. In doing this, we become whole—holy.

SACRAMENT: The traditional Catholic Church defines a sacrament as: An outward sign, instituted by Christ to give grace. Metaphysically interpreted, we can say it is something we do in the outer, inspired by Christ, from within, to uplift us spiritually. Examples can include things such as forgiveness, charity, helping others when you could be doing something for yourself. Specific activities might be participating in a Burning Bowl and White Stone service, or Communion with or without the elements.

SIN: Falling short of divine perfection—thoughts, feelings and actions that are contrary to spiritual law. All sin starts in mind. Sin is not an act of inherent evil; it is typically conscious or unconscious action, based on false beliefs. Sin is forgiven, or redeemed through realizing the error, and the cause that manifested negative effects. The most dangerous sin is fully aware something is wrong and doing it anyway. Consequences or effects for this sin will be exponentially greater. Sin is consciously, willfully and intentionally acting contrary to Principle. It is sending forth negative cause, and will receive negative effects.

SON OF GOD: The perfect idea of mankind created by God; the Christ. Jesus fully embodied and expressed the Christ within and taught us we could as well.

SON OF MAN: Is the work in progress—the part of us that is awakened to truth concepts—able to discern right from error and choose the better. This work is done through prayer and meditation as well as right thought and action. *Adam man*, is the fallen expression of Son of God, who is regaining his Sonship through transformation.

TRUTH: The absolute, eternal and unchanging—Principle. Truth is within every person. When the mind connects with Truth, what might seem to some as new, is really just an unveiling of what was there all along. It is a realization. Through a process of transformation, we all have the potential to express the perfect mind that was in Christ Jesus.

TRUTH (source of): God is the source of all Truth. Our mind is our connecting link with God, our creator. In prayer and meditation and staying focused, God projects into our minds the ideas we develop into the spiritual consciousness achieved by Jesus Christ.

WORLD: The world is a state of consciousness formed in and by our collective mind over eons. It is in a constant state of flux created by opinions, thoughts and beliefs. One could say it is defined as *the way things are*. The *world* referred to here is the material expression under the influence of the false gods of materialism and carnality. The physical world expresses consciousness. Formed by God/Spirit from divine substance, we were given dominion, or control. In order for the physical world to continue, we will need to change our thoughts and actions to support rather than destroy it.

WORSHIP: The Early English root of the word *worship,* is worthscipe, meaning to give worth. Other definitions include: to adore, adulate, pay homage. To worship God, all-good, is to give worth to all that is good. To worship, or give worth to false gods, is to give worth to that which has no foundation in Truth, such as money, sex, or personal power.

RESOURCES

Lessons in Truth–H. Emile Cady

Metamorality—Eric Butterworth

The Metaphysical Bible Dictionary–Unity

The Revealing Word–Charles Fillmore

The Twelve Powers of Man–Charles Fillmore

Christ Enthroned in Man–Cora Fillmore

A Twelve Powers Meditation Exercise–Charles Roth

SUGGESTED READING:

Psychology Today article on children and violence: https://www.psychologytoday.com/us/blog/the-baby-scientist/201801/violent-media-and-aggressive-behavior-in-children

Prophets of False Gods: Tolls, Bots and Fake News: The Mysterious World of Social Media Manipulation, Oct 14, 2017, by Samuel Earle

RECOMMENED BOOKS:

The Revelation, Our Crisis is a Birth–by Barbara Marx Hubbard

How Could You DO That–By Dr. Laura Schlessinger

Spiritual Warrior–by John Roger

ABOUT THE ATUHOR

Alicia is an ordained Unity minister, with a call from within to fill an ever-increasing gap between living lives of meaning and the limited, problematic existence so many people appear to be trapped in. She defines her writing style as enlightenment through entertainment; inspirational books to encourage readers to raise the bar in their lives, achieving fulfillment and satisfaction. While written by a minister, her works are more spiritual than religious, able to touch readers of all faiths.

She served her church as the children's storyteller prior to attending seminary, weaving Spiritual Principle into uplifting stories that appealed to church members of all ages. While in seminary she honed her skills writing sermons and inspirational articles. She has also written children's stories and articles for Unity Magazine and Contact, the Unity leadership magazine.

Alicia's first novel, Sour Grapes on Silver Platters served as a vehicle to write about her other passion, cooking.

Her second novel, The Secret of Sweetwater Stream, opens the doors of heart and mind to possibilities beyond current levels of understanding. In its pages, you will find a story of empowerment, as well as metaphysical Principles you can use to enrich your life, and the world we live in.

You can also find Alicia on Facebook at Alicia Leslie – Mundane Mystic, on Twitter @AliciaMystic, email: mundane.mystic@yahoo.com. You are invited to contact the author with questions or comments.

ALSO BY THE AUTHOR

Novels

Sour Grapes on Silver Platters

The Secret of Sweetwater Stream

Stories

The Ghosts of GrandView Manor

Spirited Stories Heard 'Round the Campfire

Other

Linea's Guide to a Delightful Dinner Party

COMING SOON

Wheel of Karma

The Bride Guide ~ A Cookbook of Sorts and Other Things

Musings of a Mundane Mystic